Can you bind the chains of the Pleiades,
Or loose the cords of Orion?
Or can you guide the Bear with her children?
Do you know the ordinances of the heavens?
Can you establish their rule on the Earth?

JOB 38:31-33

Romancing the Universe

THEOLOGY, COSMOLOGY, AND SCIENCE

Jeffrey G. Sobosan

WILLIAM B. EERDMANS PUBLISHING COMPANY
GRAND RAPIDS, MICHIGAN / CAMBRIDGE, U.K.

© 1999 Wm. B. Eerdmans Publishing Co.

255 Jefferson Ave. S.E., Grand Rapids, Michigan 49503 /

P.O. Box 163, Cambridge CB3 9PU U.K.

Printed in the United States of America

03 02 01 00 99   7 6 5 4 3 2 1

Library of Congress Cataloging-in-Publication Data

Sobosan, Jeffrey G., 1946-

Romancing the universe : on theology, cosmology, and science /
Jeffrey G. Sobosan.

p.   cm.

Includes bibliographical references.

ISBN 0-8028-4648-3 (pbk. : alk. paper)

1. Cosmology.   2. Religion and science.   I. Title.

BL240.2.S64   1999

291.2′4 — dc21   99-12919

CIP

I have known him down the days of so many years
it seems like all my life.
He dances with the spirit of God in all he does
and delights in beloved Earth more than words allow.
There is no harm in him,
yet a fierce love of life in all its forms
that beguiles him into the profoundest sanctity
I have known.
The wonder, grace, and beauty I have found
in the night sky
I have found in him, and more.
This book is for Tom,
my beloved friend of nearly 40 years.
In giving it over to him I have given nothing
compared to what he has given over to me in humor,
patience, intelligence, and a steady loyalty.
Creation doesn't always bless such a kind,
but its Creator does,
in a smile and a contentment that here,
in one life again,
there has been a love that surpassed understanding.

Contents

Preface ix

I. The Dahlia and the Spiral Galaxy 1

II. A Therapy for Narcissus 37

III. The Breath of Life 71

IV. Night Stars and the Day Star 105

V. Thoughts in the Late Hours 137

Notes 155

Bibliography 196

Index 205

Preface

There is a seduction to being alive, a fascination that sometimes breaks through the grinding tedium of life and makes it worthy. Often this seduction works on us in amazingly discreet ways, with a subtlety that only slowly moves toward passion. At other times it assails us with unnerving speed, taking us over and demanding immediate acknowledgment. All seduction, all fascination, works in one of these ways. And the desire we each have for what captivates us is always made the more profound and satisfying when shared with others. My starting point in these reflections is that this communality of desire can also have a communality of object, and that one of these objects is all around us in the night sky — which for me is but the most intense manifestation of the attraction that the universe itself holds. It is true that giving in to this attraction, allowing the endless fascination of the night sky to wrap around our minds, can issue in a conclusion like that of the illustrious Nobel laureate, Steven Weinberg, when he ends his own popular but demanding book, *The First Three Minutes,* with the sorrowful but firmly convinced words: "It is very hard to realize that this all (he is looking at the clouds and snow and land while flying over Wyoming) is just a tiny part of an overwhelmingly hostile universe. It is even harder to realize that this present universe has evolved from an unspeakably unfamiliar early condition, and faces a future extinction of endless cold or intolerable heat. The more the universe seems comprehensible, the more it also seems pointless. But if there is no solace in the fruits of our research, there is at least some consolation in the research itself. . . . The effort to understand the universe is one of the very few things that lifts human life a little above the level of farce, and gives it some of the grace of tragedy." I will not demean this perspective in what follows; in fact, I will be honoring it at various points, wrestling with its spiritually paralyzing integrity. Instead, I will be proposing that it is but one perspective, a powerful and honest one, yet still just one, and that other perspectives merit equal honor in our consideration.

There is an image we sometimes encounter in romance and love songs, and now and then in the fables of children. The image is that of stardust. It emerges, however, not just from caprice — a pleasantness born of whimsy — but from an actual physical phenomenon that appears when the moon is bright enough and droplets of moisture in the air are just the right density and translucence: the lunar light, which in truth is solar light, turns the droplets silver to our eyes, like countless miniature stars, bathing our surroundings in the way dust motes do in a room full of sunlight. I bring this up because it demonstrates the skill and subtlety of which human imagination is capable, its ability to take quite ordinary experiences and view them in a way that alters them and elicits truth, often beauty, as when some see only mist in the night air while others see a stardusted landscape. Taking this as my cue, therefore, I will be giving my own imagination a critical role in these meditations, as I hope you will give yours while reading them, because the matters we will be discussing lend themselves to such imaginative play.

The book is composed of five interrelated chapters. While I will not attempt here to give a detailed accounting of their concerns, I would nonetheless like to isolate what I judge to be the major focus of each in order to give the reader an initial taste of what lies ahead. Thus, in chapter 1 I will lay the groundwork for an aesthetics that acknowledges, describes, and pursues beauty in formulating a theological/cosmological vision, with an attentiveness to the linkages that prevail among all parts of the universe from its inception. In chapter 2 I will contend with the narcissistic spirit as the major threat to this vision, emphasizing the need to look continually beyond ourselves in order to understand ourselves; our aesthetics will become partnered to an ethics of humility.

PREFACE

Chapter 3 will take up the issue of life elsewhere in the universe, the need for imagination when considering scientific data pertinent to the possibility of extraterrestrial life as well as a theological perspective concerning divine largesse in bestowing life. Chapter 4 will tailor our conviction about such largesse to fit what we know of stability and chaos in the universe, and will explore how acknowledging each might lend itself to a spirit of docility when contemplating creation, its God and its life. The final chapter will provide a recapitulation of what I judge to be the more salient points of the previous four when attempting to wed theology and science in an appreciation of cosmology. I should also note that the theology I have emphasized throughout is derivative from Judeo-Christian traditions, though here and there I touch on others in supplementary and I hope illuminating ways. The science has been appropriated from what I believe to be the best discussions currently available to an audience not necessarily composed of professional scientists. In addressing both theological and scientific issues, I have striven diligently to make lucid and accessible to the reader ideas that might otherwise remain obscure in their detail and complexity.

One further word. This book contains many endnotes, some quite lengthy and presented in a different, more expository style than the main text. For this reason you might find them somewhat distracting if you refer to them as each appears. If so, I would suggest that you read the main text through, and then, if you wish the further exposition, return to the endnotes and read them with quick reference back to their setting within the main text.

As I write this it is very late at night, in the small hours of morning, and outside my window I can hear the plaintive and beguiling sound of killdeers calling to each other as they fly in the safety of the dark. They have been my companions during many lonely, many working nights, touches of life to stir my mind and soothe my feelings. I have often thought that if the night sky could sing, this too is how it would sound, a plaintive and beguiling melody calling us to share in the song of the universe.

I

The Dahlia and the Spiral Galaxy

There is something about the clear night sky that always works on me like the charmed talismans of an ancient sorcery. I can spend hours at a time looking up at it, and every time see something new, some configuration or sparkle of light. The experience is both aesthetic and moral. It is aesthetic because the panorama of shapes and color my eyes take in produces an experience of beauty; it is moral because knowledge of the sheer size and age of what I am seeing produces an experience of humility. There is a vastness, a differentiation in the night sky that roiling oceans, grand and eloquently silent deserts, dark and heavy mountain vistas can only hint at. When I was six years of age I began to learn of this. My father and I were in the backyard of our home and he was telling me about the various constellations we could see in the night sky. I didn't find the instruction particularly interesting since the only constellation, to my child's eye, that clearly looked like its name was the Big Dipper. But then he started talking about size and distance, and my attention became increasingly focused on what he was saying. For I was hearing new things, things I had never known before: that the stars didn't look about the same in size and luminosity because they actually were, that some stars were much larger and brighter but also much farther away; that some of the single points of light were not just one star but two circling closely to

1

each other; that all the stars were the result of a single, unimaginably dense concentration of energy that exploded 12-18 billion years ago; that we could only see about 6,000 of them with our unaided eyes in a universe that contained a countless number of them; and so on. I cannot say that these facts stirred an interest in me that would eventually issue in the desire to study the stars as a vocation. They did not, and I have never professionally done the work of astronomy or astrophysics. What they did stir in me, however, was wonder, and I have turned this wonder loose in my imagination many times as I have looked into the clear night sky. And each time I have been given joy.

Kant is often quoted as saying that there were two enduring sources of wonder in his life: "the starry heavens above me and the moral law within me."[1] I have devoted some of my previous books to meditations on "the moral law within me," books on sin and contrition and guilt. As I've grown older, though, and have read and experienced more, I have become less concerned with the intricacies of how we human beings relate amongst ourselves and more concerned with how we relate, first to the world, then to the universe around us. I owe this change primarily to my reading of the works of Loren Eiseley, a profoundly gifted and insightful man,[2] but also to my recollection of those first stirrings of interest in a creation outside myself bestowed on me one night by my father. Some might say that in this I have fallen partial victim to the so-called "pathetic fallacy." The accusation here has both a soft and a hard version. In the former it means that one has assigned to inanimate objects certain qualities that properly belong only to human beings. It is particularly ascribed to poets, especially those of European and American Romanticism: Tennyson, Wordsworth, Coleridge, and Emerson are typically cited as examples and anthropomorphism is its characteristic form of expression. In the "hard" version one is criticized for the assignment of the same importance and corresponding relationship as one enjoys with other people to animate objects, plants, and other animals that populate our lives. It is "relationship" that is the primary interest here, with the ascription of anthropomorphic characteristics a secondary expression of it. How does one wish to understand one's relationship to inanimate or animate but nonhuman creation? The pathetic fallacy emerged largely as a reaction to a defensive maneuver by scientists, especially biologists, to relieve anxiety about the morality of their experiments. Moral impunity vis-à-vis the inanimate and nonhuman world implies a relationship not just of ethical but of ontological inequality that permits us to do as we please outside the arena of our own kind. Lynn White attributed this assumption of inequality to our biblical heritage and to enthusiastic acceptance and aggressive implementation of the misunderstood assertion in Genesis about subduing the Earth and being the master of its life.[3] We now know, of course, that the passage does not imply domination but, rather, casts us in the role of diligent caretakers or caregivers in partnership with God. It is this relationship of care that will guide the reflections in this book,[4] an affiliation that not only recognizes the place, value and distinctness of all things in God's universe, but also, perhaps more importantly, seeks to learn from them. The spirit that we hope will guide us in these pages, then, will not be mastery but docility, and the primary relationship we will pursue with the inanimate while contemplating the heavens will be that of an attentive and respectful student.

I have said that I have never studied astronomy or astrophysics professionally. But over the years I have kept attuned to whatever sources of information in these areas have come my way — books, magazines, journals, television shows, lectures, private conversations with university colleagues — which are presented for the serious nonprofessional. So I have an educated layman's knowledge of such things as black holes, cosmic strings, parallel universes, and cold dark matter, each of which is a fascinating factual or hypothetical construct worth a continuing and ardent curiosity. But I think that what enchants me even more is the excitement which the study of the stars and universe obviously evokes in professional scholars and which has always brimmed over into my own mind.[5] I feel a similar, though less powerful excitement when I also read or hear of new theories or discoveries at the other end of the proportional spectrum, namely, in the arena of sub-atomic physics. There is a vitality, a freshness or newness of insight and information that makes both these fields of study energetic and enormously creative. Any overarching vision of the "created order" must take into account both the microscopic and macroscopic intricacies of what these stimulating and productive sciences are telling us about the universe in which we live.

In a previous book, *The Turn of the Millennium,* I offer a sustained argument that if Christian theology is to remain persuasive in the generations to come it too must absorb and make its own the characteristics of both these contemporary sciences: the data they are accumulating and the spirit of excitement that pervades their work.[6] For Christianity can no longer assume that the primary intellectual trait of the cultures in which it exists is philosophical. This is not to say that philosophy is no longer an effective intellectual discipline or that some of it is not still important to theology. Such an assertion would sound a note of ingratitude that is not only inappropriate but petulant. Rather, it is to say that the intense dependence of theology upon philosophy that has characterized so much of Christianity's past must now give way to a similar dependence on science; the first marriage, though not the friendship, must come to an amicable end so that a new marriage, with a new privileged partner, can take its place. Even in cultures where philosophical visions still predominate as the primary tools for assessing reality, the eventual predominance of science is inevitable. The transition may be slower but is nonetheless discernible, if only because the example of scientific success in evaluating reality in other cultures is irresistible. Some would argue that the prospects of such a union are not realistic, since a marriage between theology and science would need to emerge from a relationship whose history since the Enlightenment has been ambiguous at best, and frequently hostile. But it is not science that has suffered from the distance; theology has. So the first serious and well-reflected movements in establishing the relationship must inevitably come from theology.[7] If successful, I am convinced that such a relationship would effect an enlivening of Christian theology which has probably not been experienced since the reemergence of Aristotle's works in the twelfth century, an infusion of entirely new considerations that could restore reflective vigor and pertinence to a discipline that many, including many scientists, have consigned to the periphery of what is important about being in the world. I write this as a theologian who knows that in his own field perhaps more than any other the practice of humility is to be commended as a way of acknowledging the needed assistance of others to do one's tasks well.

Some people are intimidated by new knowledge. I can assure you

that this aversion is present even where you would least expect to find it —
among faculty at universities. We get comfortable with the knowledge we
have, warm to the values and visions it sustains in our lives and threatened
by any proposed refinement, let alone denial of them. The new knowledge comes to us like an assault on cherished idols, and the bringer of the
knowledge is often treated accordingly. At a cultural level this phenomenon is invariably and profoundly conditioned by history. By this I mean
that what one generation construes as intellectually violent proposals
against an established pattern of thought, to be met with the most assidu-
ous defensive strategies, a subsequent generation — when all the strategies have failed — will establish as its own orthodoxy. I want to suggest
that at the heart of all such intellectual revolutions lies a critical issue of
epistemology, which I would cast in the form of the following inquiry:
Does experience control thought, or does thought control experience? My
argument throughout these pages will be that the former is the case, so
that when experience conflicts with a particular style or pattern of
thought, it is not the experience that must change, since this is impossible
anyway, but the thought. Or to put it differently, I will be arguing against
all dogmatism — that desire to capture in set formulas ideas presumed to
be immutable, that is, ones for which temporality as the womb of novelty
is not a defining trait. The capacity for certainty that dogmatism assumes
does not, in fact, lie within us. Instead, we are always left with tentativeness, acknowledging that while changeless ideas might exist — and
would be equivalent to what we typically mean by eternal truths — ac-
cessing them would require among us an absolute and universal consistency of experience whose possibility all our experience in fact denies.
Even the slightest difference among us in how an experience is received
prohibits this consistency. And since such differences always exist,[8] if only
minutely, dogmatic ideas can at best lay claim to only a relative, not absolute, consistency, which in turn usually means general agreement among
the large majority of a given group. The individual either from within or
outside the group who denies this consistency through fresh data or insight is therefore typically designated a renegade. And while history certainly tells us loudly that renegade ideas are not always superior to dogmatic ones, it also tells us that intellectual advance, when it occurs, is
always born from them.

Perhaps some examples might assist our appreciation of these remarks. Three of them come immediately to mind. The first is Copernicus, whose field of study, as it happens, was astronomy. As everyone no doubt knows, Copernicus was the first to formulate in a persuasive fashion the heliocentric model of the solar system, as opposed to the centuries-old and venerably popular geocentric theory. The new model was especially attractive in that it offered solutions to anomalies and contradictions in observational data which the previous model was unable to resolve convincingly.[9] At least it was attractive to many contemporary astronomers. But it was not attractive to people at large, under the influence of a Church leadership hostile to the new model from the start.[10] As time and further observational experiments continued, however, it became obvious that any intelligent person either consented to the new model or consented to foolishness. And most intelligent people do not consciously consent to foolishness. The point is that it wasn't so much the *facts* presented in the new model that disturbed people as it was their explicit conclusion, namely, that we human beings did not live at the metropole, the center of the universe, around which everything else in "the heavens" revolved. The furor it caused was the result of the judgment that it was a direct assault on the dignity of the place human beings occupied in the universe. Even the renowned Tycho Brahe, a generation after Copernicus and the greatest observational astronomer of his time, fell prey to this viewpoint, insisting that while all the other planets revolved around the Sun, the Sun itself still revolved around the Earth.[11] Consolation was therefore sought, and found, in the assertion that even if we did not live at the center of the universe we could still find our dignity in the idea that we were the apex of the created order, brought into existence directly by the will of God. But then Darwin, with his tightly reasoned and abundantly documented data, came on the scene, arguing that the progenitor of human life was not a miraculous divine creation but a hominid derivative from the family of great apes. Again, it was not so much the facts supporting Darwin's theory that gained him and his supporters the hostility of many, but the conclusion that his model of the evolutionary process, like Copernicus's model of the solar system, was an assault on human dignity.[12] Finally, having accepted that we do not live at the center of the universe and that we are not the unique creations of divine intervention, many people sought to locate human dignity in the idea that we are nonetheless the masters of our fate, free within chosen moral constraints to be or do whatever we desired. But then, from the early to the middle decades of this century, the luminous works of Freud became increasingly influential in assessing human capabilities. We learned — though we could have done so from other people, in their own distinctive vocabularies, deep within human history — that we are not as free as we might have thought. The exercise of our freedom is often confused or made ineffective by such factors as infantile trauma, repressed but still active neurotic fixations, sexual fantasies and jealousies, generally inept self-appraisals, and the like. So we find ourselves bereft of our third source of dignity and perhaps wishing that the new knowledge gained from such thinkers as these three had not been gained at all. This is a sentiment with which it is easy to sympathize. Yet we gain nothing from it except a soft-minded sense of security which will not or cannot accept the fact that embracing new knowledge — however disconcerting or even destructive of our accustomed ways of thinking — is a greater act of dedication to humanity than refusing it.

In my view one of the primary tasks of Christian theology in the new millennium will be to identify a new or refreshed source for affirmations of human dignity. I have made it clear that if such a discovery is made, we ought not to dogmatize it in such a way that further data or insights beyond it are refused in an intellectually aggressive protectionism.[13] I have also made clear my conviction that this new vision of human dignity will need to be formulated in consort with science if it wishes to be intellectually persuasive and not merely the longing of a wishful piety.[14] I am not sure what the source of the new vision might turn out to be, but if permitted to play the prophet for a moment, I suspect it will reside not in an idea of our uniqueness or superiority in creation but more in one of our partnership within it. This will require as a major step a return to cosmology in order to promote relationships that extend beyond the immediacy of our local environments: a broadening of ecological awareness of partnership with all the nonhuman life on this planet — life we can see and touch and relate to here — and eventually with life elsewhere in the universe (a topic we will take up in chapter 3). Theology, moreover, will need to insist that the communality this partnership implies is provided not just by a sharing of those same elements that constitute all that exists in the universe, common forms of energy/mass[15] such as photons, quarks, and electrons, but by a substrate that allows these elements to relate in a fashion that produces both ourselves and all other objects we experience in the universe. This substrate is what we can designate metaphysically as God, while allowing metaphors to embroider the designation into more satisfying relational terms. In a new vision of human dignity premised on our partnership with all else in creation, God's being will reside neither outside nor among the objects in the universe, but *in the relationships* that constitute them in themselves and then allow their partnership with each other. This presence in the relationships is what we will later describe as divine love and its motivation as the cherishing of life.

Contemporary astronomy and astrophysics, like contemporary nuclear and particle physics, is hurling new knowledge at us at a breathtaking rate, and some would undoubtedly prefer that it were not so. The long-cherished image of the universe as an unspeakably grand and intricate machine, demonstrating for many the subtlety and wisdom of God, is now bankrupt. For too many anomalies have been found in the machine — from cosmic strings to dark matter to sub-atomic particles that pop briefly in and out of existence — and cause havoc in any attempt to provide an overarching and irrefutable predictability to how the machine runs. Dreams of a Final Theory within which all the physical phenomena of the universe have become comprehensible, like the individual parts of a well-ordered machine, will never come true.[16] For now it appears the universe is much more like a series of continuing thoughts, not all of them related or even coherent in themselves, than like a machine. And if this is so, the critical question becomes, metaphorically but intriguingly: Is there someone thinking these thoughts?

❋   ❋   ❋

SEVERAL YEARS AGO I was reading a series of reflections written by a Navajo teacher. They were quite striking in the way they extolled the loveliness and bounty of the Earth, and reaffirmed an impression I had that perhaps no people had built into their cultural heritage more of an appreciation of natural beauty than the Navajo.[17] And by "beauty" here, as throughout the book, I will simply make my own Webster's excellent definition: "Beauty: that quality or aggregate of qualities in a thing which gives pleasure to the senses or pleasurably exalts the mind or spirit; physical, moral, or spiritual loveliness."[18] But nowhere did the Navajo writer speak of what lies beyond the Earth. For him, all that was useful in comprising the geography of a spirituality of beauty was what was at hand on this planet, particularly the plants, topography, and climate of the southwestern United States. But this must surely produce an abbreviated spirituality — not an ineffective one, but lacking what the poet Charles Péguy described as "expansivity" of vision, the ability to shape the way we think according to factors beyond our immediate surroundings. To say this, of course, is not to censure so much as to assert the limits of the immediacy as a source for a spiritual vision. Nor would I ever wish to live without the Earth's beauty, the pleasure we can gain whenever we travel its land and waters, but which is concentrated most forcefully for me in that single view of the whole which our satellites provide. It is the blue more than anything else, that caressing color the photographs record, that for me is the source of this beauty and because of which the clouds and continental shapes become beautiful too. I have such a photograph on my office wall and have spent much time, in a type of daydreaming trance, just looking at it and feasting on the thought that this is my home.

These remarks reactivate a memory I have of a trip through the Southwest. It is of the place rather than one of its resident teachers that comes back to me now, and breaks the bonds of Earth that he did not. It was evening and I had stopped the car to look at a sheer cliff rising a thousand feet or so above the desert plain. It looked so smooth from a distance that it seemed as if some ancient god had taken a sharpened knife and neatly lopped off a part of the mountain. I knew, of course, that this mythological fancy was badly in error, that it was actually the slow action of erosion many thousands of years ago that had produced the effect. But I had already spent days among the Navajo, studying their religious traditions, and the beauty of mythic thought, its personalism and its connectedness with human activity, was still very much with me. Then while I was looking at this sheer face of rock I noticed that it began to shimmer with color and in a few moments various hues became quite distinct and intense. A geologist friend later told me this was probably due to striations of quartz or other minerals at the rock's surface. At any rate, I turned to see what the face was reflecting, and there to the east was rising the largest and most magnificent circle of the moon I had ever seen. It was what we called a harvest moon when I was growing up in the Midwest, a deep burnt-orange in color and clear as could be because there in the desert no urban light or pollution diffused it. It riveted my attention, this best known of our companions in the universe, the only one on which human feet have walked. I noted again the odd shadows that cross its surface, the way they configure into something like a distorted human face. I thought of the old mythologies too: the moon with its monthly cycles as a symbol of fertility; the sign of Minerva, goddess of wisdom; emblem of life in its waxing, of death in its waning; abode of greater and lesser deities; way station of alien yet superior life-forms. I thought also of some of the theories surrounding its origin: born from the same swirling and compacting dust as the Earth was; torn from our planet by the Sun in the Earth's soft infancy, or yanked out by some other large object passing too close; a remnant of a planet which for whatever reason was shattered; simply a celestial rogue trespassing too close and trapped by Earth's gravity.[19] I thought as well that on the surface of it the moon is not particularly beautiful, or at least not as spectacularly beautiful as Jupiter, Saturn, or, of course, the Earth itself. Yet despite this, I also knew that down the ages poets and paint- ers and musicians have celebrated the moon more than any of our other companions, even the Sun, the source and sustainer of the only breathing life we know. Possibly this is because it is so much closer to us than any of the other companions, and easy on the unaided eye. Or perhaps it is because of the light it often gives to a darkness which for many would otherwise be forbidding. Or maybe it is due to the moon's power, the strongest force, even stronger than that of the Sun, in one of the truly amazing natural phenomena we can daily observe, the pushing and pulling of ocean tides. Or perhaps it is because of one of the old yet still gripping mythologies that captivate the mind aware of it. Whatever the reason, the moon seems to inhabit the consciousness of many of us to a degree that of all celestial bodies only the Earth exceeds.

The point I want to rehearse is that while reflection on the Earth alone, something like reflection on human life alone, can produce great insight and an intellectual beauty to match the beauty of the planet and human life, our reflection should seek to go beyond these confines. We should try to discover what is of worth and beauty in forms of life other than human; we should break the bonds of *anthropocentric* concentration. And we should seek to discover what is of worth and beauty in nonterrestrial bodies; we should break the bonds of *geocentric* concentration. In this way our thought will be richer, fuller, more reflective of the universe, not just the world, in which we live. The unattractive image of the guru who devotes his rapt attention to meditation on his navel — his own life and his own relationships — can be writ larger in the person who devotes exclusive attention to meditation on his or her own planet. And so we must look outward, from ourselves and from our planet, to be made receivers of new knowledge and new beauty that we previously did not possess. If these words sound like piety, then let them be; for there is nothing wrong with a piety, religious or not, that is vigorous and investigative.

One of the great theologians of this century, Karl Barth — along with contemporaries like Rudolf Bultmann, Emil Brunner, and Dietrich Bonhoeffer — declined such a piety. A sullenness pervades his refusal, born as it was from a certainty that science had nothing to offer Christian theology, especially its doctrines on God and Christ, despite his awareness that for many believers science was quickly replacing this theology as the basis for confidence in what blessings life had to offer. In this Barth showed himself Goethe's spiritual mate, at least to the extent that both objected to the reliability that "objective" science, with its formulas and equations disattached from lived experience, could bring to the disclosure of meaning.[20] Even when he came to so scientifically pertinent a doctrine as creation when writing his *Church Dogmatics,* he relied on a dazzling display of exegesis that attended to Genesis but refused the insights of science, ignoring almost all the currently pertinent data of geology, evolutionary biology, and astrophysics. His is a very pi-

11

ous presentation of the doctrine of creation, but far from the vigorous and investigative piety we recommended above. Yet he captured a tone or approach that we find predominant even today among many Christian theologians, not so much because of a similar sullenness or antipathy toward the contributions science can make to theology, but because science seems to frighten them, both in the intellectual demands of its various fields of study and in its general hold over believers as a basis for hope in the future. While it has become popular to excoriate the great "parson" naturalists of the last century, I often admire the spirit with which they engaged the data of science not as a threat but a partner in the praise of God. Today we see a similar spirit, wedded to a much more competent knowledge of science, in very few theologians. But among them are the impressive examples of John Cobb, Jay McDaniel, Sallie McFague, Holmes Rolston, Jurgen Moltmann, and Wolfhart Pannenberg.[21] If I was right when suggesting earlier that Christian theology will be persuasive in the generations to come only if it aligns itself intimately to the data and excitement that occupy scientific inquiry, then it is to theologians like these that it must look for its guidance. The spirit Barth represents, at least regarding our present interest, must be fairly acknowledged, but then set aside.

Albert Einstein was once asked, "What is the most important question a person can ask?" With barely a pause the subtle genius replied, "Whether the universe is friendly or not." He meant by this the need to discover the order that he was certain prevailed in the universe, since its absence could only mean (for him) that the universe is constitutionally unpredictable and therefore hostile. Yet the presence of novelty pervading the findings of so much contemporary research into the universe appears to forbid from the start the formulation of any theory of its order that can endure in the way for which Einstein longed.[22] On the other hand, while we must certainly acknowledge unpredictability within the universe, this is not the same as admitting its hostility. Each of us has had experiences of unpredictability in our lives, as in the behavior of a loved one, that are by no definition hostile. Mere unpredictability does not always hold the germ of hostility, so that I suspect Einstein's answer was consequently pointing not so much to a physical enmity as to a type of intellectual one that emerges when data prove analytically recalcitrant. In this, despite his contrary theories, he shows himself a soul mate of Isaac Newton. Both were aware of novelty in the universe, and each in fact contributed newness in epoch-making ways to human thought. So it was not novelty in itself that worried them; they were enchanted by it. Rather, what caused their distress was the thought that new discoveries would not fit into an overarching, ordered, and discoverable design in the universe.

Certainly for someone like Barth, and for countless other Christian theologians, there is indeed an overarching design to the universe. But discovering it belongs primarily if not exclusively to the study of God's providence as described in revelatory traditions. For Einstein, however, and for countless other scientists, it can emerge only through the concise and insightful handling of mathematics, or more precisely, mathematical physics. It is the equations that hold the plan of the universe, and unfolding them in logical sequence as more and more data accrue provides the basis for confidence that eventually sufficient data will be available to provide a reliable mathematical map of the order prevailing in the universe. The equations, therefore, will need to be amorphous enough to include all eventualities within their compass — that is, they will need to be constructed so as to be "bendable" to new data without damaging their consistency. Or to put it differently, they will have to be inductively successful enough regarding the whole of creation to tolerate within them unexpected novelties. This is the dream of a final theory to which we previously referred, and a delicacy of thought is now required of us. Our consistent position throughout the book will be that such a final theory is beyond human talents, not just because of a well-founded suspicion that much of the novelty in the universe will be neither relatable to other data nor bendable to even the most inclusive equations, but because our minds themselves are not sufficiently competent to structure such equations even if they were possible. On this latter point in particular, theology will speak of the finitude or fallenness of our intellects,[23] though such language can sometimes obscure the more blunt and basic fact that the neural exchanges in our brains, while counting into many billions, are insufficient to process events occurring in the universe to an extent and precision that would provide an adequate basis for reliably inductive equations regarding *all* the events. The same delicacy, however, requires us also to say that at some future time novelties in our own evolution might make such intellectual competence possible, including the creation of machines that might themselves be autonomously capable of digesting the data and producing the equations, reflecting a universe now more tractable in its surprises. But this would be radical evolution indeed — of the type that usually gets described in the very loose question, "Who knows what the future holds?" — and for our reflections here can provide no pertinence.[24]

We must always remember that both Newton and Einstein, along with many other of their respective contemporaries, were profoundly religious men. In a sense they thought of their science, or much of it, as a type of theology, discovering the kaleidoscopic intricacies of God's construction of the universe as a witness to divine subtlety and wisdom.[25] They looked upon the work of science, so to speak, as the reconstruction of a gigantic jigsaw puzzle; all the pieces were available and, once found, would create a picture giving due glory to God. And so we have Einstein's famous statement, which he himself took with studied seriousness, "God does not play at dice with the universe," to which we might add as a cautionary proviso, "or if God does, the dice are loaded." Yet the God Einstein is thinking of is considerably different from the one Newton worshipped. For the latter is the God of deism, the celebrated Watchmaker who sets the primordial universe in place, provides it with initial motion, and then withdraws save for intermittent intrusions when anomalies develop and something goes awry. The problem that has always plagued this particular understanding of God — and Einstein was sympathetic to it — is that it does not accord well with Judeo-Christian tradition, in which God is not seen as sitting aloof on the island of heaven, largely indifferent to creation, but as embracing it and being actively involved in its changes and development. If *this* is the controlling image of God, then not only can the universe be open to newness, it can also, when understood as a result of God's free and intervening activity, be entirely unpredictable — though not in a way unrelatable to some encompassing intention.

There are still evident differences between the historic Judeo-Christian image of God and Einstein's deity, or for that matter (at least on my reading of it), the deity affirmed by most scientists who are philo-sophically or theologically inclined. When he was asked about his con-cept of God, Einstein replied that he believed in the God of Spinoza. This is not a particularly curious reply, since we know that people easily attach characteristics to God that reflect major concerns in their own lives — the lawyer speaks of a contract-making God; bankers and busi-ness people of an Accountant; engineers and mechanists of a Watch-maker; the poor of a Consoler; the wealthy of an Owner; etc. — and that they intermix these images in the most amazing and creative ways. Spinoza is perhaps the greatest formulator of a philosophical pantheism wherein God and the universe are identified. Einstein's driving passion was cosmology, the study of the universe, and so his attraction to Spinoza is not difficult to appreciate. Moreover, pantheism has at least three implications that are exquisitely beautiful and were enormously attractive to Einstein. First and foremost among them is that all creation must be treated as sacred since comportment toward it is the same as comportment toward God. Secondly, if one's understanding of deity is also of a purposeful and ordering presence, then the universe, too, must be so described: a matter of profound importance to the success of any scientist's craft. Thirdly, pantheism tends to obscure the alienation that can occur when God is held as distinct from the universe and claims are made that proper access to this distinctness is reserved to revelatory in-tuitions and historical events that themselves are distinct. This third point, of course, is precisely where the major departure between panthe-istic and traditional Judeo-Christian understandings of God occurs, since the latter wishes to insist, primarily from its doctrines on creation (of time, space, etc.), redemption (including incarnations of providen-tial care), and divine attributes such as eternity and ontological immuta-bility, that God is qualitatively other from everything else and thus ac-cessible only through privileged communications. Somehow, I think, we must learn to blend the beauty of the pantheistic vision into Chris-tian theology so that God's presence can be understood as ontologically inclusive of everything that is in the universe — this is what I was get-ting at earlier when saying that God is in the relationships that consti-tute everything that is, but not thereby intrinsically identifiable with the things themselves once constituted — and that this presence is oriented toward the cherishing of life as its encompassing intention. Such a view requires in turn that the notion of life itself needs to be reconceived so as to characterize everything that is and avoid any implied alienation between life and non-life. In *The Turn of the Millennium* I suggested such a reconception away from the biological characteristics of life (metabolism, growth, reproduction, and internal powers of adaptation to environment) toward others premised on physics and more congenially applicable to all that is (motion, duration, novelty, and relationship). In the same book, moreover, since I clearly wanted to assert that God too is alive, though not by the former, biological traits, I offered suggestions regarding how the four latter traits might be applied theologically. Having dealt with them there, however, and at some length, I will not repeat these suggestions here.[26]

We need not, of course, theologize the newness and unpredictability of what we observe in the universe; we need not involve an understanding of God in what we observe. The observations can stand in and of themselves, and the conclusion will remain ineluctable: there as yet appears no ordered plan into which all our observations will fit, so that any postulate of the existence of such a plan, whether theological or scientific, brings both theology and science to a similar act of faith.[27] This results in our having to endow the universe *as we actually observe it* with degrees of idiosyncrasy or strangeness as we examine its inhabitants, size, and age. But as with novelty, not everything that is strange is necessarily threatening. We still know this even in our suspicion-ridden, xenophobic culture. What is strange can frequently be a source of pleasure for us, of increased insight and more mature understanding. Traveling to a foreign country often has this affect, as does the study of strange art and languages and music. We begin to see that the neat proportionality we may have given our existence or our universe — everything in its place — can in fact diminish the richness, profundity, and excitement of both. And we begin as well to appreciate the rightness of an observation Francis Bacon once made, that "beauty lies in the strangeness of the proportion."[28] Perhaps it was because I was not old enough to understand Bacon's sentiment that, years ago, I was not able to appreciate my father's pointing out to me constellations in the night sky. I could only appreciate the Big Dipper because its proportions are so obvious; there is clearly the outline of a handle and a cup. But when he pointed out the Archer and the Water-Bearer, the Big and Little Bears, I grew listless in my attention because being able to see the beauty of these, how the individual stars related in order to shape the figure, required that I be able to see the strangeness of their proportions. But then, I was only a little boy at the time, and little boys must always be forgiven their failures of imagination.

The role of imagination has already appeared repeatedly in these reflections, and will continue to do so throughout. I would therefore like to offer some understanding of it now for purposes of clarity and deeper appreciation. The classic study of the phenomenon, in my judgment, still belongs to Jean-Paul Sartre, though in what follows I will be departing considerably from him because I wish to give the analysis a broader compass than he does.[29] In doing so I will follow very closely the definition offered in Webster's, with emendations appropriate to the clarity, breadth, and appreciation I am seeking.[30]

The dictionary begins its definition with the general phrase: "the act or power of imagining," then defines imagining as the "formation of mental images of objects not present to the senses, especially of those never perceived in their entirety, and hence the mental synthesis of new ideas from elements experienced separately." This is an extraordinarily precise description whose precision nonetheless captures exactly what I think we all experience at root as the act of imagination. What it is depicting fundamentally is the talent of our minds to draw relationships between objects that the objects in themselves neither furnish nor necessarily imply. In brain physiology this would involve above all imprinting or memory and the ability to construct gestalts or patterns from otherwise random bits of information. Both of these in turn require sophisticated chemical and neural interdependencies among molecules in the brain that allow the various imprints into close enough proximity to each other so as to permit exchanges that produce the synthesized products that at some point become neurally/chemically energetic enough to become conscious. The reader is aware that I am trying to reduce here to the greatest possible simplicity an extremely complicated phenomenon which even specialists do not fully understand.[31] What the dictionary then goes on to call "reproductive imagination" simply acknowledges what we have just called the memory or imprinting capacity of the brain, just as what it calls "creative imagination" acknowledges its ability to draw patterns from randomness. It is this latter talent that principally concerns us here. Creative imagination is defined as having three traits. The first is merely an extension of the brain's capacity for synthesis and reads, "the mental representation of that which in its entirety has never been offered to the senses." The talent here is to extrapolate to the whole when only parts are available, and in this it is similar to what is philosophically known as inductive reasoning. The second trait is described as "the power to represent the real more fully and truly than it appears to the senses and in its ideal or universal character." This is simply a proviso on the first trait, acknowledging that imagination has not just the fanciful but the real as its proper object and can achieve universally applicable statements about real objects. The final trait is defined as "the power of inventing the novel or unreal by recombining the elements of reality." This trait, coupled to the first, involves the ability to see in a random group of stars the shape of a bear or a scorpion ready to strike.

It is this last trait especially, now that I am a middle-aged man and no longer a child, that has allowed me to relish thoroughly Bacon's appreciation of beauty as lying in the strangeness of proportion. Further, my increased years have taught me that, like competence in all other things, competence in imaginative effort also takes deliberate and focused attention. The listlessness of mental effort that often characterizes our behavior, the refusal to attend to anything that is not immediately apparent or useful — what in the next chapter I will describe as the narcissistic temperament — can give way to intellectual passion only when the mind is diligently and carefully exercised over a wide variety of experiences. So now I can look into the night sky and see the classic constellations and even imagine figures of my own. I can see animal faces and pyramids, tulip shapes and trumpet horns, the outline of the United States and an angel fish. Perpetual delight is my reward for these imaginative efforts, worked out in my own mind if in no one else's. I can see a starfish sometimes, and am reminded of Loren Eiseley's hauntingly beautiful essay, "The Star-Thrower." And sometimes I can see the outline of a beautiful woman's face, and am reminded of Dante's

Beatrice, Don Quixote's Dulcinea, or the Lady of Shakespeare's sonnets. Imagination is free-roaming here, to be sure, but it is not undisciplined. If it were, all these stars would remain simply a jumble, the unsorted mess I saw when a little boy. Left undisciplined, imagination tends to become erratically overloaded and kaleidoscopically confused. It produces headaches, or better, brainaches, and a corresponding desire to suppress its activity.

Yet despite these imaginative efforts — at least those described by our third trait above: "the power of inventing the novel or unreal by recombining the elements of reality" — and the pleasurable effect they work on me, it is still the *science* that studies the universe, the facts and theories it offers, that delights me the most.[32] I will give you just one example, drawn from current theory about "dark matter," that illustrates not only this but also our first trait of the creative imagination: "the mental representation of that which in its entirety has never been offered to the senses." The theory is based on the fact that the universe we can observe accounts for less than 10% of the matter needed to suppress the universe's expansion and begin a collapse back toward a primordial condition similar to what initiated the expanding phase we are now experiencing. The postulate, therefore, is that around 90-95% of this matter is not detectable, or not easily so. Candidates accounting for it have ranged from interstellar dust to burned out galaxies to neutrinos.[33] But recently another candidate has appeared on the scene, the so-called brown dwarfs, bodies many times the size of even very large planets (like Jupiter) but still without enough mass to ignite in a fusion reaction, or barely enough so that they become just tiny and weakly luminous stars. They were initially presented as hypothetical constructs which, in addition to things like dust and dead galaxies, might help to account for the missing matter in the universe.[34] But in 1995 a group of scientists announced that they had conclusively located at least one of these dwarfs circling a small star 19 light-years from us — a few others have been located orbiting other stars since then — and that their reality, probably their abundant reality, must now be taken into account when attempting to locate and assess this missing matter.[35] Now I suspect that for many people this announcement was greeted with a yawn or an indifferent shrug saying, "Who cares? How important can this be when the Dow Jones dropped 75 points today and my car wouldn't start this morning?" Others, sufficiently educated to recognize the importance of the discovery, might be more interested. And finally there would be those, precisely because they have indeed gratified a thirst for education and interests beyond the immediacies of everyday living, who would have responded with great excitement and the satisfaction that something new, fresh knowledge, had been delivered to us — especially since one of our own planets, Jupiter, fits the description of a potential brown dwarf, an unborn second star in our solar system with a retinue of planetary satellites all its own, yet whose mass, to date, is still insufficient to ignite under the pressure and heat of its own gravity. I have some confidence that by reading this book and perhaps others like it, you too will come to share this thirst and interest.

However, it is the celestial objects that *do* ignite, the stars, both individually and as they cluster into galaxies, that seem to hold the greatest rapture for us. Our language, its metaphors especially, betrays this rapture in many ways when we describe things and experiences that populate our world and our lives. And so we call the beautifully proportioned marine animal a "starfish," and two of our most exquisitely cut and lustrous diamonds the Star of India and the Star of Africa, joined by their remarkable cousins, the star sapphires. We also recognize the Star of David as the symbol of the ancient yet still vibrant culture of the Jews. Less admirably we speak of overly paid actors and sports people as "movie stars" and "star athletes." When I was in grade school, excellent written work was awarded with a gummed gold or silver star placed on the paper near the student's name. And when we witness the behavior of two people at the beginning of their love, we sometimes say that they have "stars in their eyes." Our word "disaster" comes from the Latin meaning "separate from the stars" or at cross-purposes with them, a definition Shakespeare employed when he described his tragic Romeo and Juliet as "star-crossed lovers." Then there are the esoteric interpretive formulas of astrology, attempting to define a person's fate by the placement of stars and planets, much as ancient peoples tried to do by interpreting the position of the innards of a slain animal. Citizens of the United States take pride in their flag, the Stars and Stripes, and in their national anthem, the "Star-Spangled Banner," but British citizens take no delight at all in their once powerful but juridically self-serving panel of judges, the Star Chamber. To delight us in the Spring we have star flowers, a group of plants whose most widely known member is the primrose; to stir religious sentiment there is the woman crowned with twelve stars in Revelation 12:1. Finally, at least for this current list, there is the Star of Bethlehem, the augury to Gentiles and Jews alike of the birth in David's city of Jesus, whom Whitehead once described as "the brief Galilean flicker of humility." Many more examples, I know, could be given, but here I have provided enough to indicate our enchantment with the stars and some of the ways in which we allow this to influence how we speak.

Stars come in a variety of sizes — from many times larger than our Sun to many times smaller — and colors ranging from white to red to blue to yellow. They also emit different intensities of heat and light, depending largely on the quantity of mass being consumed in fusion reactions at their core. Fusion is the process whereby atoms, say of hydrogen, are squeezed into each other because of the gravitational pressure of the star's mass and as a result release photons, the quanta or packets of energy, massless in themselves, that carry the heat and light. These photons gradually make their way over millions of years to the star's surface, having undergone further fusion/energy release processes on their journey, until they are liberated into space; the star, we say, shines. In most stars this initial stage of fusing hydrogen continues when the helium formed by the fused hydrogen itself ignites and begins to form lithium, then beryllium, then carbon. For further ignitions to occur after this helium to carbon stage, however, the star must have a mass somewhat greater than the Sun's, since the heavier the elements involved, the greater the gravitational pressure needed to fuse them.[36] With each ignition, of course, there is an explosion that hurls portions of these elements out into space, where they move freely until again attracted by another gravitational source. If it gets that far, the process usually stops when iron is reached because it takes more energy to fuse these atoms than is released. However, if the star has initially been truly massive the gravitational collapse can still continue until its density is so enormous — and in processes only beginning to be understood — that one of two results occurs: the original body becomes either a neutron

21

star, whose gravity is so intense that electrons and protons are forced to fuse together into neutrons,[37] or a black hole whose yet greater gravity is so enormous that even massless particles like photons traveling at the speed of light cannot escape.[38] Neutron stars still shine; black holes do not. Out of this whole panoply of stellar phenomena, our Sun emerges as an average-sized yellow star roughly halfway through its 10-billion-year life span, whose mass is apparently sufficient to trigger helium to carbon ignitions but no further ones. It will eventually become a white dwarf, many times smaller than its current size, burn at this stage for billions of years, and then end its life as a cold cinder (in chapter 4 I will give further details of this process). Because of its composition, we are fairly sure that it is at least a second-generation star, meaning that in its own formation it gathered small traces of elements other than hydrogen and helium from stars that exploded before it.

One thing more needs to be said before we conclude this section. It is that before the Sun reaches its final development as a white dwarf it will have undergone an intermediate stage in which it will bloom into a red giant. This stage is critical because in the half hour or so in which it is reached the diameter of the Sun will expand beyond the orbit of the Earth. At this point the planet will be seared of all life and massively re-arranged in its contours. It is true that this will not occur for about an-other 5 billion years, and for that reason seems to many to be a fact of a ridiculously small degree of pertinence. But it is nonetheless an inevita-bility, and the Promethean mind always takes regard of inevitabilities. This is the type of mind identified with the epic hero of Greek mythol-ogy, Prometheus, whose name means "forethought." Kant may have ar-gued in the details of his logical empiricism that inherent to the cog-nitive process itself are boundaries that limit the rationally secure knowledge available to us.[39] And we know that classic Christian tradi-tion, too, has recognized these boundaries, though as already noted usually ascribing them more theologically to the mind's blighting from sin and fallenness. Still other factors, less speculative and more direct, may condition the limitation of thought: genetic inheritance, disease, accident. And there can also be a *deliberate* limiting of thought — the kind we will discover when examining the narcissistic temperament in the next chapter — that steadily refuses to extend one's experiences so as to produce new ideas or doubts about old ones. Yet to these may be added one further limit that makes all of them secondary because it establishes an absolute boundary not just to thought but to life itself on Earth. That limit is reached when the Sun goes red.

This last fact is sobering. It spells the death of all illusions that the Earth of itself, beautiful, bounteous in life, self-regenerating, wed to a reliable star, will continue forever. It spells the demise of the Earth as goddess, the final disenchantment in that whole series that began in ancient Greece and continues to this day. If the natural limit of the Earth's life is to be breached by us, not in the unanchored longings of a naive theology but in the hard reality of a science that alone has the prospect of contending effectively with the results of solar evolution, then theology, again, finds itself in need of science as a partner. For if we are to assure our continued survival — and just as importantly, that of other earthly life-forms — we need to be somewhere else before the Sun goes red, off this planet and on another one circling another star (and by "we" I mean those living forms we have genetically engineered to be our survivors or into which we ourselves have altered from genetic mutation, since it is unlikely that eons hence we will be biologically the same as we now are).[40] Other options might include the development of technologies capable of either moving the Earth itself, adequately protected for such a journey, or, if we were unable to do this, enwrapping it in a shielding mantle safe from the Sun's explosive power, with machineries generating the heat and light we need. Barring these three options, there remains the construction of some large, artificial habitat, or series of them, with similar machineries and safely distanced.[41] Otherwise nothing can provide us with the "new Earth" of which Christian apocalypticism speaks (Revelation 21:1), or keep us safe at home on this one when the Sun detonates. The ancient seer who spoke the words in a vision of the world's end, that the moon had turned to blood (Joel 2:31), was thus closer to the literal truth than he could have ever known. For in that time when the Sun turns red, our small companion, its light not its own but a reflection of the Sun, will turn red too, red as blood. But unless he or she views it from another planet, some artificial habitat, a competently transported or an unmoved but elaborately protected Earth, no one will actually see the vision come true, or if they do, the sight will last but a second's fraction. Unlike the seer's final advice, then, that we turn the future completely over to God's good providence, we prefer instead a more realistic theology born in the awareness that God tends to turn things back to us; that deity is a reliable presence seeking the cherishing of life in creation but generating a freedom that also requires life to do what it needs to cherish itself and, in our case, all else that is alive.

Let me conclude this section by noting that with the obvious and singular exception of the Sun, the stars are quite useless to us, if by usefulness we mean the capacity to directly assist or enhance our physical well-being. They provide neither enough light nor warmth to grow our food; all of them together in a clear night sky cannot nurture even a single plant. Nor, to the extent we can currently detect, do they contribute anything to geologic, tidal, or atmospheric conditions on the Earth. They cannot warm our bodies, and no matter how much magnifying power we use, they will not start a fire from dry paper. On the other hand, in earlier days they did provide guides to travelers, particularly mariners, in their journeys. But in these pages we are not really concerned with the stars as they do or do not directly assist our physical well-being. We are concerned with them, rather, in these other two ways: as they help increase our knowledge of the universe in which we live — we must dare to extend our notion of "home" beyond the confines of this planet and even this solar system — and as they nourish our need for intellectual excitement and beauty. It is the beauty that has been of special concern to me, since I believe that before we can passionately seek the truth or goodness of any experience — those two companions to beauty which the Greeks held in special reverence — we must first perceive the experience as beautiful, whether it be of God, a tigress, a tree, a human being, or the stars in the night sky. For it is the perception of the beauty of an experience that is the impelling force which drives us to seek the true things we can say of it and the goodness within it.

❉   ❉   ❉

FOR A NUMBER of years now I have kept several file folders of photographs and imaginative though fact-based illustrations of various galaxies. I am most enchanted by our own, the Milky Way, and one of our near neighbors, the Andromeda. Both are spiral galaxies, thick and bulbous at the center, then swirling their stars out from this center in magnificent curved arm formations.[42] Our Sun is in one of these arms, roughly two-thirds of the way from the galaxy's center. Like all others, the Milky Way is composed of huge numbers of individual stars, 100 billion by the best estimates, and is one of 100 billion galaxies in the observable universe. The fact that our Sun is just one of these stars in one of these galaxies prompts in us the kind of humility I mentioned at the beginning of this chapter, as well as the preying thought that with so many stars in so many galaxies perhaps there is planetary life elsewhere in our universe, a topic that will occupy us in chapter 3. There are other shapes besides spirals which galaxies take. There is the famous sombrero galaxy, which from the perspective of our observations looks exactly like its namesake. There are many ball-shaped galaxies, and some that look like dinner plates. Many, too, have no clearly identifiable shapes, being mere collections of stars relating gravitationally to each other. But for me the most spectacular of them all are the spirals. Perhaps the reason for this is that they share a shape similar to that of an Earth-bound form of life which, whenever I see it, gives me special and continual pleasure. I will return to this in a moment, after a small interlude.

With so many galaxies clearly populating the universe, it may come as a surprise that their existence is considered by cosmologists one of the major conundrums in their science. There are a number of issues involved, but two stand out. The first centers around the seeming fact that not enough time has elapsed since the origin of the universe for galaxies to have formed on such massive scale as we observe, since the primary cause of this formation, gravity, is a very slow-acting influence on bodies of mass, especially when these are traveling apart from each other at the enormous speeds instigated by the big bang. The second issue centers on the observation that galaxies tend to clump together in large numbers, with vast amounts of space between them, whereas the expectation is that they should be much more evenly distributed due to the presumed uniformity in space and time of the primordial particle(s) at the moment of the big bang and the uniformity of energy released in the explosion itself. I bring these issues up not just because they are interesting in themselves but to illustrate once more something we find over and over again in the history of science, as in other areas of creative advance: insight can resolve the most intractable problems by suddenly reducing them to the simplest of concepts or, sometimes, the simplest of images. The concept I am referring to in our current context is that of inflation, and its original formulator is one of the most creative scientific minds living today, Alan Guth. He himself tells us of the abruptness of his insight while worrying the above problems on and off for long periods of time; suddenly one night he saw their resolution in the simple expedience of an inflationary period shortly after the big bang in which the universe rapidly grew from about a trillionth the size of a proton (10^{-25} centimeters) to roughly 30 feet across. The specifics providing this growth are too complicated to go into here,[43] but the growth itself was almost instantaneous and, given the scales of size within which it operated, almost unimaginably gigantic.[44] The theory he subsequently elaborated on the basis of his insight has not met with universal approval and has been amended several times. But it appears for now that the insight itself provides the most satisfying handle on the aforementioned problems. It provides rapid enough expansion early enough to account for the time needed for galaxy formation. And once amended[45] it allows for fluctuations or "wobbles" during the inflation that produced a bundling effect permitting the subsequent clustering of the galaxies. Like so much that we experience, the mere givenness of galaxies does not provide us with a rationale for why they are there. The givenness of things can issue in but one intellectually competent response: acceptance. It is seeking their rationale, especially in how that rationale relates to other, better known experiences, that extends this competence into the work of creative imagination and insight. While he doesn't mention it, for Guth — or anyone else — a phenomenon such as the sudden expansion of a balloon when we first blow into it might be the common experience producing a magnificent insight into the origins of galaxies.[46]

Let me now return to the spiral galaxies and the thoughts suspended by the previous paragraph. My dearest friend is a gardener by avocation. He has two fairly large parcels of land behind his apartment, and on them he grows only one type of flower: dahlias. The dahlia is probably one of the least known cultivated flowers in this country. Many people have heard the name but have never actually seen the flower. They don't know what they're missing. I'm talking here about the large, not the small varieties, the latter looking very similar to chrysanthemums. Their appeal comes from the array of solid and double-hued colors they possess, sizes that range in the neighborhood of 8 to 18 inches, and above all, for me, the most intriguing of shapes. And the dahlia I favor most (coincidentally to these reflections) is the one called Bright Star. It is a lovely light shade of orange, the plant standing about 5 feet high, and the flower reaching a diameter of about 8 to 9 inches. The flower itself is remarkable. The petals remain tightly rolled, and at the center they are short and numerous, forming a thick, somewhat spherical cluster. The outer petals, though, are quite long and array themselves around the center in a spiral fashion. The first thought I had the first time I saw Bright Star was that I was looking at a three-dimensional rendition of our own Milky Way, represented in my friend's garden in a living way I had nowhere seen before. I remember being entranced, staring at the flower for a good 20 minutes, with the recurring and strengthening thought: linkages.

As I have described them, these linkages are first and most obviously aesthetic; the objects linked share beauty in common. But they are also physical. This idea still surprises many, even though science has been comfortable with it for decades. It is not to say that the dahlia and the galaxy have a direct link to each other in the sense of a string of intermediate but discernible objects between them. It is that there are fields of force (or influence), especially electromagnetic and gravitational ones, that permeate the universe so thoroughly that what happens in one place can have effects in another place hugely distant from it. In fact, many scientists are comfortable with the idea that *anything* happening *anywhere* in the universe must to some degree have an effect on anything happening anywhere else. The fields guarantee this in a type of "rippling" movement continually stimulated in them by the activity of matter or energy traveling from its source point outward in all directions, somewhat like the intermingling waves when you and a friend simultaneously throw two stones in a still pond. Aristotle is sometimes thought to have had a similar idea in his notion of the "aether" that pervaded the universe.[47] But Aristotle's aether was a physical quantity, like a very thin, invisible blanket on which objects and motions travelled from place to place. The fields of contemporary science, however, are composed of quanta or "packets" of energy whose presence is immaterial but detectible in its effects. Also, in Aristotle's aether the objects had to be in relatively close proximity to each other to produce a mutual influence before it disappeared with time and/or distance. In the fields, on the other hand, this influence is transmitted electromagnetically by the massless particles we call photons and gravitationally by the massless ones called gravitons,[48] both of which are virtually impervious to time or distance in their effects, though circumstances like collisions can alter their amounts of energy and thus the formats they can take. As we will note in chapter 4, it is considerations like these that underlie recent chaos theory, whose classic example is the butterfly flapping its wings in Bolivia causing a windstorm in New York. The fundamental insight of this theory, however, was known to poets well before its birth in scientific analysis, as with Francis Thompson when he wrote hauntingly in *The Mistress of Vision,* "Thou canst not stir a flower/Without troubling a star." A beautiful ecological awareness can be born from these fields, this chaos, a sense of the wholeness of all things contributing to each other in motion, duration, novelty, and relationship, those very characteristics we earlier suggested as defining a new understanding of life that includes the whole of creation.

In the Spring my roses bloom. They are not as spectacular as the dahlias, but I find their velveteen petals and the flush of their colors very appealing. On the other hand, the rose is also one of the most senseless members of flowerdom. It attracts countless insects and viruses to itself without defense (the thorns don't help at all in defending against the pests I have in mind, like aphids and earwigs and red spider mites), and it never has sense enough to know when the blooming season has ended. Those of you who keep roses know what I mean. However, what I think I like about the rose as much as the texture and color of the petals and the fact that it is a fairly early bloomer here in the Pacific Northwest, is that the mature bud moves so rapidly into becoming the flower. I have known it to happen in the course of a morning. Whenever I experience this, my thoughts sometimes turn again to the universe — not just a segment of it like a spiral galaxy, but the whole of it, the universe in its entirety — and specifically, how it began.

The study of cosmogony is a subtype of cosmology, which is the study of all dimensions of the universe as we currently know them. Specifically, cosmogony deals with the origin of the universe. Ancient accounts of this origin are fascinating to study, though they all fit into surprisingly few categories. The fundamental intent of all of them is to describe a cause-and-effect sequence that issues in the world we know but whose initiating event or agent is merely stated as existing. In none of them do we find unambiguously the idea of a creation out of nothingness; where it exists, it comes later as a philosophical embellishment on the older narratives (we shall deal in a subsequent chapter with this notion in its Judeo-Christian dress). The most ancient of these accounts, of course, and probably the ones still most widespread among people, are mythic/religious in orientation.[49] Sometimes the religious element is fairly well hidden, as in collections of tales that speak of a cosmic egg from which the world hatches, or a primordial womb from which it is born, or an ancestor who fished its various parts out of a turbulent sea. Other accounts, however, are built prominently upon the belief in a god or goddess, or group of deities, whose actions bring about the universe's creation (for most ancient peoples, of course, the universe was effectively the Earth and its immediate celestial neighbors seen by unaided eyesight). Of these there are four general types. The first is perhaps best illustrated from ancient Mesopotamia and involves the specific activity of deicide. Marduk, the good god, enters into battle with Tiamat, the evil goddess pictured as a cosmic serpent. Since we know something of ancient peoples, and the "lean" of their psychology, we know immediately who will win this battle; our distant ancestors abhorred the thought that evil might finally triumph over good. And so Marduk prevails. And in an act of savage victory, he dismembers Tiamat, differing parts of the serpent's body becoming various parts of the universe as it was then conceived: her textured skin becomes the land with its mountains and valleys; her body fluids become the waters of the world; her one eye becomes the Sun, the other the moon; and from her soft, malleable liver human beings are formed. An interesting effect of this rendition is the implicit ethical judgment that the universe, especially ourselves within it, having been created from what was evil, is by nature evil.

In the second type the activity is set within the context of a hierogamy. Here, instead of an act of violence being the source of creation, it is an act of love. A hierogamy is a holy marriage (the literal translation of the word) between a god and goddess whose children compose the universe we experience. Thus, a tree is never just a tree, for as the child of deities there is something of them — something of the divine — in it; so too with rivers and mice, jasmine plants, cats, pelicans, and human beings. This portion of divinity the whole of creation shares is what long and varied traditions typically designate as "spirit" or "soul."[50] As with the previous rendition, an interesting effect of this mythic formula is the implicit ethical judgment that the universe, again with special emphasis on ourselves within it, having been created from what was good, an act of love, is by nature good. Still another, and for me far more interesting effect, is that this second ethical judgment has built within it a profound appreciation of ecology, in the sense of an awareness of the sacredness of *all* creation and the relationships and responsibilities inherent therein because of the bequeathal of a common parentage. Perhaps no one demonstrated such a perspective more than St. Francis, and one of the persistent laments among ecologically committed Christians is that they cannot discover a similar appreciation in the teachings or deeds of Jesus himself. There are some indications of a sensitivity to nonhuman life: the fact that he must have clearly forbade his disciples to practice animal sacrifice, since from the beginning it was never an element in Christian ritual, and his respectful use of plants and animals in some of his parables and example stories.[51] But there is nothing we can draw from the Gospels that indicates a direct, passionate concern with the whole of creation: land, air, water, stars, other celestial entities. However, it might well be the case that this absence owes more to the concerns of the early disciples, including the evangelists, than to an indifference in Jesus himself.[52] One of my tasks here and there in the following pages will be to suggest that a number of his teachings lend themselves to this appreciation in an oblique way.

A third type is found in the first two chapters of Genesis. There are two accounts here, and while they are quite dissimilar, I will take the account in chapter 1, composed centuries after the one in chapter 2, to represent the more studied and orthodox rendition of Old Testament reflection on the origin of the universe. In this account the mechanism of creation is God's word. There appear to be two dominant reasons explaining this, both of them polemical and clearly intending to argue against contrary explanations. The first has to do with pride of place and takes the form: even if there are other deities, they are far too inferior for Yahweh to engage in noble battle, let alone in an act of love. The second has to do with an assertion of Yahweh's might and reads something like this: Yahweh is so powerful that all he need do is speak and the universe comes to be; he need do nothing else, neither engage in heroic battle nor procreative love. We may note that the common experience underlying this mechanism was likely the power all of us know words can possess, the way how we speak can create new things, specifically new thoughts or feelings in a listener, just as acts of destruction and acts of love can bring about new things. Of course, in the case of God this power is embellished to divine proportions, so that God's words create not just new interior realities in the mind, but actual ones in the world.

There is, finally, a fourth type or mechanism of creation, and it is also found in the first chapter of Genesis. I am referring specifically to the sixth day narrative and the creation of humanity. Here the type is that of an artist, more precisely a sculptor, and it is the one I myself find most appealing. I say this because built into the notion of artistic creation are certain characteristics that nicely align with proposals regarding God's activity that I will make later in the book, especially in chapter 3 — though at that point I will want to apply them to all of creation and not just humanity, just as other biblical narratives subsequently do. Awaiting this application, then, I will record these characteristics only briefly here.[53] The first is that a work of art is always the expression of a concept that first existed in the mind of the artist; this concept may be spontaneous or unaccountable in the moment of its origin, but afterwards is always pursued with conscious intent. The second trait is that as the work of art proceeds it becomes more than the mere expression of the concept in the artist's mind; in fact, it becomes an expression of the artist him- or herself, and in this may even eventually assist the artist's self-knowledge. The third is that the final work of art nonetheless achieves a relative independence from the artist; it can stand alone and be judged in its own right — much like a child after the completion of childhood can be judged independently of his or her parents. The fourth trait is that the work of art probably comes closer than anything else to the notion of creation out of nothingness, though this of course is never literally true; in the way the artist transforms the material with which he or she works there is something like a new creation where previously there was not. The fifth and final trait is that the work of art is done in a medium other than what composes the artist. As already noted, in later pages I hope to bear out these characteristics in critical ways when assessing more closely God's own creative activity in the universe.

It is also noteworthy that at the end of the account in chapter 1 Yahweh blesses all that he has created as good, thus aligning this narrative with the ethical judgment implied in creation myths based on hierogamy: all that composes the universe, including ourselves, is by nature good. I do not wish to enter at length into the ethical/theological fracas of trying to determine whether we, or less poignantly, the universe as a whole, are *by nature* good or evil. Exquisite presentations of both views have been made throughout our history. I am thinking especially of Rousseau's depiction of the "noble savage," who is innately good because free of the behavioral patterns (particularly those enforced by politics and religion) which make evil actions a commonplace, and then of Golding's novel, *Lord of the Flies,* where a properly educated group of little English boys, stranded on an island and without the constraints of parental or social authority, turn wicked in their behavior. On this issue I will offer only three very brief comments. The first is that I am in sympathy with the older creation narrative in Genesis 2, which I think is more in accord than Genesis 1 with the dominant biblical position: that we judge whether we are good or evil on the basis of what we do, not through a surreptitious insertion into our ontological makeup of some innate proclivity. The second and related point is that only in this way can we be held to full account for our behavior, having achieved proper age and education in this regard, without benefit of alluding to some uncontrollable tendency that robs us of proper praise when acting well and proper blame when acting badly. The third point is that this interpretation frees us from the awkwardness of describing the good or evil we do as a type of heroism of virtue or vice in which we must conquer our own nature. Yet enough of these ethical issues for now. For in any case, none of the creation accounts we have described can serve as a basis for how *science* understands the origin of the universe. Clearly, this is not to say that scientists are therefore atheists; no doubt some are, but many are not, just like people in any other walk of life. Rather, it is to say that in the doing of their science, as trained and objective practitioners of it, they cannot employ the concept of deity as a usable postulate in shaping analyses of how the universe occurred, anymore than an architect would in shaping a building, a baker in shaping a cake, or an accountant in shaping a budget. They bind this usefulness only to what can be materially observed. On the other hand, while a mature understanding of deity requires some sympathy with this viewpoint, since deity in itself is not materially or directly observable, the following caveat is clearly also in order: some objects which science, particularly subnuclear physics, postulates as existing are also not materially or directly observable; instead, they are said to exist because of their effects on objects which are observable.[54] Could not a scientist who is also a theist argue similarly, as religions have often done, regarding the existence of God?

At any rate, when we turn to science, especially astronomy and astrophysics, and ask about the origin of the universe, we garner what appears to be a general consensus modified (depending on the scientist) by some particularities. The general consensus is that the currently observable universe originated 12-18 billion years ago in a massive explosion of primordial matter, the big bang.[55] Estimates of the size of this "piece" of matter generally assume it to be many, many times smaller than a single proton, a dimension where talking about it as "matter" becomes quite ambiguous. There also appears to be a consensus that whatever its size or content, and whatever the mechanism of explosion, this matter fairly quickly formed elementary particles (quarks and electrons especially), with these eventually fashioning atoms of hydrogen, followed by deuterium, helium, and perhaps a few heavier elements (as noted earlier, most of the heavier elements in the universe are formed in stars). How much mass this matter possesses is still a debated issue, with two viewpoints predominating. Proponents of the closed universe theory suggest that there is enough of it so that the universe will achieve a certain size and then begin to collapse gravitationally on itself, ultimately disappearing into a singularity. Whatever characteristics this singularity possesses must forever remain beyond experimental analysis. Nor have theoretical suggestions of its nature achieved anything close to consensus, except to say that its temperature and density are likely infinite, and that when it is achieved all the laws of physics must break down — one of the principal reasons being the supposition that it is utterly simple, that is, there is nothing against which it can be measured or aged, or more generally, dissected and compared.[56]

The second of the two dominant theories is that of the expanding universe, whose proponents suggest that there is not enough mass in the universe, and thus not enough gravitational force, to cause it to contract again. Here the universe will simply dissipate over the course of countless billions of years, breaking down eventually into elementary particles and pockets of energy, ever thinning and distancing themselves from each other in an infinity of space and time — the heat death of the universe.[57] This theory, however, is growing weaker among some scientists because of the continual discovery of new sources of "dark matter (or mass)" previously unknown, like the brown dwarfs described earlier, neutrinos, black holes, together with the increasingly larger estimates of the amount of cosmic dust and gas present in the universe.

A third suggestion, the so-called "steady state" theory, though once of considerable popularity, is no longer considered feasible by the vast majority of scientists. It requires a universe that maintains basic uniformity for eternity — thus, no big bang — and must therefore postulate the spontaneous creation of matter to guarantee this uniformity over the undeniably large-scale expansion of the universe. The theory was finally put to rest, among other more esoteric reasons, when a clear temperature ambience for the entire universe of about 3 degrees on the Kelvin scale, assumed to the residual heat of the big bang, was discovered in the 1960s.

My own current disposition is toward agreement with proponents of the closed universe. To this, however, I would add a proviso. It is that while many proponents of this model suggest that the contraction will issue in a stable singularity, and at that point the universe will end, others propose the possibility that this singularity will in fact be unstable and will explode again in a new cycle of expansion.[58] The question at this point almost inevitably becomes whether or not these cycles or oscillations can continue indefinitely,[59] and if so, how would they relate to each other? The major argument against affirming the idea of indefinite continuation is the law of entropy (the second law of thermodynamics), which states that in time all closed systems eventually become disorganized, breaking down into their constituent parts and gradually dissipating through loss of energy into a type of evenness of distribution — which would effectively prohibit the concentrations of mass needed for gravitational collapse. An example would be a bottle of perfume uncapped in a vacuum; over time all the molecules would be more or less equally dispersed throughout the enclosing container. Another example would be the heat death of an open universe described previously. The only currently perceivable way this objection could be overcome is through the hypothesis that the law of entropy does not in fact hold unflinching sway throughout the universe, or that at intervals in the cycles, in a physics we do not yet fully understand, it is suspended. This is not as fanciful a suggestion as it may first appear, since if physics has learned anything in this century it is that even its most cherished theories and laws are susceptible to qualification or outright rejection.[60] The second part of the question is often answered in a roundabout way by noting that no succeeding collapse could ever be *absolutely* identical to the one(s) preceding it, and so could not produce in subsequent detonations identical universes relatable to the previous ones. But this is really no objection at all, since it is presumed that the novelty operating everywhere in the universe would operate on the universe itself as it collapses and then re-explodes, and that relatability between two things does not depend on their being an absolute identity between them. A *similarity,* in other words, can be fairly expected, since all phases would share something of the content of each of them individually.[61] There would be linkages. This theory appeals so enormously to me not only because it is adjustable to the hard facts as we are gathering them in ways that permit an elegance of interpretation but, more importantly, because it acknowledges the reliable rhythms we find in movement everywhere, from the change in seasons to the motion of tides to the spiraled dance of galaxies around their cores to the human heart as it expands and contracts in the preservation of our lives. I will be taking this notion up again at further length in chapter 3.

The rose again comes to my mind as I close this chapter. Of a day it suddenly explodes into beauty, just as of a "day" our current universe did. And so too, over time the bloom fades and shrinks in upon itself, just as it appears the universe will. But then, for as long as it exists, the rose returns in a newness of bloom every year, just as the universe, for as long as it exists, seemingly will. The rose and the universe, like the dahlia and the spiral galaxy: these aesthetic linkages cause me to wonder if there is not more than mere piety in the old religious myths telling us that all the constituent parts of the universe are the product of a creative love that refuses their annihilation, and in ways we have still to imagine, are all related. This wonder: it will occupy us again, at points with great urgency, in pages that follow.

II

A Therapy for Narcissus

I n Hindu mythologies the theme of the dance appears like a rhapsodic refrain. Great Shiva, the feared and honored lord, does the dance of the universe, of birth, death, and re-birth. It is the dance of grains and granite, flies and the flamingo, of men and women, stars and galaxies, of all that is. This image of the dance of creation is not confined to Hinduism, however; it appears here and there in other cultures as well, and in the musings of poets.[1] Yet circulating beneath all of them is the question of the nature of this dance. Is it like a minuet, with all the movements carefully planned and expected, or is it more like a free-style dance, where you are never quite sure of what will happen next? Some insist that it is indeed like a minuet; they wish for what happens in the universe to be predictable and well-ordered. Otherwise the dance is not entertaining but too easily becomes a dance macabre. Others, though, take delight in unpredictability, and wish to be entertained in the manner of a free-style performance. I am in the latter category, even though I am often able to appreciate the appeal of neatly programmed movement, such as the chiming of a clock or the risings of the Sun and moon. I think it is the suddenness of the unexpected that grounds its appeal for me, like knowing that a man sitting for months upon a mountain in Chile suddenly witnesses the supernova explosion of a star in the Great Magellanic Cloud — such as happened in 1987.[2]

You are that man. Your theory, of course, has predicted that supernovas occur, but you also know that the most recent record of one goes back to Johannes Kepler, who died in 1630, and its reliability has often been questioned. And there you are, on this devastatingly lonely and cold mountain, with a somewhat aged and battered telescope, and you are the first to report what no one has seen in over 350 years. We can all gain at least a glint of that man's excitement, when what had not been there before suddenly appeared in the night sky.

These supernovas: I have isolated them as an example of the unexpected because their occurrence is essential to the development of biological life as we know it, and the one observed in 1987 settled most suspicions that even the great Kepler did not really see one, but something else — perhaps a closer, smaller, and less critical explosion called a nova. But on that friendless mountain in 1987 the theory that such monstrous detonations happen was confirmed in a way that the rest of history can never doubt. They occur only in the evolution of stars possessing several times the mass of our Sun, and result from the intense gravitational compaction of this mass until a point of such enormous pressure and temperature is reached that they explode. Intense electromagnetic radiation is produced, much of it in the form of light, and it scatters quickly and far from the originating star. In fact, so much light is produced that for a while the supernova is brighter than whole galaxies, increasing in brightness a hundred million times in a matter of days and maintaining this brightness for a month or more. It illuminates the dust and gases it swiftly passes through in sometimes startling and beautiful ways,[3] as with the Crab Nebula that resulted from a supernova observed by Chinese astronomers in 1054. What remains of the parent star is still disputed among scientists, although the center of the Crab Nebula indicates that pulsars are strong contenders. These are densely packed and rapidly spinning neutron stars whose spin produces a lighthouse effect of exquisitely precise radio pulses, so precise that they are the most perfect clocks known to us.[4] But it is what does *not* remain that justifies the previous statement about supernovas being essential to biological life as we know it. For under the influence of the tremendous gravity the parent star produces, the simple elements of hydrogen and helium found in all stars compact even further into heavier elements that must also be present for biological life to occur, such as carbon, magnesium, and oxygen. While less massive stars might also produce these elements, they tend to remain locked in the stars' interior because the smaller mass cannot compact far enough — build up enough pressure and temperature — to explode these interior regions into space. The stars that can do so, producing huge clouds of these elements to roam through the universe, thus become the seedbeds of biological life as these elements are gradually gathered together to form still other stars, such as our own, and their retinue of attendant planets. A geologist friend tells me that the gold you might find pan-sifted from a stream of running water may have partly originated in the interior of the Earth, propelled upwards by volcanic or tectonic action, but most of it is from stars grown heavy and old elsewhere in the universe, and then in a final heaving sigh sharing themselves with the likes of us. I will be returning to some of these phenomena (supernovas, neutron stars, the production of carbon, etc.) and the physics underlying them in later pages.

But there are far more common events that occur in the night sky which can cause a similar, if not as rare, excitement as supernovas. Many times, for example, I have seen meteor showers, when small chunks of matter enter our atmosphere, sparkle for quick moments and then dissolve. And I have seen great comets, those lone and long-haired (from the Greek *kometes*) voyagers that ancient minds often feared as preludes to tragedy. I have seen harvest moons and lunar eclipses and, once, a lunar rainbow. When I was travelling far north into Canada as a young lad I was left gaping at an aurora patterning the horizon in hues I didn't even know existed. In the evening I have seen Venus, the small red point that is Mars, many times great Jupiter and, though not its collars, Saturn. And all these I have seen with the unaided eye. Never have I had the benefit of looking through more than an amateur's telescope, though even that experience opened up a much vaster tableau. To my examples many of you could add others. The point is the commonness of the beauty always available, one that does not hide itself in secret places nor show itself only to an elect.[5] And our imaginations, too, coupled with hard-won but reliable knowledge, favor us greatly, for we can create portraits in our minds of still further beauty which our eyes have never seen. In all these experiences, however, much of the worth is for me not just in the seeing or imagining of what is happening, but in its suddenness — not its uniqueness, but its unexpectedness. That is where full excitement is born.

Of the whole variety of experiences I have mentioned, it was the sight of the lunar rainbow that was of particular importance to me. I had just completed one of my books and was enjoying a small vacation on the island of Maui. I had never been to a place so consistently and breathtakingly beautiful in my life, and my contentment was doubled because I was with my oldest and most beloved friend. The rooms we were staying in were on the eighth floor of a building and were situated so that one whole wall of the living room was clear glass and looked over eight miles of water to the island of Molokai. On the night in question we had gone out to taste something of traditional Hawaiian cuisine and had returned after dark. I entered the room first, and before I turned on the light I glanced through the window toward Molokai. That was when I saw the lunar rainbow. I froze in what at first was complete confusion, then walked slowly toward the window and entered a type of rapture at what I was seeing. The experience lasted about two minutes, during which the rainbow faded and disappeared. The confusion came from the fact that I had never seen a lunar rainbow, and had never even heard that such things existed. Later, when talking to others about it, I found only one person who had heard of the phenomenon, and no one else who had actually seen one. In its composition I don't suppose it could be called beautiful; it had the arch but not the colors of a solar rainbow, being rather drab in differing shades of gray. No — the rapture came from the fact that it was there at all; that it was something unimagined that had entered my life without warning and without effort on my part; and that despite its common shape and drabness of color, it was still a rainbow and so carried with it all the atavistic memories of ancient promises between creature and Creator, of Noah saved and blessed. It was within an hour after the experience that I knew my passion for study had shifted. I knew that the person of Jesus would still remain its center — I am a Christologist by doctoral training — but that a whole new context now had to be pursued, one that would take me into partnership with the natural world and there seek ways to apply the meaning of his life and teachings, not just regarding our own kind but for a creation that included lunar rainbows and, surrounding them, the stars. I had been reading that great and luminous master of the New Testament, C. H. Dodd, and I remembered a telling passage he wrote about the parables of Jesus: their realism "arises from a conviction that there is no mere analogy, but an inward affinity, between the natural order and the spiritual order. . . . Jesus therefore did not feel the need of making up artificial illustrations for the truths he wanted to teach. He found them ready-made by the Maker of man and nature. . . . This sense of the divineness of the natural order is the major premiss of all the parables."[6] In short, I wanted desperately to learn what place the divine had in regions of existence that were not human but that could provide the context for a covenant with God.

The ancient Greeks employed a distinction in their understanding of time that might help us here. They spoke of *chronos* as everyday time, the way we ordinarily fill the hours and days of our lives with the simple business of living the way we do. This is, as the word itself indicates, chronological time; its contents are predictable and therefore reliable. But then the old masters recognized that there are also moments in time when something out of the ordinary happens, some event or experience that has the potential of altering the pattern of how we are living chronologically. Such a moment they called a *kairos*. All of us have experienced such kairotic moments. They come upon us suddenly, without bidding, and they are powerful. As such they have the character of what Schopenhauer called an *apercus,* or what we more commonly call insight, that is, an "opening" in experience that provides novelty in how we contemplate previous events or evaluate previous patterns of thought.[7] Subsequently we also become aware that remaining faithful to this experience will mean changing accustomed behavior. Yet because domesticity, settling into a patterned routine in life and not wishing to leave it, is such an easy temptation — perhaps the second easiest, after denying God's existence, which can be done, after all, while sitting in an armchair sipping a martini — this fidelity can be quite demanding on us.[8] So it is, for example, at the moment we suddenly realize we are in love with someone and wish to make that person an everyday companion in our lives. Any mature understanding of what has happened here brings with it a simultaneous awareness that one's life must change, possibly in drastic ways, precisely because it is now being shared in an intimate fashion with someone else. So too with someone, even when religiously trained from childhood, who suddenly understands the repercussions of faith in the God of Jesus and how this must influence ordinary behavior; or someone else whose years of courting music finally issue in a passion that must henceforth control time and energy, decisions regarding how to go about living. Many more illustrations could be provided, of course, and one of them would include a man standing at a window on Maui seeing a lunar rainbow and knowing from that moment on that the natural world must be included in formative ways in any adequate understanding of his God.

There is a sense, of course, in which every moment is a *kairos,* not just in its brute temporality — everything moves continuously from one unique moment of time to another; there is no such thing as a point where this movement ceases — but in what it carries over from one moment to the next. This is usually obscured in discussions of macrocosmic events, where chronological time prevails and the kairotic moment tends to stand out in the way described above. But when it is examined at microscopic levels, particularly the atomic, nuclear, and sub-nuclear, we discover that the easy passage of chronological time becomes less and less reliable in the content it carries over from moment to moment, and that what reliability remains has become thoroughly statistical in nature. We are in the world of quantum mechanics here, where the behavior of electrons, for example, constantly eludes all attempts to predict it. At any moment an electron can move in ways that appear utterly random and, when set within our expectations of its statistical normalcy, unexpected, or kairotic.[9] While usually presented as a modern "discovery," this idea can actually trace its roots back to the "atomists" of ancient Greece, especially Democritus and Leucippus.[10] The former is famous for arguing that all of reality consists of atoms and the void, and that the distinctions between all things derive from the way the atoms relate to each other and then to the void. To afford a greater precision of explanation it was suggested that the atoms are intermittently capable of a "swerve" in their movements that allows for collisions and consequent groupings that explain the clear differences we note among objects in the universe. Normally we can define things with reliability according to type or genus only because these swerves are in fact intermittent, or too small to be noticed, or smooth themselves out as the atoms gather to form macroscopic objects. While clearly many of the details of the atomists' explanation can no longer be accepted — among other things, they spoke without benefit of a modern experimental technology that has divided atomic structure into various parts — they nonetheless seem to have hit upon one of the basic tenets of quantum mechanics. The contemporary scientist, too, will say that swerves exist among atomic particles, though he or she will speak more comfortably in the equations of quantum indeterminacy, but that they occur at such a remotely small level of material reality, momentarily and individually, that they ordinarily disappear among the whole gathering of these tiny components when orchestrating the universe we experience. Only when they do not disappear do we encounter something fundamentally new. In other words, while it is true that at quantum levels kairotic moments might prevail, once we leave these levels chronological moments do, and the universe begins to appear ordered and intellectually manageable. A universe in which quantum effects prevailed throughout would be a madhouse; one in which they didn't exist would never change. Something like this same process also describes the activity of thinking, where normal patterns of thought are suddenly interrupted by a new idea whose effect is to alter the previous patterns. Whether such sudden insights actually result from quantum effects within the physical substructures of the brain, from more macroscopic behavior in cells, or from some ethereal talent within the interstices between these structures — the activity of a soul or spirit — is still an issue of great controversy among theorists both inside and outside professional biology. Such speculation is not, however, especially pertinent here. What matters, rather, is that the general description of the process in both physiological and cognitive phenomena appears to be much the same.

As implied from our reflections in the last chapter, if there is a single *kairos,* a moment that has exercised primordial as well as absolute control over our patterns of existence, or of anything that exists, it is the origin of the universe. And if the theory of the oscillating universe is correct, with the universe continually exploding, growing, and contracting only to explode again, then the kairotic moment in which this par-

ticular universe of ours was born might be only one of an indefinite series. Of course, to speak in this way of a kairotic moment at the
beginning of the universe cannot have the same meaning it did in the
personal examples I gave above. For one thing, we can ignore a personal
kairos; the unexpected insight that insists we change, the sudden conviction of the rightness of a relationship that demands we alter, can be
refused. For we have control over the influence these personal experiences will work on us. But we have no control whatsoever over a universe born in an exploding moment eons ago, save for our tiny bit of it,
the Earth and its immediate environs. There is a degree of fatedness to
everything that exists, in other words. To deny it, no matter how strong
the impulse to do so, always reduces eventually to foolishness. In the
kairos that set the universe on its course we have the most basic stricture
on what we can become, followed by others in a sequence leading to our
galaxy, solar system, planet, and what all of these working together can
finally produce by way of biological life. This fatedness in turn establishes a destiny, that is, an arena of choices that describe what becomes
of anything that exists within the confines of its fate. Here enters the notion of hierarchy in creation, though not in the sense of an intrinsic superiority of some things over others — the way its classic illustration in
the concept of a "great chain of being" usually reads — but simply in
recognition of what I would call an "expansivity" of will. By this I mean
that while all things possess will, some things clearly exercise it within a
larger context of possibilities than others. It does not seem intellectually
abusive, for example, to speak of electrons as possessing will when we
examine the unpredictability of their behavior. Yet it *would* be intellectually abusive if we refused to recognize that the range of possibilities
over which this will is exercised is infinitesimally small when compared
to the range of behavioral possibilities presented to human volition. We
are undoubtedly more free to select a destiny within our fatedness than
electrons are, or, as far as we can currently determine, anything else is.
On the other hand, our will appears to be effective when absorbing
something into a chosen destiny only when it lies relatively close to us
spatiotemporally. When the context is the universe as a whole, therefore, or even our galaxy, we have no more freedom right now than an
electron in the choices we can make toward controlling them: they de-

termine what we can be, but we have no say at all in determining what
they can become for us. Yet as we get closer in from the galaxy, closer in
than even the solar system, we finally do come upon a presence in the
universe quite thoroughly subject to the effectiveness of our will. We
come upon the Earth. And here the possibilities of creating a destiny
within the context of fate — for the Earth still does impose defining restrictions on us[11] — are abundant. I would like to spend a brief moment
on this point.

In the last half century especially, we have exercised increasingly
comprehensive control over the Earth, developing more and more techniques and devices to oversee it. Fortunately, many of these developments have been positive, such as water pumps that can quench ravag-
ing fires, irrigation systems that can make barren soil fertile. But many
have been negative, like fungicides and insecticides designed to destroy
other lives to improve our own,[12] or earth-movers bigger than dinosaurs
to gouge the land for its minerals and useful ores. Most frightening of
all, of course, are our nuclear weapons, those monstrosities of an evil
which is Satanic in its proportions. On this particular issue I myself had
a sudden kairotic experience while reading Jonathan Schell's terrifying
volume, *The Fate of the Earth*. Until then I had thought of nuclear destruction very abstractly. I had seen films of nuclear explosions, knew of
the horrors of Hiroshima and Nagasaki, had heard lectures on the effects of fireballs and radiation. But for some reason all these things remained at a distance from me; I was too confident, I suppose, in the virtue of human decision-making on issues as serious as using such
weapons in warfare. My confidence has since dissolved. Schell's book
also brought home to me, in a way my previous knowledge never did,
the effects of a full-scale nuclear exchange, the fact that when all its effects took hold it might well leave alive only some species of grasses, insects, deep-sea marine life, bacteria, and viruses. His words were so
lively, challenging, even accosting, that they metamorphosed my attitude toward these weapons into one — the one I still have — of pervasive, nightmare-breeding dread. And for some reason while reading the
book a memory from my childhood, one causing increasing aggravation
as I read, kept emerging. I recalled how I was just a tyke in the early
years of grammar school and how several times each year we would

have air-raid drills just in case the Russians managed to drop an atomic bomb nearby. And what did our vivacious but ignorant teacher tell us? "Just get under your desks, children, and you'll be alright." These words: perhaps their deceit, intentional or not, was the catalyst to the dread I experienced as I read Schell's volume. Whatever it was, though, I also remember how I began to appreciate Oppenheimer's sentiment, which he drew from the Bhagavad Gita and which undoubtedly represented a kairotic experience of his own while witnessing the explosion of the first nuclear device: "I am become Death, the shatterer of worlds." In Hindu thought and mythologies, I have said, the theme of the dance appears like a rhapsodic refrain. But the dance can turn deadly when Shiva, its mighty lord, casts a cold eye on us.

These remarks remind us of a parallel often drawn between the power of our nuclear weapons to release energy and that of stars. Both are drawn from fusion processes between atoms,[13] though the energy released in one of the weapons, or for that matter all of them, is barely a hiccup compared to even a microsecond's burst of stellar energy. Our Sun alone, for example, a medium-sized star, pours out the energy equivalent of more than 10 billion (10^{10}) megatons of TNT *every second*.[14] We are further reminded of the parallel by the fact that the universe is a violent arena as well as a beautiful one, and that beauty therefore is frequently inaccessible to moral judgments. Whitehead claimed that the fundamental evil in creation is destructiveness; that we find it everywhere we look, including manifold forms of human behavior; that its purpose is brute, non-creative obliteration; and that in itself it is a metaphysical rather than an ethical category, that is, not yet subject to judgments of right and wrong. Certainly the fusion between atoms that in both stars and nuclear bombs produces detonations, when taken merely in itself, provides an illustration of this evil as two independent entities join, release energy, and in the process destroy their individuality. On this issue, too, perhaps the ancient wisdom of Empedocles is a complement to Whitehead's. The Greek sage argued that two things prevail above all in creation, love and strife, but that strife is the stronger.[15] For it can even overcome love of self, since at a certain point of intensity it can cause an individual to choose self-immolation as long as this guarantees the destruction of the other. And this is as true when we are speaking metaphorically of the self-immolation chosen by atoms or more literally of that chosen by ourselves. This is worlds away from love, of course, where the self-immolation of the one is pursued not for the destruction but the increase of the other, as when the Baptist says of his relationship to Jesus: he must increase, I must decrease (John 3:30). The fact that the destruction occurs as the result of intimate contact is likewise illuminating. When things are far from each other and relationships between them are obscure or need mediation, this very obscurity or mediating requirement provides a buffering element that prohibits direct contact, and so diminishes the potential of mutual destructiveness. Again, this is as true of atoms as it is of ourselves, guiding much of the study of science when examining very small atomic structures as well as much of the advice of psychology when examining the structure of human relationships. But diminish the distance or dissolve the mediation, and the result can be catastrophic. Little imagination is needed, therefore, to picture what is going on at the center of stars as atoms are pushed into kissing distance of each other, or even more at the origin of the universe when all matter and energy was confined to distances the size of a proton or less.[16]

The Bible opens with the well-known words, "In the beginning God created the heavens and the Earth."[17] We are told nothing of what was happening before this event, only that there existed formless matter, from which the deity shaped the universe.[18] The biblical authors would not have made sense of the later Christian doctrine of creation from nothingness, which we'll touch on below and again in chapters 3 and 4, and would have been more in sympathy with what I think is the overwhelming view among contemporary scientists, as it was among the ancient Greeks: "there has always been *something* in existence, since only nothing can come from nothing." At any rate, what we have in these words from Genesis is the initiation of a religious account of the origin of the universe not unlike that of science, at least to the extent that each suggests the suddenness, the kairotic character, of this origin. "God created" gets at this in the religious account; the explosion of an unimaginably dense and hot mass/energy object, the primordial singularity, gets at it in the scientific account. There is also nothing in the biblical tradition that would prevent the deity from bringing this universe to an end and replacing it with another, over and over again, by the deity's own, ineluctable will, or what in scientific jargon we have been describing mechanistically rather than voluntaristically as an oscillating universe. In fact, I would argue, there is much to suggest just such a possibility. Furthermore, at least within Judeo-Christian tradition, there is the recurring idea of providence, the belief that the deity is guiding the contours of the evolution of the universe toward a boundless cherishing of life ("life" understood according to the physical attributes we gave it in the last chapter, so as to include everything that is) with an understandable if questionable emphasis upon that segment which we ourselves are. Combining all three of these observations — on the origin, recurrence, and life of the universe — finally brings us, therefore, to a second and for our purposes concluding difference between personal kairotic experiences and the kairotic event that initiated the universe. For we can now say on the basis of our small excursus into religious tradition as it greets contemporary science that not only can we not refuse the originating event of the universe — we cannot refuse the fact *that* it happened, in the way we can a personal kairotic experience — we also have no control over *how* this origin is unfolding in space and time,[19] as we do over the effects we allow a personal kairotic experience to exercise in the evolution of our lives.

Because it has intermittently played an influential role in the structuring of Christian theologies, we should perhaps attend to some further brief comments on the idea of *creatio ex nihilo* before closing this section. We have already noted that it appears to have emerged primarily to safeguard the unique dignity of God, the concern being to avoid all notions that there was anything co-infinite with God upon which God was dependent to work divine will. This was a noble and reverential gesture to make, and we should certainly honor its historical influence. But as we said, it always collides eventually with the fundamental perception — one seemingly innate in human consciousness — that from nothing, nothing can come.[20] The choices in this situation can be generally reduced to two. We can say that there must indeed have been something co-infinite with God, however amorphously described, upon which God acted in creating the universe: something like what preceded the initial conditions that generated the big bang. Or we may say that it is from the divine itself that the universe emerged. This second is the choice I would make, though it requires some readjustments in very old and much esteemed conceptual preferences regarding divine nature, such as its utter simplicity, impassibility, and non-partakability, and certainly goes against all methodologies insisting that what we can say of God can only be said in negatives (e.g., God cannot be a physical body, God cannot be limited in space or time, and so on) since there is much that can be said affirmatively about the universe. Yet in working out this second option we also discover that at some point it must inevitably merge with the first, in the sense that what we say of the universe and what provided its initial conditions we now say not of something distinct from God but of the divine itself. The divine, for example, must have within itself infinite energy, the capacity to persuade it in particular ways, and the ability, as their source, to remain within the relationships that evolve from these particular ways that energy is persuaded. Matter, of course, is one of the forms these persuasions of energy take, in accord with Einstein's energy/mass equivalence equation. As noted in the previous chapter, this is not a pantheism that I am recommending. I am not saying that God *is* the universe, but only that in the relationships constituting it — between photons, quarks, electrons, atoms, molecules, etc. — there is always something of the presence of their origin. A scientist would find this description more congenial by speaking of the singularity underlying the events that produced the universe, and whose presence continues, though deeply subliminal, in all that is. Also: as with the nature of the singularity, which is impenetrable because the laws of physics break down at its doorway, so with God's nature, with regard to the laws of logic governing the certainties of our reasoning minds. Or to put it more succinctly: God and the singularity can be known only in their effects, not in themselves. Or more briefly still, and with due caution: God and the singularity are epistemologically synonymous terms. The singularity, in other words, is not a particular object, anymore than God is. Rather, it is always what lies further than we can seek in determining with completion and exact certainty the origin of the universe. This epistemological stance — what we can know — thus provides a metaphysical barrier to God and/or the singularity that separates them from everything else that is. To confront this separation, then, cannot gain us metaphysical certitude — what is, as it is in itself — but only metaphorical approximations.

Here and there throughout the remainder of the book, as already in the previous chapter, I will be touching again on issues raised in the previous two paragraphs, though since I have examined them with some thoroughness in other works,[21] I will continue to do so only lightly. For now I would like to close this section by simply noting once again that we can learn many things looking into the night sky, and what we see can lead to trains of thought not only about the universe we inhabit, but also about ourselves, and about God. In the foregoing reflections I have briefly followed one of my own trains of thought when contemplating what the poet Charles Péguy called "the speckled heavens," the one that has often led me to questions about the source of what I am seeing. But there are many more thoughts as well, and in these pages it is my purpose, and good fortune, to share some of them with you. But they are all based on the singular experience of wonder when I lift my head and look at the stars mantling the Earth. And one of the things I wonder about is why other people do not take the same delight in this experience as I do.

NARCISSUS IS the person who does not look into the night sky and wonder. Narcissus: the name given the youth in the famous myth Ovid records in his *Metamorphoses*. He is born beautiful beyond telling, and as he grows becomes a rival even to the comeliest of the gods. He is treasured by all, the object of their constant gaze and attention. Wherever he walks conversation ceases, so pleasant is he to behold, and one hopes selfishly that he will walk toward oneself. His effect is hypnotizing; others would willingly do anything for him, should he but ask. For his will and intentions are presumed to be good, so god-like is his beauty and so pervasive the misplaced judgment that what is beautiful is by definition good. The prejudice of all is in his favor. The figure of Narcissus, therefore, while the product of mythic imagination, is not at all unfamiliar to us. Each of us has likely met someone with a beauty like his, whose beauty taps feelings from us which other, less beautiful people do not.

Our history is replete with this theme. Think, for example, of Helen of Troy, Caesar's Cleopatra, and Abelard's Heloise. Here beauty catalyzes a response that an individual otherwise would not make, namely, unguarded rapture of another person, a compulsion to allow him or her to control one's thoughts, one's actions. My argument in the book is that looking into the night sky can have a similar effect, since objects of rapture need not be limited to our own kind. For every Abelard contemplating his Heloise, there is an Einstein contemplating the heavens.

In the response others make to Narcissus we are observing the psychological phenomenon known as obsession. The term has an interesting etymological source. It derives from the intensive prefix *ob-*, plus the Latin verb *sedere,* meaning to sit. When you put the two together obsession has as its root meaning the refusal to move from a position, to want to stay there permanently and to resist any attempts at alteration. Psychologically this means an unrestrained preoccupation with something, or an attention to it so concentrated as to obscure the presence, even existence, of anything else. The object exercises a compelling authority over the individual. In two very important instances this state of obsession may be positively assessed. The first pertains to knowledge, since profound knowledge of any object of study is directly proportional to the extent one allows the object to occupy one's consistent and concentrated attention. This helps create a spirit of docility, that is, a receptivity to the knowledge that wishes to gain both a wider and more intense content than is available to a less involved acquaintance. The second consequence pertains to virtue, since the obsessive state produces a loss of self that is always spiritually healthy when the alternative is self-infatuation. A two-sided caveat must of course also be entered here. For the healthiness of the obsession is directly related, on the one side, to its content. We would not consider healthy an obsession that plots the murder of an irascible neighbor, or one that concentrates on the trivialities of life. But we would consider healthy an obsession with excellence in refining one's contributions to the world. Furthermore, on the second side, the obsession must not be allowed to obscure other responsibilities that also populate the individual's life. An obsession, however virtuous it might be, even an obsession with God, should not becomes one's *whole* life, since the healthy life is always multi-faceted,

51

shaped in ways that procure from whole varieties of experience their richness and wisdom. An obsession that takes over one's life necessarily narrows this richness down, sometimes to a thinness that might gain an unparalleled expertise of knowledge but in the process sacrifices its fecundity.

But there is also a worm at the core of Narcissus, and we must seek to discover it. Clearly it cannot lie in his consciousness of his beauty, the knowledge that he is god-like in demeanor. For he cannot be justly faulted for an appearance that was not his to control: it was a grace, a gift from the gods. Yet perhaps not precisely this either, when we are thinking clearly. It was more like a decree of the gods over which he had utterly no control. For he could not refuse his beauty, as he might refuse a true gift. It was there, a part of him, born with him. He was no more responsible for it, and the enduring response it drew from others, than he would have been were he born clubfooted or cleft-lipped. Short of a willful, blind obstinacy, or a pretentious and false modesty, he could only affirm of himself what he heard all others say. No, the worm at the core of Narcissus lies neither in his beauty nor in his recognition of it, but rather in the attitude it engenders in him. It lies in what the knowledge of his beauty does to Narcissus. For this knowledge makes him vain and arrogant, what the Greek dramatists described as "overweening" and their philosophical counterparts discussed in terms of *hubris,* the pride that invests itself only in oneself. His beauty becomes like a weapon in his hands, with which he uses and abuses others. He comes to exult in the power it gives him over them, the way it allows him to bend them to his will.[22] And he delights in the freedom with which he can afterwards shed them from his life, scorning any further relationship. Does such a description strike a familiar chord in the mind; are we closer to home than we care to admit; is there not a touch of Narcissus in each of us? That he is wrong in his behavior never dawns on him; that he should regret and amend it is something he has never considered. Does this fact make the familiarity somewhat strange to us, then, the closeness more distant, the touch only slight? If so, it appears that while Narcissus might seek to breed in us, we do not share completely his contentment with the way things are, his self-satisfied resistance to a change in attitude. For while acknowledging that at the same moment fate gave him beauty it gave him power over others, we do not fully believe, as he does, that it is his right, even his obligation, to put this power to the service of his self-concern. It might occur to us, but it never occurs to Narcissus, to employ it in the service of others. And so to the saying of Jesus, "I am among you as one who serves" (Luke 22:27), Narcissus, and anyone in whom his breeding has been triumphant, can only respond with incomprehension, or gales of laughter.

The obsession we previously discussed has changed, therefore, from having its object outside oneself to having oneself as its object. This is so-called "classic" narcissism, the kind that has occupied analysts of human behavior for millennia, and in modern times perhaps no more brilliantly than by Freud and especially Erich Fromm.[23] If the first type of obsession leads to self-loss, this second type concludes in utter self-infatuation. For this reason the love it demonstrates is always essentially erotic, not in the usual exclusive sense of sexual but in the deeper sense of a love that has its motivation in self-interest, concerned that the beloved (1) remain lovable according to the lover's standards of lovableness, standards that might or might not include sexual attractiveness, and (2) that the love given be returned at the very least in the same degree and fashion. But in the self-infatuated contemplation of the narcissistic individual, the only beloved that can guarantee these two qualities is the lover him- or herself, so that lover and beloved become one and the same. Psychoanalysts are nearly unanimous in agreeing this is a personality disorder of the severest type, and at a certain point becomes incurable. As we would expect, it manifests itself preeminently in the inability to give love — with its attendant virtues of compassion, generosity, humility, etc. — to anything outside oneself, with secondary characteristics such as the inability to feel guilt and a stylized romanticism used to seduce others into securing one's will over them. The world has no value to the narcissistic individual except what it offers for purposes of pleasure and self-aggrandizement. This is the philosophy of idealism in its worst-case scenario, when the meaning of all that exists is directly dependent on our having bestowed it; nothing has value, or beauty, in and of itself. And yet because beauty, as we said, is so often misjudged as being by definition good, the narcissist thinks that he or she is also by definition good; that his or her behavior is the standard of all behavior.

The typical disposition of the narcissist, therefore, is the very disposition that drew the harshest criticism Jesus ever directed toward the people of his own day — that of self-righteousness, or what St. Paul calls boasting: the use of one's own goodness as the criterion for judging the goodness of others. (The narcissist, of course, will hear nothing of this criticism, convinced from the start that its motive is envy.)

The gods of Narcissus, however, judge his behavior much differently than he does. They are the gods of the Greco-Roman pantheon, swift to anger at human pride, and quick to punish according to the offense. They are the same gods about whom it has been said that they created the universe as a joke, the stars and galaxies as mere entertainment for themselves, and they are ingenious in dealing with Narcissus. Enticed one day to the edge of a still pool, his eyes fall upon his reflection in the water, and yes, in an instant he sees there what all others have seen in him, his irresistible beauty. Like them he becomes riveted by the sight and cannot take his eyes off the reflection; he is immobilized. And thus the tragedy begins to unfold. To be sure, at first Narcissus is delighted; he could spend all his time kneeling there at the pool, before himself in an act of self-adoration. But after awhile he begins to tire. The image that first enraptured him begins to lose its drawing power, and his contemplation of it becomes less and less satisfying. In fact, it begins to become painful, because kneeling there, unable to move, he realizes he has lost control of himself, his life. He has become, like Lot's wife, a pillar of salt, frozen in a vision of himself and completely unable to dissolve the meaninglessness he is now experiencing. By that pool Narcissus deserves our pity; he has looked into his self-infatuation, his too self-centered vision of life, and seen its barrenness.[24] But too late, much too late, for his fate is already decreed, and his gods give no ear to a last-minute repentance. Still breathing, still thinking, still speaking, Narcissus has already returned to the dust from which he came, the deadness of a life too limited in its concerns.

We can conclude from this analysis that narcissism is finally a self-destructive attitude, that it is psychologically harmful in the sense that Fromm analyzes it in his volume, *The Anatomy of Human Destructiveness,* and that its measure therefore is not the degree to which the narcissist is extolled but the degree to which he or she is debased. What is at the heart of this violence toward the self? If we examine Ovid's narrative, the answer seems clear. It is boredom, the enervating condition or state of mind produced when unrelenting and tedious repetition prevails over one's experiences. Boredom emerges from lack of novelty in life, and even the most conservative spirit, like Narcissus at first, who wishes to maintain a set of circumstances as long as possible, eventually becomes its prey. For we are built to receive the new; there is something in the way our consciousness preserves its vitality that requires freshness of experience. This is why rapture or ecstasy, whatever its object, can remain healthy only if it remains momentary in life, a still point or parenthesis in an existence that otherwise must be available to the unexpected and unrehearsed.[25] In this context it is also interesting to note that it was Nemesis who represented the gods in punishing Narcissus. Her name comes from the Greek verb meaning to deal out, and she is the goddess of retributive justice. But in stories of her the retribution typically has a clever slant: the offender is punished according to the character of the offense, so that the boredom Narcissus feels toward all others becomes finally a boredom with himself. Above all, therefore, the myth is driving home the truth that the individual self is not sufficient in either establishing or maintaining a meaning for life that will not desiccate in self-absorption. Perhaps the Greek mythmakers were right, that the gods created the world for entertainment. We find the same idea in Hindu mythology, where it is said that Vishnu created in order to play (lila), though to play as children do — so totally that they pass into it.[26] But if this play is indeed at the heart of creation, it endures as such only if characterized by novelty, regular and robust novelty. Otherwise, as any child will tell you, the play becomes rote, and finally deadening.

Narcissus, of course, represents an extreme case, an exemplar of what happens to any individual overwhelmed by an excessive self-concern or on any solitary concern at all. His life becomes void of a richness of meaning because it has been too singular in meaning. Yet, unwilling to admit that the responsibility is his own, he will blame his gods, his family, his companions, his upbringing, anything or anyone handy at the moment. But never does he blame himself, until it is too late. Contrition, a change of perspective, would once have saved Narcissus; but he never learned its importance.[27] He does indeed deserve our pity — not because of his brutal gods, however, whom we can dismiss, but because of what he is: blind unto death to the self-imposed limits he has set within himself. Furthermore, in a culture like ours that encourages a similar narrowness of vision, where even advanced education pursues a policy of strict expertise that often denies the learner even remote knowledge of anything outside his or her field, this narcissism can become not just a personal but a pedagogical phenomenon. And from there it can become a cultural one. I offer this comment because my own career is that of a university teacher, who teaches those who themselves will one day teach others. Fortunately, I am at a university where an appreciation of a broad mixture of knowledge governs the core curriculum of all undergraduate students, so that they emerge, not so much with a comprehensive as an articulate awareness of the humanities and sciences, along with a more specialized one in their majors. The university, in other words, is catholic in the strictest sense, that is, accessible in its required curriculum to the many ways that human intellect and wisdom have manifested themselves in the best of past and present thinkers. I am not saying that this type of education prohibits a cultural narcissism, since there are many pressures working toward it — especially, but not exclusively, career expectations — but it certainly does not contribute to it. On the basis of this personal experience, then, and in a wish-filled play of the mind, I would like to recommend that from the first years of the primary grades to those initiating graduate level work there be an emphasis on three areas in order to assist overcoming as much as possible structured limitations on how students are educated, both formally in schools as well as at home. The first is anthropology as the study of ourselves; the second is ecology as the study of our environment, from the immediacy of a local habitat to the universe as a whole; and the third is theology, not as a justification of particular creeds but much more inclusively as an assessment of what might lie beyond the first two areas that yet touches human concern, and as a catalyst to appreciation of the role imagination plays in the life of the intellect. In all three areas there should also be a deliberate attempt at relating them to each other, along with an emphasis on the contemporary and historical data pertinent to each as these are discussed in reliable scholarship. Finally, though even in our best schools and homes it rarely receives sufficient recognition, the aesthetic dimension of all three areas of study — how it is they demonstrate beauty as we have been defining it, namely, that which pleasurably exalts the mind or spirit — should be underscored. While in such a milieu narcissism is not guaranteed a demise, there is the strong possibility that it will choke to death on the many foods now nourishing our thought, and then, hopefully, our behavior.

I have dwelled on the figure of Narcissus in the last few paragraphs for two fundamental reasons. First, because I think there is something of him in each of us: a desire to set limits, sometimes severe limits, on our interests and concerns seems woven into the fabric of human existence. It is what tends to give us restricted perspectives and insights, what contributes to degrees of narrow-mindedness, refusing to embrace new ideas or entertain new experiences. I can't imagine anyone not existing to some degree under the conditions of this description. This is what Reinhold Niebuhr meant, in part, by the "fault" laced throughout our spirits, or what Paul Tillich called our "finitude." What we must do, then, is strive to break through these limits, though we cannot succeed completely — because whether by fault or finitude, we are always to some extent limited intellectually, emotionally, and spiritually. And at this point we come to the second, and for me more important, reason why I have dwelled on the figure of Narcissus. For I think he offers us, in what he did *not* do, a type of therapy for partially dissolving the limits of our self-concern. It takes the form of contemplating the heavens, particularly the night sky. I would put it in the following way, adding my own to the concluding words of Ovid's rendition of the myth. For let us say that had Narcissus but for a moment turned his gaze from the pool toward the heavens he would have realized at once his immense insignificance and perhaps been saved from his fate. For the stars would have outstripped him in beauty, and their magnitude would have obliterated his sense of self-importance. They would have taught him humility and powerlessness, that strange serenity which comes from knowing that creation would be as wondrous had he never existed, and that his existence is therefore a blessing. Untouched, unscarred, unmoved by human life, the sky gives wonder and humor to human life. And only Narcissus, or someone like him, cannot respond in gratitude. And so he dies, made isolated and humorless by his self-imposed limits. Alone, he cannot see beneath these limits, into himself, and laugh, nor beyond it, into the heavens, and be thankful.

This lack of gratitude, then: it is the key to the undoing of Narcissus. For gratitude always implies the recognition of someone or something other than oneself, and that this other has acted in one's regard in a way that has produced benefit. It is the recognition, in other words, that not everything one cherishes has been self-generated or controlled, but that much is derivative from sources that lie beyond oneself. Moreover, gratitude includes the recognition that the benefit has been unearned; that it has been freely bestowed. As such the benefit takes on the character of a gift, a true gift in the sense that there is no accompanying demand for equal recompense, nothing exhibiting a spirit of condescension in its bestowal, and no feeling that a disparity now exists between oneself and the giver.[28] This thankfulness, too, becomes more intense when the gift has been unbidden or unexpected, simply and suddenly there in one's life as something surprising — as when for the first time you look into the night sky and are captured by its beauty, aware that it has always been there but until that moment unappreciated. And while there is undoubtedly a sense of obligation engendered here, it is imposed not by the gift's source but by oneself, and reads something like this: Faced with the gift's reality, I must make myself worthy of what is already mine. In this it is like the gratitude a child may sometimes feel in the days or weeks before Christmas. She knows that she will receive the gift asked for; she may even know through diligent spying that it is already present in the home. So, to prove herself worthy of what is already hers, she adjusts her behavior to please her parents. When gratitude does this — impelling conscientiously good behavior — it sloughs its usual status as a lesser virtue and becomes a great one, surely of equal importance to such practices as compassion, generosity, and humility as they all conduce toward a sanctity that narcissism knows nothing of, since it thrives on the conviction that everything one has, one deserves.[29]

I will conclude this section by noting that one of the goals I have for this book is to provide the reader with heuristic assistance in contemplating the night sky. "Heuristic" is a technical term usually employed in theories of education, and it means a method of teaching or demonstration which seeks to lead a person to continue investigating an issue by him- or herself. The book has been written, in other words, to provide a stimulus for initiating or continuing contemplation of the night sky as a way of putting the limited concerns of our individual existence into a broader perspective. For we can find beauty there when we find it nowhere else in our lives, or forms of beauty we would otherwise not experience. And we can find power and purpose there, too, serenity and even godliness when these too seem absent from our lives. An aesthetic which is also heuristic attempts to encourage ways of looking at the universe, and not just our limited place within it, that promotes an independent seeking of experiences that bring wonder, entertainment, excitement, and meaning into life. If I succeed at contributing to such an aesthetic in this book, then the book is indeed a success. So, for example, if you can look some night through a telescope at the magnificent Ring nebula, with its old star at the center surrounded by a halo which for all the world looks like a smoke-ring, and this drives you to discover how such a thing could be, then the heuristic purpose of these reflections has been met. Or if you have the chance to look at great Betelgeuse, the red-giant star in the constellation Orion, and seek to find out what it might tell us of the evolution of our own Sun, then again this purpose has been fulfilled. We can delight in Albireo, part of the anchor shaping the Northern Cross, in which one star colored gold and another colored blue dance around each other. But if the sight does not lead us to further investigation, then the experience remains aesthetic, to be sure — but it also remains sterile, producing nothing beyond itself.[30] We have come close to the trap of Narcissus, not going beyond the immediacy of our delight, and must step away.

❋   ❋   ❋

MY USE OF the phrase "ways of looking" in the preceding paragraph was meant to lead us into an appreciation of the *visual* tradition that undergirds so much of human thought, above all in its assessment of beauty. Especially in the history of religious thought, however, or at least those parts of it with which I am familiar, this tradition has typically been placed second in importance to the hearing tradition. In Judeo-Christian cultures, for example, the emphasis in both theology and spirituality has consistently been on the written (scriptures) and preached word. In the prologue of John's Gospel the divine incarnation is even called the Word. While I certainly don't wish to gainsay this hearing tradition, it still seems apparent that experience, including religious experience, increases in worthiness when a hearing tradition is partnered equally with a visual one. And from days beyond recall this appears to be so — from religion again: when people first began hearing each other's words about the existence of deity, more often than not, I suspect, they pointed to the night sky as a forceful support for this existence, its beauty, and, for them, its orderliness. This was the beginning of cosmology, the attempt to give meaning to the birth, evolution, mechanics, and purpose of the universe. It is the visual tradition that far predominates here, for when at last the universe was able to be "heard" by our machines, it gave back only confusing hisses and whispers, like the sounds of a mumbling person who is asleep.[31]

The key player in this visual tradition — aside from our eyes, though giving them intellectual credentials — is geometry, the study of lines, angles, curves, and the casting of appropriate equations to describe their relationships within and among themselves. By the time of Kepler, and mostly under the influence of Platonic speculations, it was thought that there were six "perfect" geometric solids, and that the movements we observe among celestial objects, particularly the orbits of planetary bodies in the solar system, could be analyzed to explain spacings and order among them. A perfect solid is one whose faces are all identical: a sphere, a cube (six faces, all squares), a tetrahedron (four faces, all equilateral triangles), an octahedron (eight faces, again all equilateral triangles), a dodecahedron (twelve faces, all pentagons), and an icosahedron (twenty faces, all equilateral triangles). Kepler constructed the most amazing models showing how all these solids nested with each other to structure the movements we observe in the solar system.[32] Unfortunately they proved to be idealizations — as much science that derives from Platonic influence does — that simply didn't fit with further observations. It was largely under the influence of this failure, coupled with the enormous success of Newton's later equations describing and predicting celestial movement as the result of gravity, that geometry as a tool for investigating astronomical phenomena became embedded in the study of forces, and thus somewhat secondary in its importance. All this, of course, changed with Einstein, whose general theory of relativity in 1915 re-established the primacy of geometry by demonstrating that space itself could be described in terms of curves because of the presence of mass within it.[33] Space bends wherever mass is present, so that the planets were now thought to orbit the Sun because the latter bent the space around it. In a common image, the Sun is like a bowling ball resting on a stretched rubber sheet (space) and the planets, as long as they maintain a certain acceleration, are caught within and revolve around the dent the Sun has made. Gravity, in other words, is not so much a force in the universe as a geometric characteristic of it; or perhaps better, combining both vocabularies, a geometric force. Countless experiments since have demonstrated that this basic insight holds good throughout the universe; even light will detectably bend in its travels when it passes close enough to an object of sufficient mass like the Sun.[34] The germane point I wish to make from all this is that in his later years Einstein used to lament that he was no longer capable of visualizing phenomena in geometrical contexts, and that this was the Achilles' heel in his theoretical work, especially the construction of a field theory uniting in a single set of equations the then known forces of nature. In short, being able to visualize phenomena, especially those accompanying the amazing acrobatics of scientific imagination, appears to play a critical role in the process of creating, analyzing, and explaining them.[35]

I once had a conversation with a Russian Orthodox priest, during which I mentioned my enormous admiration for Ukrainian and Russian iconography. He was an old man, gray-bearded, with a face treated by sorrow and eyes blinking loneliness. I asked him to explain his religion's history of icon-making. He looked closely at me, almost, I thought, as if searching out the degree of sympathy and understanding I would have for what he was about to say. Apparently he concluded I had enough, and replied, "We do our theology not by reading but by seeing." With these words the centuries slid away for me, and in this old man I could imagine one far older, one of the first cosmologists, saying the same thing. I thought to myself that over the years I had heard many preachers, some tough-minded, screeching divine fury, others tender-hearted, speaking divine love, and in between all the mediocrities. But the words of this old man touched me in a special, a serious way; for they reminded me of my father, and that long ago night when he spoke to me about the stars in the sky. I remembered him pointing out beautiful Arcturus, which later, in a telescopic picture, I saw bathed in its lovely orange cloak, and tears filled my eyes. The old man stared at me, and an atavistic response, not gained from my parents but from my peers and teachers, took hold and I felt ashamed, because men were not supposed to cry. But then I thought: these tears, sad ones for my father who died too young, grateful ones for the vision of Arcturus — they were not causes of shame; they were a baptism by God.

There are three types of blindness. The first is physical, a deprivation of eyesight. The strongest memory I have from my grade school years is the day we were asked to blindfold ourselves for one hour to experience something of what physical blindness is like. We were carefully supervised, but the experience was still profoundly disturbing; I could not engage it the way many of the other students did, as a game or whimsy. I remember two things especially about the experience. The first was the absence of color, and the second was the insecurity of movement, even in a room I knew quite well. This deprivation of both aesthetic delight and confidence of personal safety seemed at the time utterly disastrous for a satisfying, protectable life. Now I know that other senses — hearing, touch, and taste — can develop more exquisitely in a blind person and help assuage the lack of visual pleasure, and that unchanging room arrangements and paths of travel, the assistance of companion animals and various detection devices, along with the other heightened senses, can assist feelings of safety. But still, since that day in the classroom the one impediment I have feared above all others is physical blindness, and my admiration is boundless for those so afflicted — for the courage, confidence, and love of life they so often exhibit.

The second type is what I call "experimental" blindness. The area in which I am most familiar with it is that of cosmology. What it means is that there are whole areas of cosmological interest about which no experimental procedures can be constructed to test theories since it is impossible to duplicate the needed conditions in our laboratories. Of the newborn or dying universe, for example, just the heat we would need in order to generate simulations prohibits evidence for any empirically reliable conclusions.[36] And yet the drive to knowledge is so potent, its need to round itself off in completeness so challenging, that scientists will spend years grinding at their theories to provide what at best can only be tentative proposals never experimentally provable. In this they are close kin to theologians who speak of God. According to some, such experimental blindness makes the work of these scientists and theologians (like the blindfold experience in my childhood classroom) a game or whimsy that cannot be taken seriously; to others, however, it represents a work of intellectual courage, confidence, and love of knowledge that merits gracious appreciation.

The third type of blindness is moral or intellectual. It can owe to simple ignorance, gradually, if never fully, redeemed through education and advancing experiences in life. But it can also result from willful refusal, an obstinacy born of intellectual or moral comfort with the ways things are that deliberately turns its back on novelty. This blindness creates a mind that feels itself continually threatened by alternate ways of thinking or behaving, so that to perpetuate its comfort it must ignore them.[37] While the first two types of blindness, when handled well, can draw our admiration, this third, willful type brings us back to the character of Narcissus, and as such merits an aggressive yet patient therapy. We must strive to open the blind ones' eyes and set them moving.

Nietzsche once remarked that only one Christian has lived since the time of Jesus, and that is Francis of Assisi. Saint Francis preached to the birds and gave thanks to his brother Sun and sister Moon, much like his only (but much lesser known) "kindred saint," Saint Seraphim of Moscow. Both these men understood the importance of the visual tradition, the conviction that deity is discovered and known at least as much, if not more, in what we see as in what we hear. And they also teach us not to concentrate our sight in a permanent exclusiveness, like Narcissus with his image in the pool, blind to all else, but to look widely, at everything around us, to take it all in as indicators of deity's presence. They are right. But even if we are not seeking deity in what we see, or have not discovered it there, the seeing itself can still touch us in extraordinary, even metamorphic ways. I have had this happen to me on a number of occasions, most of them privately cherished, so that from my own experience I can endorse the idea that the wider you cast your eye, including your mind's eye, the more thoroughly you are able to appreciate not just the beauty but the intention of what you see. By "intention" I mean why something is the way it is and why it is moving in the universe the way it does. And then to this perception of intention you can apply the interpretive ability of imagination, so that now you can look into the night sky and see in the configuration of stars whole shapes that perhaps no one else has and which, therefore, are in a sense personally yours. In a way perhaps nothing else does, such imaginative attention proves that there resides in you a spark of creativity. Or you can cast your eyes about the Earth and see a mother cat brooding and nursing her kittens, and in that sight learn more about the meaning of care than all your reading and conversations have taught you. Or you can look upon Botticelli's *Venus* or Michelangelo's *David,* and deeply appreciate for the first time what you have always heard about the grace and attractiveness of the human form. It is the *seeing* that matters in all these examples, and the play we allow it in our minds.

If, on the other hand, our enthusiasm for visuality seems excessive in these remarks, and we sense a needed tempering, this is because vision is also frequently deceptive. We are each familiar enough with this experience. Much of the time the deception happens because of the speed with which things are moving; for while normally successful in detecting the motion of objects, at certain speeds our eyesight is not precise enough to register the lineaments of the moving object correctly in the brain. The object, we say, becomes a blur, or even unseeable. Physical deterioration of the optic system can likewise mislead us in accuracy of vision, as can something as common as weariness. The context in which an object is set can also be a factor in deception. We are all acquainted with those drawings which on a first look appear to be depicting one thing, say a vase, while on a second look seem to depict something else, say two faces staring at each other. It is in the context of this particular deception, of course, that we discover centuries-long repercussions in contemplating the heavens, since nearly everyone was deceived by the same context in which they were seeing things. Two prime examples come to mind. The first is that for all the world it seems the Sun revolves around the Earth; this is what our eyes tell us on immediate observation. The second is that in the night sky all the stars appear to be a similar distance from us, with only slight differences in luminosity. Obviously both these visual observations are wrong; once the grossness of their immediacy was refined by further, more meticulous observations, they were abandoned. The importance of such examples, however, is not in the mere correction of faulty data but in the insight they provide for how vision is to be used if we are employing it to secure accuracy of observation, namely, that we must look at things close up, in the details.[38] This, moreover, serves not just accuracy; it, too, can promote our appreciation of the object's beauty. From a distance a dahlia is a beautiful flower, to be sure. But as we approach it we begin to detect specifics about it, refinements of texture, color, petal arrangement, that only serve to enhance this beauty, and with it, we must now add, our wonder over its existence. And while it is certainly true that in some instances a closer approach might in fact diminish an object's beauty — as when we look at the specific chips that make up a mosaic, or some of the details of the human body — it rarely diminishes this wonder at the exactness of what we are now seeing, particularly in how the parts relate to each other. Vision may easily deceive, but when healthy, alert, and willing to examine closely, the eyes are the primary sensory vehicle to truth about creation.

Helen Keller, a woman born blind and deaf, was once asked which of all the things she had never seen did she miss not seeing the most, and she replied, "the stars." I remember that when I first heard about this years ago, I was quite astonished. I would have expected her to name something more Earth-bound: a rose, a mountain, a rainbow, a baby, a human face. And then, if memory serves, she was asked why and said something like, "because in the stars I would be able to see the shapes of everything else." Perhaps in this her expectation was exaggerated, but the response rings true of what the sight of stars would have let loose in her imagination: seeing them she could have rejoiced in the wondrous contours she had given them, the names she would have bestowed, the favorites she would have selected. This old woman, so bludgeoned by dumb fate from the beginning of life, could smile in pleasure at just the thought of what she would never see. There is a grace here, a costly grace which some of us experience a few times in life, some of us not at all, that looks into the ugly maw of despair and refuses to be swallowed. Yet not just refuses, but refuses with a wonder-filled joy. It is precisely this that someone like Narcissus, impeded not by the frightening absence of sight and hearing in his life but by the petrifying absence of wonder, cannot do. In this he is worlds away from Keller — not just her, however, but even more from Jesus. For the Nazarene saw the wildflowers, the flock, the mother hen, houses being built, the farmer in his field: he cast his eyes widely and in wondering over what he saw gave the world fresh insight into the ways of the Earth and dwellers on it. And while from a different tradition Aristotle tells us that wonder is the beginning of philosophy, we are not hard pressed to find Jesus making this truth his own. For philosophy is defined as the loving search for wisdom, and from Jesus' own tradition wisdom describes the ability to gain from life what one desires without breaking the law. What is this law, this obligation? I am suggesting throughout these pages that when reduced to its fundamental ingredient, it is the cherishing of life. And what is it one wishes to gain from life? This can issue in many responses, but I would gamble that a common element constituting all of them would be beauty. So when gathered together these various descriptions seem to be telling us that wonder is most properly engaged when it seeks beauty within the context of cherishing life. Or that wondering about the way we might cherish life is fundamentally beautiful. Or that cherishing life creates beauty as a catalyst toward wonder. In whatever way we choose to describe it, however, this interplay between wonder, beauty, and the cherishing of life seems always assisted when we look intimately at the world around us, away from ourselves toward all else that is.

It is a commonplace in religious piety to encourage the individual to close his or her eyes during meditation. It is easy enough to understand: visual stimuli can be a major distraction when you wish to become absorbed in concentrated attention. In chapter 4 I will argue this same point when discussing the meaning of obedience as undisturbed concentration on a proposition or experience in order to achieve a conviction regarding its truth or meaning. Where I think the encouragement begins to go awry, however, is in the excessiveness with which it is often taught, so that an individual begins to think that the only proper context for successful meditation is darkness, literally or figuratively. This appears to preclude the possibility of meditative intensity with one's eyes wide open, drinking in all that can be seen, or attending for awhile to the sight of just one thing, like the swirl of a dahlia's petals. There is, in short, a time for silence, darkness, and withdrawal from the world to contemplate our experiences. But there is also a time for a ready openness to all that nature offers us, for being wide-eyed and receptive to those experiences which stay with us precisely because we have *seen* them — and which we then judge to be worthy of further pursuit in quiet and darkness. So as we look among the stars and see Aquarius, the Water-Carrier, the sight is not a picture of a fancied nourisher in the night sky but is itself a source of nourishment to us, bringing to memory all the different ways our bodies and minds have been fed down the years. Or we can gaze at Sagittarius, the centaur-shaped guardian with his bow arched and ready to strike, and begin meditating on the pains we have both endured and inflicted. The visual tradition is served whenever what we see becomes the source of our greatest talent: conscious reflection, and with it, both its parent and child, imagination. The hearing tradition is served whenever we make the effort to capture this reflection in words that affect others. Only pitied, paralyzed Narcissus, seeing but one thing he has ever valued, himself, is left without words, because no one who has failed to look beyond his or her self-concern, the confines of just one existence, has anything truly worthwhile to say.

In almost all religions, then, we find due recognition given to both a hearing as well as a visual tradition, particularly as the former gets expressed in the preached word. This is certainly true of Christianity, which from its inception saw the need for effective preaching, in and out of liturgical contexts, and in the Johannine community, as already noted, even saw fit to emphasize this importance by utilizing the Greek term *logos* ("word") as a designation for Jesus (John 1:14). Whatever else we might wish to say about the meaning of this term — and the history of its interpretation in Christological studies is enormously complex[39] — one thing we may surely say is that by identifying it with Jesus the community was ascribing the highest authority to the requirement to preach well, both what Jesus himself preached and what the community desired to preach about him. It is the first part of this requirement, attributed to Jesus himself in the great "commissioning" mandates toward the end of each Gospel, that interests us here. And of the many things we might note about his own preaching, two relate especially to our current interest. The first we have already described as his reliance on actually looking at what went on in the world about him to draw inspiration for his preaching. The second pertains to his appreciation of wonder. This is perhaps exhibited nowhere more clearly than in his statement, "You have heard it said . . . , but I say to you . . ." (Matthew 5:43-44; the context is hating or loving your enemies). The first part of the statement refers to a well-rehearsed teaching drawn from previous generations, the second to the novel one he is about to offer. What went on between the two was an act of wonder whereby he questioned whether the received teaching should maintain its authority or be replaced by another that he first imagined, then became convinced was more reflective of God's will. So he might have thought something like, "I wonder what the world would be like if we assumed that in God's own activity love always presides over anger, and then made this the control on our own behavior."[40] In a much different context a similar process must also have occurred in the first person who realized that the stars in the night sky shared comparable luminosities not because they were all somewhat the same size and distance from us, but because some were much larger, or more radiant, but much further away. In both cases, one in the territory of Christian faith, the other in that of empirical science, wonder produced a truth needed to guide all future activity in those territories. And in both, too, we learn that we must see well, wonder well, hear and speak well — in whatever sequence they might occur — if we are to engage well this guidance.

I end the reflections in this chapter with a final cue from the myth of Narcissus. The specific sin which merited his gods' anger was his spurning of the beautiful Echo, a nymph who withered away for love of Narcissus until there was nothing left but her voice speaking over and over the lament of her longing. One of the things we might learn from this is that when there is nothing left but voice, nothing but words, there can tend to emerge a monotonous repetition in how one thinks, much like one's echo resounding across a mountain valley, a self-mimicry where one says the same things endlessly to oneself. But sight (including the sight of the mind's eye), throughout the seasons and wherever one looks, holds always within it the possibility of novelty, emerging often with that suddenness we spoke of at the beginning of this chapter. In seeing the world around us, and then in trying to understand it, we recognize as well, often unexpectedly, the possibility of our own creativity, ourselves as the image of God. Emerson's question, finally, becomes our own: "Do you *see* the same truth?"

III

The Breath of Life

Everywhere in the history of human reflection we find the awesomeness of the universe attested. It is one of the two most enduring sources for the veneration and curiosity that have goaded thought to its limits yet have never been satisfied when these limits are reached. The other is God. Even in ancient times when the compass and complexity of the universe went unrealized and its confines extended to little more than the Earth and the airy territory surrounding it, we find this awe. Today it is even more fearful, more curious as the true extent of this compass and complexity are gradually being revealed through our technology. We have already noted its age, its extent, the enormity of its matter and energies, and some of the intriguing ways these are configured. All of them stun our minds, even our imaginations, and leave us searching for words, precise yet complicated ones as in the tracts of science, simple yet allusive ones as in the musings of poets. All of them seem to speak of the smallness of our human ways within this immensity, their final powerlessness should the universe decide to act against us in any one of countless ways. A relatively small meteor crashing our atmosphere would destroy our life,[1] as would a large enough solar flare (or "prominence") gurgling forth from the Sun's surface.[2] Should a day soon arrive when either comes to greet us we could do little more than stand dumb, or scream our impotence, and await our end. Any consolation sought in the idea that for these four billion years life has endured on this planet despite all other catastrophes provides only a weak thread on which to secure our hope; simple thought brings awareness of what the universe could throw so easily at us even if it has not yet done so.

There are some who think that conceding our lack of control over the universe is a betrayal of our talents; when theologized they believe it manifests ingratitude toward the God who has gifted us with intellects that appear boundless in their capacities. Various media are filled with this protest, as if advance must continued untrammeled, or that there are no such things as aporias: points beyond which thought or physical capacities cannot go. The bruteness of this assertion of our talents, though, is frequently little more than a coping device, a way of easing out of our spirits the humility that any recognition of limits requires. Humility has never been fashionable among our kind. And so, for example, we have a proposal like that of F. Tipler in his book, *The Physics of Immortality*. Here the very fate of the universe — not just parts of it, our planet and its environs, say, or our individual lives — is seriously introduced as being in our hands. If we act soon in beginning to populate the universe with intricately programmed and self-replicating Von Neumann probes, cyborg-like objects able to endure environments hostile to us and grow intellectually more adept from their experiences,[3] eventually enough energy could be harnessed, concentrated, and directed by them so as to permit the appearance of a final universal computer — which Tipler calls Omega or the Omega Point, sometimes God[4] — capable of reproducing everything that has ever existed in such exquisite detail that simulation and reality become one, with all sources of pleasure and pain capable of being edited in or out at the computer's discretion.[5] I wish to spare Tipler the harsh comments he frequently directs toward theologians for their lack of enthusiasm in assessing human talents, though he himself blunders into the other extreme, one where there are very few limits to these talents at all. His vision is mildly enchanting in its peculiar way — though sometimes one feels like Alice must have while traveling through Wonderland — and certainly a child of its times. But it represents an obsessive need for control, if not directly then in the workings of the computer "children" we bequeath to the universe who one day will tame its power to their will. For many of us his proposal is too much, an excess that breaches the intuition that the universe cannot be chained in this way, that its nature includes its unpredictability, and that this unpredictability will stymie any attempt to seize an absolute control over its course.[6] And so we look elsewhere, toward more immediate surroundings, more reliable behaviors, to satisfy this need for control.

I know a woman, a colleague of mine, who is a serious gardener. She sows the seeds, cares for the sprouts, and nurtures to bloom the mature plants. The cycle fascinates her, and she is content in being a part of it. Like a spirit let loose in ancient times, she claims this cycle is the closest she can come to notions of renewed or resurrected life — which means no more to her than that there is value in a life beyond its particular expression at any point in time. Furthermore, there is a sense of achievement, of contribution to the world, in finding a flower where not long before there had been only a seed, fragile, ugly, and when left alone unburied and baking in the noonday sun, amounting to nothing. Because of her the seed gains its purpose. It becomes what it was meant to be: a thing of beauty providing pleasure in sight and scent. She is, therefore, the savior of that seed, its deliverer, ensuring that it will meet its final destiny: she, and no one else. This is a luxurious feeling for her. It pulls the sting from her moments of loneliness and provides a small sense of meaning to her life, a feeling of power and the right to call something all her own — sentiments that only intensify when others praise her accomplishment. Her motive as a gardener, in short, is far from selfless. She does not work for the sheer love of the work itself and what it will produce, nor simply for the enjoyment of natural beauty or wishing to give others pleasure by it.[7] It is a work with another motive, one not selfless at all but quite self-oriented. And it makes our judgment of the joy she feels in her garden turn somewhat dark, our estimate of her success somewhat sour. The desire for power, possession, and praise, the basic self-centeredness of it all: these are the blots we see on even the most beautiful and wondrous plants she might grow, the thorns that make us wary. We learn that the converse of St. Athanasius's lovely belief — that every saint keeps a garden — is not always true.

Kept confined, of course, there is nothing to cause serious concern in her thoughts and feelings. Any of us might give them free rein in a garden; they may indeed be part of the personal delight from all the time and labor, the bent back, dirtied, punctured hands and arms, the sunburned flesh that has produced from barren ground a place of beauty. There is no need for recrimination if the individual is here self-affirmed to some extent, taking pride and praise in what he or she and no one else has done. Humility and selflessness, after all, are not meant to be petty; in such matters as a small garden the individual need not confess dependence on others, or lack of power or merit. That would be to trivialize truths better seen and understood in larger, more important contexts.[8] No one need muddy in a garden the truth of our status as dependent beings, or, for many, our lack of power before divine will. It is another matter, though, as soon as we step out of the garden or, to put it differently, as soon as we begin to make the garden an analogue of our life and world, even, as Tipler seems to do, our universe. It is then, as I said, that the pleasure we might legitimately feel in the limited sphere of the garden turns somewhat dark, and the taste of success there somewhat sour. For now we have exceeded our limits, committing the archetypal Greek fault of *hubris* (excess),[9] indicating that the attitude we have in one circumstance conveys a truth about ourselves that extends everywhere — thus stretching a judgment to a breadth broader than it can bear and so falling prey to the classic error of all inductive logic. From thinking that I am the sole master of my garden, I begin thinking that I am the sole master of my existence, that it is entirely within my control.

With this thought, this *excessive* thought, there is marked the beginning of that feeling of autonomy which seduces us into thinking that we are the still point of our world, the final arbiter of values and destiny. With enough effort, and perhaps a little luck, we can be whatever we wish to be, do whatever we wish to do. All we need is that our will and desire be strong enough. For what we are, we assert, is self-willed, not given. And thus the responsibility for what we become is all ours, so that the praise — and the blame, though we rarely think this — is all ours too. We have moved perilously close to the character of Narcissus, for whom everyone and everything else, all the universe, are only players in a drama of which he alone is the creator and director. Yet we must be careful here. We are not talking about a desire for knowledge but of control. The confident and energetic quest for knowledge represents one of the noblest traits of human longing. It is what guided Einstein's trust that a Unified Field Theory could be found for all the forces of nature, capturing in simple and consistent equations all that would allow us to know what impels the course of things. It also marks Stephen Hawking's on-again off-again conviction that at least physics is capable of rounding itself out in a so-called Theory of Everything that would give us the same explanatory knowledge that Einstein sought. Neither of these men is naive enough to think that their goal is to know omnisciently.[10] They do not fall into the Newtonian trap that Laplace did: that given Newton's laws of motion and gravitation we can both predict and retrodict the course of the whole of creation, every particle within it, and to that extent control it. Both are too sensitive to the restraints imposed on such a task, Einstein by his modesty before the complexity of the universe and Hawking by the unpredictability imposed by quantum mechanics. Neither would say, for example, that given the knowledge Laplace longed for, he could know exactly what you will do at 7:05 tomorrow morning. It is not this omniscience that they seek but rather the source that allows for the complexity and unpredictability. Narcissus knows as surely as the Greeks who created and preserved his story that knowledge is power. But he thinks that this power can manipulate the world to secure his will. Einstein and Hawking know the same truth about knowledge but realize that its power resides primarily in its talent for deepening and expanding itself, though even here they acknowledge points of aporia in this process that we cannot go through but only around.

One of my reasons for offering the above remarks has been to address an attitude that has recently emerged within segments of the scientific community. It is peculiar in that it seeks to reestablish the Earth as a unique entity in the universe, somewhat like the opponents of Copernicus, but for different reasons since these scientists obviously know the Earth is not at the physical center of the solar system, let alone the universe. The attitude is engendered in what is called the Anthropic Principle.[11] On one reading of this principle we are told that everything which has evolved on Earth has as its central purpose the final emergence of human life; that in fact this is true not just of the Earth but of the evolution of the entire universe, though not necessarily, some of these theorists concede, of alternate universes, should such things exist.[12] To support their claim the proponents offer an amazing array of data: the oxygen content of the atmosphere (a few percentage points one way or the other would prevent the sustenance of human life); the orbit around the Sun (not too close, yet not too far); the evolutionary process itself (the "discretion" of the selection process which chose only certain possibilities among countless others); the current failure (due, say the hard proponents, to the impossibility) of detecting indications of intelligent life-forms elsewhere in the observable universe; the precise strengths of the four major forces governing matter (the strong and weak nuclear forces, electromagnetism, gravity), and so on. In previous remarks, and in differing contexts, I have already implied what my response is to the ideological uses of ideas like the Anthropic Principle. Most, perhaps all, of the data cannot be denied, or more exactly, cannot at present be proven false. Yet it is not the data that I find bothersome; it is the interpretation, the species-centricity of it all, the ethics and aesthetics it implies. There is something distasteful in saying to the rest of creation that it all exists solely to produce and nurture us. It is saying that all other things are mere waste products — like the bits and pieces a sculptor casually tosses aside while producing his finest work of art — or, what amounts to the same judgment, necessary but only contributing components in the process leading to the evolution of human beings. This is too much, too insolent, the unkind result of a reductionism untempered by the entertainment of other options of interpretation.[13] It puts me in mind of debates over the nature of divinity, such as those between deists and theists at the time of Darwin,[14] whose major result is a hardening of propositional beliefs into mere dogmatism.

This is not to deny, of course, the tremendous heuristic application the Anthropic Principle also provides. As previously defined, a heuristic device is anything that stimulates further investigation; good teachers are particularly adroit at using them when trying to encourage students to pursue a line of inquiry on their own. The fact that we are here, human beings alive on Earth, is the fundamental datum undergirding this application. For it tells us that the universe, especially our immediate environs, must be constructed in such a manner that we became possible. We know, for example, that we would not exist if in the early evolution of the universe stars did not compact and then explode, releasing elements, like carbon, that could only have been created in sufficient abundance under the enormous heat and pressure within the star. We also know that we would not exist if in this process it was boron and not oxygen that settled on the surface of this planet as its most profuse chemical element. The examples could continue, but the point would be the same: from a knowledge of how we are constituted we can gain knowledge of what the universe at various points in its development, as with the Earth itself beginning some 5 billion years ago, must have been like. Such knowledge, rightly understood, is not a means to control the universe, nor to reduce all of our understanding of evolution to ourselves, as if it could have had nothing but ourselves as its product. Rather, it is a knowledge whose intent is simply to detail the way this evolution must have proceeded to have had us as one of its results, with no undue claim as to our relative importance in the evolutionary scheme. For the universe of itself does not tell us what is and is not important; it only tells us physical facts.

Reductionism in this context becomes particularly offensive when it is theologized, when one claims that deity has orchestrated all the needed components to bring us into existence as the only creatures capable of relating religiously to the universe. But for those differently attuned to the presence of deity — those sympathetic to Darwin's sentiment that we human beings have a proclivity to reserve everything important, even God, to ourselves — this claim puts an unacceptable stricture on the largesse of divine creativity, especially the willingness of deity to bestow life, including intelligent life, throughout creation. It would speak far more fully of the glory of deity if life were broadcast throughout the universe than confined to just this one planet. It would also speak more thoroughly of the humility appropriate to humans. It is noteworthy that humility shares its root meaning with humor; humor directed at oneself requires a degree of self-abasement and an ability to smile at how easily we think of ourselves in terms of a prominence, a centricity in the universe, that we simply cannot justify.[15] The hoarding mentality that can be implied in the Anthropic Principle is like that of the little girl who prefers to let her fresh-baked cookies go stale before sharing them with anyone else, or the little boy who meanly sequesters baseball cards without letting curious playmates see them. Perhaps such behavior can be excused when the spirit of possessiveness begins to emerge in a child, but it is not nearly as excusable in an adult, particularly in one who seriously asserts the activity of a benevolent and vital presence in the universe beyond, as John Baillie once put it, our ken and control.

There is one further point I wish to make before closing this section. It is captured in the outrage of the deity's question to Job when Job is lamenting his pain and seeking an accounting of events to explain it. The deity asks, "Where were you when I laid the foundations of the Earth?" (Job 38:4). The question, obviously meant to elicit a response of self-abnegation, is a demanding one since it seems cruel to remind Job in his suffering that his counsel was unsought when the world was created, its freedom by God's pleasure shaping events toward both pain and joy. The silence with which Job greets it (Job 40:3-5) speaks well of the growth toward humor/humility within him, so unlike the indifferent or contemptuous silence, let alone the adversarial response, that others might offer.[16] Yet what the deity asks also has repercussions for how we assess our ability to know the universe. For the inquiry clearly begs the response that we were nowhere. Or more to the point: there is no way we can re-create the universe so as to examine its entirety; it is, in the manner of scientific jargon, an unrepeatable experiment. It is this experimental unrepeatability that provides an absolute limit to what we can know for certain about the universe as a whole, what keeps our knowledge confined to bits and pieces of it where experiments are repeatable and regularly disconcerts our desire to go beyond this. This is not to say that theory is impossible — inductive extrapolations regarding the whole on the basis of what we know of the parts — but that such extrapolations can always and only be tentative. Scientists who lament this stubborn fact, and many do, like theologians who lament that God has never submitted for perusal an exhaustive curriculum vitae, must learn the beauty of the silence of Job.

❀　　❀　　❀

WE NEED TO exercise sensitivity toward the universe, both in how we engage its facts analytically and its possibilities imaginatively. Some of the facts we have already entertained, and some of the possibilities too. Of the possibilities — which will be our primary concern in this section — we have mentioned the theoretical proposal of parallel universes, variously understood as side by side with our own universe, interpenetrating it, or encompassing it. For awhile the discovery of anti-matter particles seemed to support this proposal, especially in its suggestion that universes interweave with each other: for every electron negatively charged, there is one positively charged, and so on.[17] In this context there are also some scientists who propose that black holes are actually exit ports for stars and galaxies which have collapsed in our universe and are entering others. Also intriguing is the suggestion of a Nemesis star, a companion to our Sun which at lengthy but regular intervals returns locally to cause massive environmental changes in our solar system (many scientists disregard this hypothesis, however, saying that if our solar system is indeed a binary system, one having two stars, the second star is more likely Jupiter, which, from lack of sufficient mass, has so far failed to ignite). Then there is the recent proposal of so-called cosmic strings, wispy filament-like objects that stretch billions of light-years in length, possessing, among other things, enormous concentrations of gravity, but whose possible role in the universe still remains theoretically enigmatic.[18] And as a blow to the near sacred ideas that the universe is more or less isotropic (appearing the same in every direction) and homogenous (smooth in its density distribution), there is the growing evidence of gigantic collections of matter here and there — with correspondingly massive voids — that serve as "great attractors" luring huge clusters of galaxies toward them.[19] But most intriguing of all, to my mind, and most wondrous, is the possibility of life, particularly intelligent life, elsewhere in the universe.[20]

Defining intelligence requires considerable caution since it incorporates such diversity and ambiguity of behavior. Yet an effort is required since we have just assessed its possibility elsewhere in the universe as a primary source of our wonder. I have again elected to rely on Webster's definition, with a few amendments to assist precision. The dictionary says: "Intelligence: the power of meeting any situation, especially a novel situation, successfully by proper behavior adjustments; also the ability to apprehend the relationships of presented facts in such a way as to guide action towards a desired goal. 2) The obtaining or dispensing of information." The amendments I would add are as follows. The power spoken of at the beginning of the definition presumes an organ like the brain sufficiently developed so that it can present options of behavior in given circumstances, that is, choices assessed as actualizable. The "proper behavior" mentioned implies a criterion on the basis of which the choice is actually selected. I would suggest that at the most elemental level this criterion can best be described as anything that improves the richness of life; that this does not necessarily include brute survival — since martyrdom as an expression of loyalty to causes, beliefs, and other life-forms actually overrides the survival imperative — but that it does involve a seeking of fresh experiences. The phrase "to guide action towards a desired goal" enhances the meaning of these first two amendments by assuming a teleological component in the definition, or what we might otherwise call a talent for forethought. The second part of the definition presumes two fundamental developments, language and logic, as well as the ability to implement these effectively so as to best achieve the power to enact choices that will enhance richness of life. This implementation, particularly through various forms of technology but also in satisfaction of such spiritual needs as beauty, is perhaps the most elementary consideration for establishing hierarchies of intelligence. Presumed also in this second part is the establishment of some communality between the individual and the surrounding environment. While I would never contend that this description is exhaustive, I think it is an adequate rendition of what constitutes intelligence for our purposes here.[21]

When seriously entertained, the idea that intelligent life exists elsewhere than on Earth is one that generally prohibits a middle-ground stance; it either enchants or frightens people. Frequently the latter group engage in tasteless mockery in their descriptions of what such intelligent life would look like (bizarre), what the ethics of such entities might be (bad), or their possible behavioral patterns in such activities as breathing, eating, and procreating (disgusting). Their ridicule paints images of lizard-like creatures with armored scales and sabre-length fangs, molelike beings living underground, avian ones flying through the atmosphere, and, of course, the nearly ubiquitous image of anthropomorphic freaks and miscreants — all of them at least as intelligent as human beings, and therefore as dangerous. Of course, we use equally disparaging descriptions of each other, especially in times of war: the American Indian becomes a "red devil," the German becomes a "kraut," the Italian a "greaseball," the Japanese a "slant-eyes," the Vietnamese a "gook." Even among ourselves we slip easily into a vocabulary which not only demeans but dehumanizes the enemy or stranger we fear.

On the other hand, there are those enchanted by the possibility of other intelligent life-forms in the universe. This group is frequently lyrical when describing what such life-forms might look like (exquisite), what the ethics of such entities might be (definitely good), their behavioral patterns in such activities as breathing, eating, and procreating (fascinating). If a fantasy film like *Aliens* abhors them, they take immense pleasure in ones like *Close Encounters of the Third Kind,* where the entities are peaceful, benevolent, and sometimes even humorous. They are more like long-lost but loving and beloved family members than the malevolent creatures presented by the first group. And while this whole discussion is not formally endorsed by most scientists, save as sheer speculation done in off-hours, what is important to our present concern is that it allows diverse and playful imagination that can spark wonder, even excitement in our minds, and possibly enjoyable discourse with others. In this, it shares much in common with our discussions of God.

Of course, the only thing we have to rely on regarding the issue of extraterrestrial intelligence *is* our imagination, coupled to whatever pertinent information we have that makes our imaginings realistic in the universe we currently observe.[22] We could become indifferent to the issue, to be sure. But since indifference is never interesting, it is not worth considering. So it is to our imagination that we must look, asking what would be the proper imaginative stance toward the possibility of extraterrestrial intelligent life. Two options have already been mentioned: by any ethical standards we can generate, these extraterrestrial entities might be irredeemably wicked or sanctifyingly good; by aesthetic standards, they might be monstrously repellent or beguilingly attractive.[23]

But I think a more prudent if less spectacular option would be to build our imaginings on the knowledge we possess of the most intelligent beings we have yet experienced, namely, ourselves. In this context one of the certain things we can say is that most of us are neither unredeemably wicked nor sanctifyingly good — though all of us can probably think of some people who come close to fitting these categories — but a composite of degrees of both. We are Janus-like in our behavior, with one face contemplating and doing the good, the other contemplating and doing what is evil. For those with any moral delicacy the clear hope is that the first set of thoughts and deeds is far more frequent than the second. At any rate, if I were to imagine the morality of non-Earth intelligences, it would be along these lines, all the while recognizing, however, that the specific constitution of good and evil might be considerably different among the different groups (what we think good, they might think evil, and vice versa). In fact, it is probably this very recognition that largely accounts for the xenophobia that affects many of us when we contemplate an encounter with a stranger. It is born not so much from aesthetic revulsion at how they might look, nor even the conviction that they are irretrievably wicked — though these can surely play a role — but that what they do, no matter how wicked, might in their own minds be good and thus justifiably pursued. Xenophobic responses, in others words, tap the self-recognition that we too are capable of the passionate conviction that what we are doing is good even when all around us others are speaking of its evil. Such responses refuse to recognize that initial malevolence might be blundering and therefore redeemable and instead see it as indicative of a whole way of life that is morally compelled.

A further issue on which we might also indulge some imaginative play concerns the degrees of intelligence we might encounter, according to something like the definition of intelligence we offered above.[24] There are three obvious choices. The first is that the entities in question might be more intelligent than we are. This judgment would be based preeminently on the sophistication of their technology as this demonstrates success particularly in mathematical analysis and physics. Clearly, for example, if any of the descriptions of UFO sightings are true, we have encountered an intelligence superior to our own, at least technologically. The same would also hold if their minds had developed extensive telepathic or telekinetic or empathic abilities. The second choice is that the entities might be less intelligent than we are. This presumes that our own current technology, particularly in the area of optical and radio telescopes, has become far more powerful and exact if our observations are Earth-based, or that we are flying manned or unmanned UFOs of our own to the home planets of other beings (it strains imagination too far to think that anything biologically alive, no matter how intelligent, could dwell within a star).[25] We might also note that in either of these two choices the entities encountered might require an atmosphere quite different from ours. It is, after all, theoretically possible for life-forms to exist which are not dependent on an Earth-like mixture of oxygen, nitrogen, and other gases. In this case contact would always have to be mediated by a device or structure that guaranteed the safety of the respective atmospheres. The third choice is that these extraterrestrial entities are at about the same level of intelligence as we are. If such contact were to happen in the near future the contact would undoubtedly be made through some form of radio and/or light transmission, decipherable messages being sent back and forth, obviously over long periods of time.[26] In a more distant future both groups may have developed technologies that would permit a more immediate contact. But again, until the speed of light can be far more closely approximated by our vehicles — it appears to be an intractable constant that can never be breached — very long periods of time would be needed for such travel, and if manned, very precise and detailed accommodations for survival during the journey. We have no evidence, for example, that even the star closest to our Sun, a "mere" 4 light-years away, supports a planetary system capable of nurturing any form of life. And the existence of such theoretical constructs as controllable "time warps," "folds," or "wormholes" in the universe which would allow almost instantaneous transportation to any desired locale is still largely undiscussed or dismissed outright by most scientists.[27] All of which means that, save for the first choice, communication with nonterrestrial intelligences, or the discovery of *any* type of biological life elsewhere in the universe, is currently a rather remote possibility. But for many of us, thinking about this possibility is still very tantalizing.

Aside from the theological bias that divine largesse would indicate an abundance of life elsewhere in the universe, there is the brute conclusion of its likelihood drawn from statistics. The best estimates we currently have tell us that there are about 100 billion (10^{11}) stars in an average galaxy, including ours, and probably the same number of galaxies in the observable universe, with a rough total, then, of 10^{22} stars. If just one percent of that number — 100 billion stars — are similar to our Sun, and just one percent of these have planetary systems that include just one planet like the Earth, there would be one billion Earth-like homes for biological life as we know it. Hydrogen and oxygen are the first and third most common elements in the universe; when appropriately combined they form water, and together with other gases such as nitrogen and carbon dioxide they could constitute an atmosphere almost if not effectively identical to our own. It seems extremely likely to me, so probable as to be virtually certain, that of the billion Sun-Earth combinations, many millions of these would also have such atmospheres and so be conducive to life-forms such as those that populate the Earth, including our own.[28] The supposition is that the course of evolution on these planets would likewise show a predilection for the same sort of biological advantages that developed here, with above all a similar development in stages of brain growth and complexity. This is based on the further supposition that evolutionary survivability (in Darwin's ugly phrase, the survival of the fittest) would encourage this type of development in the course of species mutation. While it might come as a shock to many, especially those seduced by ideologies of anthropomorphic uniqueness, to find that extraterrestrial life is a reality, to others of us it would come as a shock to find that it is not.

How communication with such beings might be established we can again only imagine. Some theorists suggest that those of greater or similar levels of intelligence would possess a profound appreciation of mathematics, and indeed that certain types of mathematics, geometry in particular, would likely be the medium of our initial communications. Others suggest music, though they tend to view music as simply the most universally accessible format that mathematics takes. Still others suggest some type of pictoriography. Their proposal is that unless the development of the two groups has been almost miraculously parallel, the differences in their mathematics (disregarding what appear to be certain universal mathematical constants such as the speed of light and some geometric functions in two and three dimensions) and music would preclude these as starting points for conversation; that some sort of pictoriography would better serve the purposes of initial communications.[29] Such a view was implicitly recognized a number of years ago when a voyaging satellite was sent into space bearing among other things an indication of what we ourselves are like by the stylized drawing of a nude male and female form. What aesthetic marvels such other intelligences might have in areas like the plastic and fine arts, architecture, music, spoken and written language, or whether they possess such marvels at all — imagine how intellectually enriching and spiritually nourishing such a mutual discovery of each other's understanding of beauty would be. And imagine, too, the consolation that might come from the knowledge that we are not alone in the universe, freaks of an aberrant twisting of circumstances such as the "hard" Anthropic Principle or any other anthropocentric vision of the universe proposes. At this point we need to exercise both an ethic and aesthetic of humility.

Whether or not there are such things as universal (mathematical or physical) constants in the universe is a fiercely debated issue among scientists. Most wish to affirm that there are, and beyond examples such as the speed of light and certain data and equations in geometry (like pi denoting the ratio of the circumference of a circle to its diameter), they will also cite such hard data as the apparent identity of electrons everywhere, the universal equivalence of mass and energy (Einstein's $E = mc^2$), the predictable strength of gravity between two masses, and so on. While these constants do in fact seem absolutely reliable, a proviso is always required. It can be formulated variously, but each formula would have at its heart the idea that these constants, as John Barrow says, "may be artifacts of the type of representation chosen."[30] In other words, it may be that we have imposed them on the universe because of the way we have chosen to observe it within the confines of the logic of our mathematics and geometry. Or it may be that we are inherently limited by the structure of our brains in a way that precludes our analyzing the universe in any other, perhaps more accurate way. In either case we must be sensitive to the caveat of Whitehead that the laws of nature within which we incorporate our confidence in these constants should never be absolutized so as to prohibit a novel perception of what they represent or how they are to be understood.[31] In this regard it is interesting to note that the very word "nature" is an English translation of the Greek *physis,* whose root *(phyo)* means "to bring forth," and the Latin *natura,* whose root *(nascor)* means "to be born." On these readings, therefore, nature has embedded conceptually within it the notion of generative power, and this in turn always implies that something new can occur.[32] Given this, perhaps those who contend that pictoriography in its visual immediacy is the best way to initiate conversation with extra-terrestrial intellects are right after all, providing the latter have something identical or analogous to our eyesight and the objects it contemplates.

In various theologies and psychologies we are encouraged to appreciate the experience of waiting. In his wonderfully allusive little volume, *Stories of God,* Rainer Maria Rilke tells the tale of a child to demonstrate this appreciation. The child has been told by her father that in the next several days a very great visitor will be coming to their home, and that he might well bring marvelous gifts for the family. The child is ecstatic, and for the intervening days allows her imagination free play as to what the guest will be like. It is an experience of wonder and delight for her, structuring all types of different scenarios concerning what her response will be when she first sees and speaks to him. The day comes when the guest finally arrives. And while he is certainly a wonderful man, the little girl feels a tinge of disappointment upon meeting and speaking with him. The point Rilke is making is that the waiting itself is what is important, and the time it gives her to exercise her imagination about the visitor in appealing and exciting ways. The actual meeting, then, produces a response in her somewhat less than she expected, though she finally begins to realize that in such experiences it is indeed the anticipation that matters and the realm of possibilities it can create in the mind.

But the waiting is not merely a passive experience. It is also active. By this I mean that there is preparation for the arrival, not just in the growth of excitement mentioned above but in external ways appropriate to what is being anticipated. Our little girl would have engaged in selecting a wardrobe and worrying a hairstyle, meditating questions and topics of conversation, perhaps assisting in cleaning the house, choosing a menu, and deciding tableware. On a more profound level this is the type of preparation the first Christians also engaged while awaiting the coming of their risen Lord, the anticipation that led them to an intensity of excitement and a sense of being privileged scarcely met at any other point in Christian history. The child and the disciples are both trying to manifest behavior that shows they are worthy of the presence of the one who will arrive. Yet both understand that this honorable and exemplary conduct is required not only to demonstrate their worthiness but also as a way of expressing an appropriate gratitude for the presence about to be conferred, what it will bring of novelty to their lives, particularly in its potential for joy. Here gratitude and the theological concept of grace join hands, both deriving in part from *gratis,* meaning a favor bestowed with no expectation of recompense.

It is thoughts and feelings like these that I find engendered in myself and many others regarding an eventual encounter with intelligent nonterrestrial beings. And I assert this because of a conviction that such beings do indeed exist — I use the term conviction here as a synonym for faith — and also because the waiting for initial contact itself possesses value. There are those, of course, far less sanguine on this issue than I. Yet perhaps if they allow the experience of Rilke's child to touch the child in them, they too will experience more of the lively excitement which imaginative waiting can bestow. It is such waiting that Simone Weil also speaks of in her luminous volume, *Waiting for God,* and the same waiting that dissipates some of the dreariness of the tramps' lives in Samuel Beckett's *Waiting for Godot.* It is the quality of our waiting, what we invest it with, that is important here, and how this investment not only makes us think but makes us feel. For our cultural idolatry of rationality, having the "hard facts" before giving rein to the freedom of our minds, must be tempered by intuitive feelings which allow us to anticipate potential future realities in the *whole* range of possibilities lying before us, including the one that proposes the existence of intelligence beyond this Earth.

❀   ❀   ❀

IN COUNTLESS theological and philosophical traditions, and especially in mythological ones, we find the idea that deity is the giver of all life, and that this giving is profligate. Frequently, then, particularly in the mythological traditions, deity is described as female, more specifically as bounteous Mother. I myself have no difficulty with this imagery, though I am aware of how thoroughly images of patriarchy have dominated other traditions: it is the Father who is the source of life.[33] I have no difficulty with this imagery either, since gender considerations seem to me somewhat irrelevant to the fundamental assertion that there is a source, deity, to the life we experience, and that this source is unbounded in its life-giving generosity.[34] Yet most of our traditions have also aggravatingly insisted that while we acknowledge deity's profligacy in bestowing life, nonetheless life — at least biological life — exists only on this planet. This basic stance is no different, though the reasons for arriving at it may be, than that of the hard Anthropic Principle. A more consistent position would result if greater fidelity were paid to the fundamental faith statement about divine largesse without attempting to modify it because of anthropocentric conceit or failure of imagination.

At this point a clarification is needed that we have been presuming throughout these pages but have not yet articulated directly. It is the distinction between metaphor and metaphysics. Every reader knows that most of our language about God is cast in terms of metaphor, that is, it attempts to utilize descriptions that literally denote one kind of thing or idea in place of another by suggesting an intimate likeness or analogy between them.[35] The presumption is that these descriptions are more effective because they are more familiar and thus intellectually easier to grasp. A successful metaphor, however, always abides by the integrity of the two terms being linked: that there is something recognized in each that betokens a mutual likeness that is more than just fanciful. One of the abiding tasks of theology, therefore, has always been to continually assess metaphors to guarantee this integrity and to demonstrate the vigor and imagination to suggest alternatives when the integrity appears threatened. This task can be quite thankless since metaphors are often ground so thoroughly into cultural consciousness that their familiarity and, often, antiquity tend to give them a patina of permanent truthfulness toward which the proper response is unquestioning reverence.

This effect can in turn be so powerful that it even overcomes the influence of new experiences that deny the likeness between the two terms of the metaphor. In other words, how one thinks controls what one experiences, no matter how serious the discrepancy between them. I have been implicitly insisting throughout these pages, however, that the relationship should be the other way around: that what one experiences must control how one thinks, and that this inevitably means that thinking always has a certain degree of tentativeness built into it since novelty is a perpetual possibility in all experience. Much of contemporary Christian religion, for example, is distressed because timeworn metaphors of God's justice issuing in hellish condemnation is at odds with our experience of a forlorn and absurd universe; that experience creates an ache in human hearts for a God who never abandons but always embraces creation. The traditional metaphor of God's justice, therefore, needs to change because it offends our experiences. A Christian theology that does not reflect this fact — to say nothing of Jesus' own witness of God's abiding love[36] — is betraying its responsibility.

Metaphysics, on the other hand, is an attempt to analyze an experience or object in and of itself. Insofar as metaphors attempt to say that the being of this thing is like the being of this other thing, they share the task of metaphysics. Yet their respective languages are typically quite different, with metaphysics striving for a degree of abstraction that, if applied to metaphors, would weaken the impact of the comparison. Metaphysics seeks to take the mind away from the incidentals that circulate around the description of an experience or object, wanting to get as close as possible to the defining elements without which the experience or object would not be what it is, whereas metaphors rely for their strength precisely on the richness of these incidentals that link — far more loosely than metaphysics prefers — the experiences or objects being compared. The metaphor of God as Mother or Father is a case in point. Each of us can bring to the metaphor an abundance of specific or incidental characteristics drawn from experiences of our parents; and the more we find these experiences in common with those of others, the more successfully the metaphor can function as a language/cognitive bond between us. Metaphysics, however, might proceed by isolating the generation of life as the defining element in parentage, seek what this generation could mean when applied to divine activity, then analyze the quality "life" such that it describes both the generator and the generated. In this process it might lose the richness of association that metaphors provide, but it gains precision regarding what exactly is being claimed. The same distinction might be made between the two by saying very generally that metaphor is where theology feels while metaphysics is where it thinks, as long as considerable slippage between the two is also acknowledged and allowed. In later pages we will touch on some of the metaphysical implications that our reflections on cosmology in this book might have for an understanding of God. For now, though, I would like to return to the metaphorical application of the theme for this section: God as *bounteous* Mother or Father.

All of us have received gifts, and we know that much of what we feel at the time depends on the attitude of the giver. If he or she is surly, clearly begrudging us the gift, our response might be one of sadness or embarrassment or anger strong enough to refuse or dispose of it immediately. If he or she is indifferent, showing no personal interest or investment in what is being given, our response might be one of shame or a feeling of belittlement. But if the giver bestows the gift happily, we are happy too; and if it is also given without restrictions, our happiness is doubled. We know as well that gifts take many forms. There are material and financial gifts, of course, the kind we are accustomed to getting on birthdays, wedding days, anniversaries, many of the festive commemorations we celebrate at regular intervals. Surely everyone has felt a surge of delight when opening a happily given envelope or wrapped package on such occasions; it is one of those experiences blessedly not confined to childhood. Yet there are also other types of gifts that we can't put our hands around or place on a shelf or invest in a bank. These are gifts like mercy, peace, a sharing of experiences, a sympathetic touch, a reassuring smile, and a common prayer. All these experiences of giving are positive and self-affirming, assuring us that at least in some other lives we matter. They are all at heart gifts of beauty, and as such please the senses and/or exalt the mind.

But what each of them requires as a preliminary is the gift of time. I have suggested elsewhere that this willingness to give of one's time represents the finest expression of the messianic trait of generosity described so exquisitely in Second Isaiah's Songs of the Servant,[37] and that it includes time spent in both thought and action. Within the general context of this book, and now in a specific discussion of gifts of beauty, I am convinced that the night sky ought also to draw from us a generosity of time such that we give ourselves over to activity that will instruct us in its character and compass — reading, attendance at lectures by the knowledgeable, travel to places of clean and clear night air — and then to thought that can alone guide this instruction toward an appreciation of the night sky's beauty. This in turn will bring our thinking, if it has been diligently engaged, back to further activities of the kind that initiated it. And in the whole process the mind becomes exalted. I am not speaking here of the intensity of activity that we find in the professional astronomer or cosmologist — that is not needed — but rather of a persistence that seeks whenever possible to engage these activities out of commitment to the sheer beauty itself: the desire to spend time with the beauty, to get to know it as much as our other commitments permit. An orchestration of our lives is called for here, a discipline that weeds out the wastefulness of time that can too easily slip into our days and begin to characterize too large a part of them. For no one can doubt that the most profound expression of our gratitude toward a gift is the extent to which it becomes a part of our lives.

We have noted, on the other hand, that receiving gifts can also be a negative, distressing experience, which we seek, or should seek, to flee. We provided a couple of examples of this, though one we did not mention is that sometimes, when we have received the same gift as someone else, there is jealousy: we think that we are more worthy of the gift than they are, or worthy of a superior one. I remember in my own life that one Christmas — I was just 9 years old — I had asked for a silver signet ring. It was the gift of greatest importance to me, and on Christmas morning it appeared beautifully wrapped under the tree as a present from my parents. I was delighted, slipping it on my finger and every few minutes looking at its brilliant shine and my emblazoned initials. But then in the middle of the afternoon my closest friend came to visit. And before we had scarcely said hello, he pointed to his finger and said that the beautiful silver signet ring I was seeing was his Christmas gift from my parents. Until that age it was the most disconcerting experience of my life. I thought that if the same gift was given, the same value was demonstrated; that I was of no more worth to my parents than this other little boy. I withdrew into my bedroom for most of the rest of the day, distressed, with tears and anger. It was only many years later that I came to appreciate the words my parents spoke to me, both on that Christmas day and several days thereafter: that my friend was from a much poorer family than ours; that the most concern his mother ever showed him was when she complained about his dirty fingernails, the closest his father ever got was at the end of a strap whistling down in punishment; that he was lucky if he received a single cheap present from his parents on Christmas day. In those later years I began to see in this personal experience an illustration of the Nazarene's parable of the eleventh-hour workers (Matthew 20:1-16), wherein a landlord gives the same salary to those who have worked twelve hours as to those who have worked only one. If the landlord in the parable is a metaphor or symbol for God, as he surely is, then Jesus is telling us that in God's activity generosity, like mercy, presides over justice and questions of fair play. Unfortunately, we typically like this teaching only when we are the ones who have worked the single hour; we don't like it at all when we have worked the twelve, thus demonstrating the peculiarities of our understanding of the relationship between justice and generosity as well as the odd twists our self-concern can take.[38]

We live in a solar system that took shape roughly 5 billion years ago, with the Sun forming slightly in advance of the planets. We know from its chemical constitution, however, as well as from normal stellar evolution, that the Sun is a second-generation star, the heir, that is, to the heavier elements that previous stars emitted when they exploded in a supernova: stars which themselves may have existed for billions of years with their own retinue of planets. We have fossils indicating that biological life first began to emerge on Earth roughly 1 billion years after the planet was formed, and that for another 3 billion years it remained quite stable in its format, confined to simple forms of algae, bacteria, and the like. About 1 billion years ago this life suddenly began to diversify and complexify at an enormous rate, eventually giving rise to all the more complicated genera that would finally produce, somewhere around 4 million years ago, the direct lineage that would lead to us.[39]

The point I wish to isolate centers on the inclination we might have to view ourselves as recompense for all this evolutionary development, this massive cosmic effort that a lesser effort could not by any standards, including scientific ones, reasonably recompense equally. Here we take the side of the twelve-hour laborers regarding proper payment for their labor; the payment is us. The flaw in such reasoning, of course, is twofold. First, we have no knowledge whatsoever that a similar process, perhaps even over much longer periods of time and a more complex evolutionary history, has not occurred elsewhere in the universe. I indicated earlier in the chapter that a simple account of brute statistics regarding stellar and planetary populations in the universe persuades us almost certainly that it has. Secondly, we have no reason to think that the expanse of time needed to generate our life on Earth has in fact been needed elsewhere. For it may be the case that a more intense temporal development could have issued in at least as qualitatively a rich result as here on Earth, where a cold eye might fairly see the development as somewhat roundabout and careless. The twelve-hour workers might complain, but the fact may be that the one-hour workers produced as much as they, and better. We are all certainly familiar enough with this phenomenon in our own everyday lives. Mere quantity of time and effort are frequently not indicative of quality of result.

I have offered these brief reflections on how we receive gifts into our own lives and the lives of others, along with a use of Jesus' great parable, not only because I hope they have value in themselves but because I think they have some pertinence to how we receive the possibility that intelligence might exist elsewhere in the universe. We can accept, as with the parable's landlord, that deity takes no account of the "worthiness" of life's recipients, whether or not they each abide in a similar ecological atmosphere or are chemically parallel or have a selectively defined evolutionary history. Or we can take the attitude that no one else in the universe is as worthy of the gift of life as we, either chemically *or* theologically, and that therefore we possess the only created life, and certainly the only self-reflective intelligence, that exists. And always, of course, there is the option of mere indifference. Furthermore, I would like to suggest that each of us also has a likely indicator of how we would respond to non-Earth intelligence in how we care for the nonhuman animals inhabiting our planet, especially the remarkably intelligent ones like the cetaceans and primates, but also those that more ordinarily populate our lives like dogs and cats. Some of us are outrageously brutal in our attitude toward these animals; we see them as mere objects for scientific experimentation to better our own lives, or to clothe ourselves decadently, or to feed ourselves indiscriminately.[40] Others are far more tender-hearted, seeing these creatures as presences to be protected and cherished and, as we communicate with them, possible sources for our own education. Still others, again, are indifferent, jailed in the tight little world of their self-concern, interested only in what affects their immediate lives — so that while they might indeed show enormous care for their personal pet, they show no interest at all in other animal life. These, along with those in the brutalizing category, are the type of people who would far more readily crush a moth out of existence in their living room than make the small effort needed to capture it and set it free outdoors. Every presence in their lives, save that which induces feelings of well-being, tends to be perceived as either inimical or unimportant. We can easily imagine how these people would greet the presence of non-Earth intelligence: they would attempt to destroy or utterly demean it. And so it is to the people in the second category, the tender-hearted and sensitive, that we must look for guidance in how to construct a humane and virtuous response to the possibility of non-Earth intelligence, as it is to them that we must also look for guidance in how to treat our animals. The attitudes of the brutalizers and the indifferent provide us with nothing of value.

Christianity, it is clear, both in its biblical foundations and its long doctrinal traditions, has very little to offer us on this issue. The Bible knows nothing of extraterrestrial intelligences, save for angels, demons, and of course God. The worldview of its authors and their science, to the extent they possessed the latter, confined the material universe to the Earth and its immediate environs, with little accuracy regarding the times, distances, and possible habitations, the chemistry and physics that we now know characterize the universe. There was the Earth, beneath it the abyss, and above it the vault with its lights of various magnitudes. This worldview was immediate to the senses, and because of this very immediacy it remained dominant for generations; it is the type of worldview, as we've noted before, that every child, left to untutored observation, possesses or that any of us might have if we were uneducated. As to the attitudes it engenders toward nonhuman earthly life, the witness is quite clear: animals have no value and consequently no rights in and of themselves; whatever they possess of these they do so as the property of human beings. The Genesis mandate that we are to be caretakers and caregivers to the rest of Earth's life has gone completely unheeded. The preference to redefine this mandate by substituting "dominion" for "care" still shows up regularly in the translation of Genesis 1:26, where the terminology is almost never understood as indicating a kindly dominion but rather a form of mastery permitting us to do with this life whatever we wish. With very few exceptions, notably among the wisdom books and some of the prophets, the only redeeming element in this whole scriptural tableau occurs when we reach the witness of Jesus, and it is not much.[41] In the temple incident, when he overturned the tables of the sellers and money-lenders, he set the animals free that were caged there for purchase in sacrificial rituals. Further, as noted in chapter 1, nowhere in his teaching, and nowhere in the orthodox theology of Christian tradition, is the sacrifice of animals practiced or countenanced. But outside this single context of animal sacrifice, and with the rare exception of someone like St. Francis, we can read in the texts of countless teachers and ecclesial authorities — Origen and Aquinas, Calvin and Luther, Barth, Bultmann, and two millennia of popes — that moral impunity prevails in how we treat animals. It is a long and thorough tradition,[42] and it screams unpleasant things about how we would treat nonhuman life, no matter what its intelligence, from elsewhere in the universe.

There is a final consideration. A number of years ago Alvin Toffler wrote his brilliantly insightful volume, *Future Shock*. In it he describes how our technologies have rapidly outpaced our ideologies. Novelties of all kinds are entering our lives so quickly that we don't know how to think about them, and consequently are stymied about how to control their use and influence over us. A spirit of wariness toward the new has therefore arisen in many, accompanied by its correlate, suspicion. Yet this wariness and suspicion has had no effect at all on curbing further novelties, especially technological ones, from being continually poured into our culture. This word processor I am now using is one such novelty. And while it makes my work easier from a mechanical standpoint, I am still wary of the control it possesses in the process of my writing: correcting my typographical mistakes, losing its memory if the electricity goes out, eliminating or readjusting material if I happen to hit the wrong code keys. One can imagine, then, how this wariness and suspicion of future shock might escalate to become genuinely neurotic in proportion as one entertains the possibility, let alone the discovery, of non-Earth intelligence, or its prelude in primitive life-forms. Talking of the life-giving generosity of deity does no good, neither does speaking of further knowledge gained or new resources of beauty. Given all the other experiences of future shock that come our way, this is one we may well wish to avoid. For we find it difficult enough to deal with what intelligence has produced on Earth, and certainly have no desire to deal with the possibility of what it might have achieved elsewhere in the universe. And so whatever wonder we may have had initially about this possibility quickly metamorphoses not just into wariness and suspicion, but into fear. A therapy is needed here, one encouraging excited waiting and anticipation for what the future may hold, a therapy for the imagination in which newness becomes a friendly companion, not an antagonist, to our minds. This, however — as with other attitudes and feelings I encourage in these pages, and as with the birth of anything new — is far easier in the description than in the action.

Let me close this section with the following brief reflection. When we look at lovely Sirius in the constellation Canis Major, many light-years away from us though still the brightest star in the night sky, it is hard not to think that on a planet dancing around that star there might be intelligent life. And as we gaze it is equally hard not to think, in a manner going back to the most ancient of our forebears, that deity is somehow involved.

SINCE I AM a theologian by profession, many of my intellectual partners, though certainly not all, have also been theologians. And in common engagement of our tasks we frequently find that we are at odds with each other, sometimes over quite serious matters. This disagreement is no surprise (it occurs in all walks of life) and is often the seedbed of new insight, whole new schools of thought. With a poignancy I have never been able to shake, I remember one of these disagreements with a mentor of mine, an old priest who had lived richly, contributed brilliantly to his own specialty in theology, and now at the close of life had given himself over to what he once described as his first love, the study of the stars. I met him in a garden one evening, where he sat by his beloved telescope, mulling over the heavens, with a look of ineffable sadness in his eyes. I asked the reason, and he responded in typically well-tailored phrases — he always said that half the work of theology, though accomplished by few theologians, was casting ideas in effective, "moving" words. And his phrases began breaking my heart. He spoke of the beauty of the universe, the intricacy of its design and the intimacy of its mathematics, the grace of its abundance, the curiosity of its beginning and end. But in striving after this beauty, the knowledge and aesthetic delight born from contemplation of the night sky, his mind had taken a savage turn years previously toward the damning conclusion: the universe is void of meaning. You might imagine the toll this would have taken on a priest. It left him without a God, or with an indifferent one unworthy of pursuit, and a knowledge and beauty chased to a blank wall. He was like a man who had fallen in love with the music of a violin, but could not play three notes successfully; the beauty of the music remained, but could only be observed. And for this man, ultimately, it was a grief observed, one born from a sense of loss and disorientation — the kind of grief C. S. Lewis described so eloquently of the days remaining him after his wife's death. The music of the spheres, like that played poorly on a violin, had become for him discordant, a cacophony of abusive sounds.[43]

When I left the old man and was walking home, I looked up into the night sky. As always, it worked its enchantment on me, a compelling beauty that was difficult to abandon. Yet on that evening the old man's words were like a gauze on the beauty, weakening its impact and blurring its clarity. The seeming randomness of it all: this was his lament, wedded to the suspicion that any order observed was human doing, an imposition on the universe that had no justification beyond itself. He obviously knew, as I did, that a thoroughly objective appraisal of what we can see in the movements of the universe — what Yeats called casting a cold eye on things[44] — indicated seeming chaos, the universe held together by little more than nuclear forces, electromagnetism, and gravity, with explosions and collisions the order of the day. And he was as deeply touched by the overpowering character of the numbers involved: the age of the universe, its extent in space, the quantity of stars that compose just a single galaxy, let alone the quantity of galaxies we can observe, the sheer amount of dark matter needed to prevent an endless expansion. But at a certain point, we know, a difference in quantity becomes a difference in quality. This point had been reached in the old priest, in his knowledge of the overwhelming vastness of the universe linked to its unpredictable relativity, after which the quality of the universe no longer spoke of divine presence but almost of an amoral, renegade, and blind will. In a previous chapter I noted that Einstein was once asked, "What is the most important question one can ask?," to which the luminary responded, "Whether the universe is friendly or not." My old mentor, in the final, failing, needful years of his life, would have answered no, the universe is not friendly, and he would have done so with glistening eyes.

I am now a much older man myself than when I walked with my mentor. And I have come to see that his melancholy was misplaced. For only on one reading is the randomness we find so evident in the universe a basis for judgments of confusion, misdirection, and absurdity — all the baleful designations the old priest had given a home in his mind. On another reading, it is precisely this randomness that becomes the seedbed of novelty, the reservoir of possibilities that includes within it the possibility that what has once occurred can occur again, not identically — since nothing can be reproduced identically, not in all the details of its motion, duration, and relationships — but similarly. And these repetitions can be many. This, in fact, is exactly what underlies the resurrection claims about Jesus, and the old man's forgetfulness of this when we talked only served to demonstrate just how profound his melancholy was. For this claim means nothing if not that the dissolution of Jesus' identity that death initiated was overcome in the novelty that permitted a similar life to emerge randomly and quickly. Theologically, of course, this is attributed to the persuasive power of God over the elements composing his body and their reintegration into recognizable form.[45] But this persuasion has as its context the randomness of these particles, rather than their fatedness to behave only in certain ways upon death, that permitted their reconstitution into this recognizable form: Jesus, now designated risen from the dead. At the beginning of a metaphysical defense for this theological position one may simply note that even on scientific investigation the randomness in the universe is repeatedly overcome in organized matter, and that the impetus toward this organization needs to be explained as somehow residing within the elementary constituents of the matter itself. What exactly is it that provides photons, quarks, electrons, etc. with the stimulus to enter into organized relationships with each other in ways that define electromagnetism, the strong and weak nuclear forces, and, especially in large-scale organizations, gravity? If the scientist wants to speculate in his or her own jargon on these issues, whereas the theologian speaks more confidently of God, does the difference in language indicate a difference in the reality being discussed? I do not think so. By whatever designation you choose, and however you derive it, there is something in the relationships that constitute the universe we experience which accounts for organizing energy and matter in fashions that at times are unexpectedly novel, though never completely unrelated to what already is, and at other times remarkably similar to what has already been.

While it is certainly not discussed in this fashion, I would suggest that something like this initial metaphysical defense underlies the claim that such novel reorganization occurred not only in the rapid transformation of Jesus from life to death to life — though maintaining enough similarity that it is clearly Jesus who is experienced as raised — but will also occur for everything else that is alive. This second part of the claim appears to have had its initial formulation in some of St. Paul's letters, though he unnecessarily confined its application only to life defined as biologically human. This was likely due to his desire to emphasize resurrection more in the context of ethics than metaphysics, that is, as an inevitability that issued in either blessing or damnation on the basis of one's conduct. This particular approach isn't useful to me, for two reasons. The first is that the ethical has in fact overridden the metaphysical in Paul's viewpoint, since there is much else that is alive that is left out of consideration because ethical criteria are not applicable to it — not ethical criteria based on subjects that contemplate decisions within the confines of a moral code. St. Paul apparently never imagines that a butterfly might be raised from the dead. The second reason is the more personal assessment of what God is like, which for the Christian inevitably involves an appraisal of Jesus' teachings. For me the issue is clear. The God whom Jesus teaches always cherishes life and never condemns it; as already noted, in those places where he seems to say the contrary Jesus is employing a literary technique to emphasize the utter seriousness of what he is saying that he does not intend the listener to take literally. In other words, all are raised for blessing.[46] If there is to be condemnation and punishment for evil committed, therefore, this is something we do to each other in an attempt to purify behavior. It is not something that God does — except in our poor metaphors that try to make God act as we do — because the presence of God in the universe is fundamentally a metaphysical, not an ethical one, even as we strive to apply the cherishing of life in ethical ways that demonstrate our understanding of what the cherishing means.[47]

There is more. We clearly need to delve a bit more deeply into how we are using the words "cherishing" and "life." In its most usual meaning to cherish something means to hold it dear, to nurture it with care, to keep it in mind, or to cling to it. These definitions make it primarily an ethical term describing a specific type of responsiveness to an object, person, event, or memory. What I wish to do is intensify this meaning to the extent that a difference in degree will again become a difference in kind, that is, to deepen it so as to allow the notion of cherishing to transmute from an ethical term to a metaphysical one. My suggestion is that underneath the ethical description we find the more fundamental metaphysical assertion that to cherish is to affirm, or, more precisely, to cause something to be. When applied theologically this becomes the same as creating;[48] when applied scientifically it captures what it is in the structure of forces and particles that permits their relationships to each other and thus the organizations that we designate as reality. Yet the ethical cloak around this metaphysical meaning still does appeal and has its place. For it is what allows us to move into those metaphors that describes the creating activity of God in terms like nurturing and care and faithfulness (the "clinging to" in the above definition), and what allowed Einstein to ask whether the universe is friendly or not. In the context of this metaphysical meaning "life" then becomes a companion term. Because cherishing is now understood as affirmation or causing something to be, the phrase "cherishing life" must consequently be applied to all that has been caused to be or, less awkwardly, to all that is. This is the heart of the reason I have previously suggested that we need a new definition of life that breaks the bonds of mere biology and becomes applicable to all that is. I proposed that this criterion is met when the characteristics we assign to life are motion, duration, novelty, and relationship. Since all things that exist share these characteristics, all may now be understood as alive. God breathes the breath of life everywhere in creation.

There are at least seven consequences that are embedded within such an outline of the metaphysics underlying the notion of cherishing life. The first I would describe by adverting to classical Greek tradition and the works of Aristotle; it pertains to the issue of methodology. Many readers might know that in the standard listing of Aristotle's works, the treatise on metaphysics comes after the one on physics. In the usual interpretation this order is dismissed as simply a fluke in the way the various treatises have been put together and published. I believe, rather, that the listing — probably assigned by the great philosopher/scientist himself — clearly intends to indicate that metaphysical positions achieve their most persuasive statements when they are able to absorb as much as possible the findings of physics, or as we might say more generally, science. This is certainly a stance I have taken in these pages. Of the remaining group of consequences there are six, and I will describe them within the context of Christian religion. The first we are now familiar with, and reads: the claim that God cherishes life must apply to everything that is, not just to human beings. The second is that if this cherishing is never rescinded because of the consistency (or faithfulness) of divine activity, then death becomes merely one format that life takes, and in time this format can itself alter into a repetition of previously identifiable forms. The Christian claim that Jesus came alive again in a form identifiable by others, supplemented by the suggestion that this destiny is shared by all that is, does not preclude further death as itself a repetitious format that life can take; nowhere do the Gospels say that Jesus can only die once.[49] The third is that the phrase we used above, "in time," must allow for an infinity of time, and because of what physics has been telling us for decades, of space as well — an infinity of spacetime. Only within this infinity, now understood simply as endless-ness,[50] does the repetition of identifiable life-forms become virtually inevitable; a spacetime that will end cannot guarantee this.[51] The fourth is that what Christianity classically describes as resurrection must therefore be a repetitive or continuing experience as all that is alive comes alive again in identifiable ways through an infinity of spacetime.[52] The fifth is that the universe needed to secure this circumstance must be one that itself goes through varying but identifiable formats in an infinity of time: what we described in chapter 1 as an oscillating universe.[53] The sixth is that at the source of all these events lies a presence that in itself is impenetrable to our analysis but originates them and guarantees the energy (or power) allowing them to endure. Physics calls this presence the primordial singularity;[54] theology should not shy away from appropriating this singularity into a metaphysics of what it calls God.[55] In this way, too, through all these consequences and their preamble in a metaphysics of cherishing life, I think we achieve a better grip on that marvelous doxology St. Paul uses in his letter to the Romans, one that I now acknowledge has repeatedly animated what I've said in this section, and indeed throughout the entire book: from God, through God, to God are all things (Romans 11:36).

A number of the preceding suggestions and their consequences are speculation. I am not hesitant to acknowledge this. In fact, I take heart in this acknowledgment, for a reason I would like to mention briefly here. It is the conviction that the active mind, scientifically *or* theologically, never succumbs to dogmatic slumbers. Instead, it stays alert and alive precisely in its speculations, its reworkings of the old and anticipations of the new. The dictionary gives as good a definition of this intellectual activity as I can discover either in my own musings or those of others. It reads: "speculate. 1. to contemplate; see mentally; 2. to ponder a subject in its different aspects and relations; meditate; especially, to theorize from conjectures without sufficient evidence." The first part of the definition is simply providing synonyms; the second part is the definition proper. For many the task this definition describes is an uncomfortable one; of what possible use is theorizing from conjectures "without sufficient evidence"? Underlying this discomfort is the assumption that the intellectual investigation of the universe, or of God, can achieve sufficient evidence for a full, systematic, unquestionable, and novelty-prohibiting description. But this is an impossibility, not only because there will always be doubts regarding what constitutes evidence itself, especially whether or not it is sufficient, but more importantly because the freedom (or novelty) built into the universe makes such an attempt itself speculative. Our ever-doubting, inquisitive minds are in this sense a complement to the nature of the universe itself. The latter produces the former.

Let me conclude this section and chapter by noting that for me a Christian vision has as one of its fundamental purposes the opening of the mind to all that the universe contains, the nurturing of a spirit of receptivity toward the known and the still unknown. This is a risky venture, and its initial wonder may lead to confusion, then that sense of meaninglessness ("there is no discernible order in all of this") which the old priest experienced. The universe here becomes monstrous, too huge and irregular to hold onto conceptually or emotionally; at an extreme it becomes terrifying. Now the night sky looks like a kaleidoscope, a helter-skelter of lit objects where no rhyme or reason prevails, and dumb paralysis, like that of the baleful victims gazing upon Medusa's face, is the result. When I have experienced such moments, perplexed and somewhat frightened by the enormity and apparent disarray of what I am seeing in the night sky, knowing that this is but an immeasurably small fraction of all the universe contains . . . at such moments, when I am perhaps blind to the presence of deity, its cherishing of life in eternal renewal, I again take consolation in those singular words of the remarkable Francis Bacon, that beauty lies in the strangeness of the proportion.

IV

Night Stars and the Day Star

Our vision is always foreshortened, and this fact accounts for much of the distress we experience in life. We know that if we could only see the entirety of an experience, an event, its purpose would be clear to us, or if we could only know another person completely, the meaning of his or her presence to us would be reliably secured. But such things are not possible; as we attempt to establish the meaning of any event or relationship there is always something that will slip us by. This is what Gabriel Marcel spoke of as the "mystery" of existence, arguing that it is nothing other than our own personal involvement in the event or relationship, our inability to step away from it to achieve total perceptive objectivity.[1] It is not unlike what physicists mean when speaking about the relativity of our observations, or what Augustine was getting at in his famous metaphor of creation as a mosaic: because it is I who am observing the mosaic, and because I cannot achieve a distance sufficient to see the whole thing, my assessment of it is always only partial, and thus insufficient. Such remarks, of course, do not imply that we cannot achieve *some* reliability in our knowledge. If we lived on a planet circling Arcturus, two plus two would still equal four and electrons would still swirl around their nuclei. The point is that while we can be fairly confident that there are certain reliable constants that prevail throughout the universe, especially ones drawn from physics and mathematics, they are not many, and we have no idea how they might express themselves — what they might mean or imply — beyond our current observations. It wasn't too long ago, after all, that the possibility of a piece of mass compacted so tightly that not even light could escape it would have been considered not just scientific heresy but ridiculous. Yet researchers, basing much of their work on the theoretical physics of Einstein and its further extension by Stephen Hawking, have established with fair certainty the existence of such objects, which we commonly call black holes.[2] As noted in the last chapter, it was probably similar discoveries in his own time that led the great Alfred North Whitehead to admonish that many of our so-called "laws of nature" could in fact be contradicted in varying circumstances elsewhere in the universe; that they are not as indelibly stamped on creation as we might think.

Yet within the confines of scientific study at any given point in our history, it appears necessary to postulate some constants, or axiomatic presuppositions, to guarantee a basis for theoretical coherence. For the impulse that drives science has always been the conviction that there is a detectable order in the universe, even if what composes this order gets regularly reassessed. The first great formulator of this idea was Aristotle, though he argued it equally on the basis of observational data as on the superiority he assumed philosophical reflection possessed in revealing the nature of creation — as in the idea of the "least imperfect of all forms" (the circle) that he was convinced *had* to be mirrored in planetary orbits if they were to provide, as he thought they did, premier examples of this order.[3] We have also seen that it was a similar conviction that made Einstein so wary of quantum mechanics and the inherent unpredictability it argued as characterizing the behavior of atomic and subatomic particles. For him this proposed a condition of uncertainty too close to the heart of things. And so, as one of his consolations — the other being his Spinozan theology — he took particular delight in arguing the absolute constancy of the speed of light, even among these various particles. And indeed the speed of light appears to be a constant of nature. Hypothetical particles capable of breaching it, like the so-called tachyon, have remained unpopular among most theorists because there exist no experimental procedures that can demonstrate their reality.[4] Yet advocates of these particles often prefer to assert this reality, even if unprovable, as a particular expression of their own loyalty toward the conviction of order in the universe, this time an epistemological one — that is, the certainty that the universe is so ordered that it cannot prohibit the endless expanse of knowledge. For if light's speed is indeed a constant, *and* an absolute barrier, it puts strictures on the amount of knowledge available to us from the distant recesses of the universe since there will perpetually remain a distance beyond which no information will have had time to reach us.[5] Furthermore, this same constant tightly limits the extent to which we can explore the universe even well within its boundaries. Just the delivery of a message to the other side of our own galaxy would take around 100,000 years, and any possible reply the same time in return. This makes any productive communication virtually impossible, and even more so, any human travel to such places. Theoretical proposals such as wormholes or tunnels in spacetime that might permit much quicker progress from point to point, even if they allowed for objects much larger than a small molecule to traverse them (which most don't),[6] have largely gone the way of the tachyon, and for the same reason.[7] Effectively, therefore, we must indeed deal with constants in the universe, even if their number is not particularly large and we remain always alert to Whitehead's admonition. Ultimately there is a tentativeness to our knowledge of everything that occurs in the universe; but pragmatically we possess sufficiently reliable data to continue the researches of a productive science.

A critical element in what defines such a productive science, particularly regarding its theoretical competence, resides precisely in the above-stated reliability. I am referring specifically to the predictive aptitude of the theory. If there were no reliable constants at all, science could do little more than analyze specific sets of circumstances whose intellectual utility would be confined to a mere gathering of historical data with no confidence that they pertain to future events. This would define a completely disorganized universe in which prediction could amount to nothing but a fanciful gamble. But it is because the universe *is* apparently patterned according to certain reliable constants that an incisive theory is able to calculate how these constants will apply in a given set of future circumstances. In fact, just such prediction is generally regarded as an essential component in determining whether or not a theory is taken seriously. And for the theory to be taken very seriously, the prediction must come true.[8] In this respect scientific theory is functioning not unlike biblical prophecy. In a previous book[9] I identified nine traits of the biblical prophet, four of them quite common in other religious traditions — wonderworking, counsel, predicting the future, rapture — and five of them more or less distinct to biblical tradition: the call, the authority, the criticism, the political involvement, and the reluctance. While in this scheme predicting the future does not have the same distinctive role as the final five traits, in practice it was utterly critical to whether or not the people gave the prophet their trust. What the prophet foretold had to come true or the prophet quickly slipped into disregard. Furthermore, the most effective prophecies were not the result, as is sometimes proposed, of the manipulations of talismanic or incantatory magic but of the incisiveness of the prophet's mind in analyzing the constants of a given sociopolitical or religious situation. When Isaiah predicted that Assyria would attack it was not because he had consulted animal entrails but because he was a competent student of the constants in Assyrian foreign policy, especially represented in the character traits of the Assyrian king, and correctly deduced behavior based on them. In this way too, scientists predict not on the basis of arcane mysteries in their craft but because they have disciplined themselves in the knowledge appropriate to the context of their prediction.[10] But in both cases, whether of religious prophecy or scientific forethought, our point is that some degree of constancy is needed as the basis of the prediction.

Like science, therefore, theology — and, we will now add, philosophy — has concerned itself in its "prophetic" role with the issue of constants. Additionally, however, theology and philosophy have also involved themselves in the question of whether a *singular* constant exists that endures perpetually and establishes the reliability of the others. For the most part their positive response to this inquiry has been far more robust than that of contemporary science. Two questions have been of particular concern, and each involves a key term that we have used repeatedly throughout the book, as in the previous three paragraphs. First is the basic question, "Is there in fact such a constant in the universe?"

By the word "constant" we have meant something that in its entirety or in part remains always the same. The issue concerns absolute ontological integrity, and the nearly unanimous response has been to assign such integrity to God. The second question has a related but somewhat wider scope and can be put as follows, "Is there reliability in the universe?" By the word "reliability" we have meant changes that are predictable or coherent with what preceded them. The issue here is whether or not the ontological integrity of deity overflows — if not absolutely, nonetheless definitively — into creation. Again, the nearly unanimous answer is yes: God is the guarantor of predictability. In Judeo-Christian cultures the first question has especially exercised the discipline of philosophy, while the second has found an ancient and comfortable home in theology (not that these are exclusive domains). In answering the first question philosophy has tended to emphasize the immutability of deity, while in answering the second theology has tended to emphasize deity's faithfulness.[11] Finally, in further response to the first question deity is typically described as independent from creation, a still point outside the universe, while in response to the second deity is typically described as actively involved in the universe (as reflected in doctrines of providence). But in the response to either inquiry, the common postulate is obviously the existence of deity.

Two further, related points should also be made. The first we have already mentioned in previous pages, though it now needs further embellishment. It is that throughout its history science has likewise frequently utilized the concept of deity in its musings, most often as an explanatory device handily available to fill in the interstices of theories where data or logical sequencing breaks down. This is the famous "God of the gaps," and represents an intellectual convenience when harmony in an explanation is prized more highly than the silence which the data and logic by themselves demand. More subtly, it often represents a simple refusal of ignorance on the part of the theorist, an absence that is met by employing a conceptuality that occurs at no other place in the explanation and consequently stands out something like an interloper. It is this intrusion that during the Enlightenment became so intellectually unnerving that science began to demand of itself a more diligent search for data, along with a more uncompromising logic, to purify and strengthen its explanations of reality solely from within the rigors of its empiricism while simultaneously establishing its autonomy from other disciplines, especially the humanities, and particularly theology.[12] Here begins that dismal history that has eroded the longstanding friendship between science and religion through a mutual and insistent hostility or indifference. Only recently, and among relatively few thinkers, has that great divide begun to close. The second point is that with this new rapprochement we have begun to see among these thinkers, both scientists and theologians, the emergence of a new stature for deity, now no longer as a device to fill in explanatory gaps but as the finest or terminal expression of appraisals of reality as these are secured through scientific investigation. Among others, for example, Stephen Hawking thus speaks comfortably about knowing the mind of God in creation through the rigors of experimental and theoretical excursions into the universe, its beginning, end, and current composition.[13] And theologians like John Cobb and Jurgen Moltmann share the same sentiment. God, it seems, can bridge the gap between science and religion to become a singular constant that, like the universe itself, provides this constancy by simple presence, even if what the presence means is a subject of diverse and ever-changing assessments. Above all, then, this is an *aesthetic* approach to deity, one that finds a beauty or loveliness or consistency in creation within the flux of its component parts and identifies their ultimate source as divine.

In chapter 2 we noted Whitehead's remark that the pure conservative is someone who tries to deny the essence of the universe, which is change. It is a marvelous description, and it captures a sentiment we all share to some degree: a longing for stability. We have met with this longing repeatedly in previous reflections. Ancient observers, we know, thought that the universe was remarkably stable, the stars and constellations gently moving around the Earth in minutely predictable patterns. They saw this as a testament to the precision of divine creative power. In the late twentieth century, however, we are reluctant to hold to such a vision. Our observational technology tells us that the universe appears stable only when macroscopically viewed, when we look up at the sky and take in the whole panorama of what we see. But as we look more closely through our various types of telescopes we discover that there is much unpredictable disarray in the universe, broken symmetries every-where.[14] We find, for example, that our Sun that seems so smooth from a distance roils and erupts on its surface in ways that distort its shape and disorient our confidence in its enduring sameness; that a panorama seemingly etched in permanence on the tableau of night is now unnervingly different because a star has gone supernova; that entire galaxies are not carved in a still beauty but move and wobble and collide. Ancient observers did not have our sophisticated technology — they only had their unaided eyes — and so we can understand their conclusions. Even a human life, when looked at from a far distance in time or familiarity, can take on an observational smoothness of interpretation that the life itself, while being lived, did not possess.

The two sides of this dichotomy in viewing creation reached their most sophisticated expression in the ancient world in the philosophical visions of Plato and Aristotle. The former thought that at the heart of reality resided not only the reliability of cycles that brought confidence in their essential sameness, but in a transcendent world where eternal Forms, above all the Good, remained statically the same while providing the genesis for their imperfect expressions in our experience. It was an extraordinarily powerful viewpoint, explaining why the beauty we encounter is never quite perfect, nor the truth, the good, a flower, a butterfly, anything and everything at all. Yet at the same time it did not deny that such perfection existed, or that it could be enjoyed. It could: in the proper methods of contemplation. Plato offered his world an escape from imperfection, and the correlative suffering it engendered, through the workings of a meditative mind. Aristotle, on the other hand, though he revered Plato, was not as comfortable with this bifurcation of reality, and sought instead to concentrate much of his formidable attention not on what we presume exists in some transcendent space and time, but on what exists in the world of our everyday experience; that this is what merits our devotion and provides the terrain in which happiness must be sought. We know that Aristotle wrote a treatise on physics, and gave serious attention to botany, medicine, and zoology; it is hard to imagine Plato doing the same.[15] From the entirely different context of the history of Buddhism we discover a similar contrast in viewpoints. Commentators frequently align Buddhism with Platonic doctrine, seeing the former's emphasis on *maya* — or the world as illusion — as similar to Plato's ideal Forms as these get distorted in the actual world and thereby lose something of the truth of their reality. But this commentary represents only one strand of the Buddhist doctrine, an errant one in my judgment. For in other strands we note that *maya* does not mean that the world is literally an illusion, a chimera possessing no true reality, but rather that the reality of the world is tricky to comprehend, an illusion in the sense of the deceptions of a master magician. The task, then, is to examine the world closely, searching out the truth of the reality that is there but cloaked in obscurity or concealed by the misdirection of the senses. And in this, of course, we are more in the home of Aristotle and his fellow scientists than of Plato and his mystagogues. Our immediate neighbor, moreover, is a vast majority of the biblical traditions.[16]

Nonetheless, we can sympathize with the Platonic viewpoint, even if we are not particularly astute philosophically. For many of us lead lives of remarkable stability — we engage fundamentally the same behavior whenever we wish to play, eat, sleep, study, pray; our lives amble on through events and experiences that seem to specify remarkably well certain overarching patterns.[17] Yet if we are perceptive, we begin to notice the differences too, especially as time endures and age encroaches with increasing haste: the recreation that has delighted us for years becomes boring or too vigorous, the food is too demanding on digestion, sleep requires new body positions, study is more tiresome, prayer less passionate. Ancient observers also noted such metamorphoses as well, just as they began to see that the stars in truth are not perfectly stable in their courses, that there are notable irregularities in the seasons, that many experiences are unique, and that birth doesn't guarantee growth but is often cut short by death. Consequently there begins to seep into consciousness the notion of disorder, unpredictability and the rule of chance. Chaos begins to emerge as an operative category in assessing what goes on in the universe, and poets begin to speak of being victimized by an unreliable and uncaring fate. Things go wrong, events happen unexpectedly, and too many of them are tragedies that ridicule the stability of existence. The stars in the night sky: they are supposed to remain the same. Yet one likely exploded in the century of the Nazarene's birth, another ten centuries later, another six centuries after that, and one in 1987 in the Great Magellanic Cloud. The distress felt is like that toward a timepiece we have relied on for years but which suddenly runs amok. We are disturbed and, if religiously alert, begin to think that one of the noblest products of human generation, Einstein, was wrong: deity does play dice with the universe. And we become sympathetic as well toward the old Greeks when they finally accorded the three sisters of their mythology a power even greater than that of Zeus — the *Moirai,* the Fates, by name Clotho, Atropos, Lachesis, and by task, the Spinner, the Weaver, and the Caster of Lots, whose wills were irresistible yet governed by whim.[18]

In the ambience of such a spirituality we can easily enough appreciate the appeal of the Platonic viewpoint. When experiences overwhelm us with their disarray and we begin to believe that this is not just a transient anomaly but a condition of existence, the thought that transcending it is a realm of implacable stability where chaos gains no foothold and beauty is perpetually at hand becomes nearly irresistible in its appeal. This perhaps gives us a clue as to why the Platonic vision and its various offshoots gained such thorough influence over the spirituality of many early Christian thinkers. The world they lived in could be catastrophically hostile; they were frequently shorn of civil rights, economic security, professional opportunity — and oftentimes their health or their very lives — at the hands of local or imperial rulers. In such contexts the appeal of a Platonic empyrean where hostility has mutated into the peaceful contemplation of the Good, or God, can become psychologically overpowering, particularly if this somewhat abstract description is further dressed out in the heaven of common Christian piety so as to become little more than a garden of earthly delights. In later centuries, while Platonism still held sway over much of popular Christian devotion, since life was still experienced by many as catastrophically hostile,[19] Christianity had become far more secure politically and economically and so in its formal theology could attend more thoroughly to the this-worldly perspective of the Aristotelian viewpoint: the sciences began to emerge under this impulse, supplemented by knowledge of the works of Aristotle himself as these, and brilliant interpretations of them, filtered into Christendom from Islamic cultures. Aristotelianism did not emphasize escape from the chaos of worldly life in a heavenly one, though this is how it was frequently presented when blended with Platonism,[20] but confronted it head-on in order to understand it. If this understanding could not heal the chaos, at least it provided comprehension that made acceptance of it an option more faithful to the world we experience than the intellectual rebellion, ridicule, or indifference that popular Platonism often encouraged.

Let me conclude this section by noting that the word "chaos" comes from a Greek noun meaning confusion or disarray, and in mythology was used to describe the condition of the universe before order and form were imposed. Interestingly, it was also used as the proper name for the most ancient of gods, overcome and defeated by others stronger than he who subsequently imposed the order and form.[21] This brings the Greek view, therefore, along with its analogue in other cultures, somewhat in line with that of ancient Hebrew mythology, wherein what precedes Yahweh's creative activity is matter without form, the *tohu-wabohu*. In all these mythologies the common substrate is the conviction that creation is a symbolic activity (from the Greek verb *symbolein,* to bring together or unify) rather than a diabolic one (from the Greek verb *diabolein,* to sunder or break apart). While from this conviction, therefore, especially as it is shared in Christian accounts of creation, we might not wish to describe the universe as a whole as chaotic or diabolic, there nonetheless exists in such phenomena as exploding stars, colliding galaxies, and meteor impacts something of these traits. And for many it is exactly these traits that are the worm at the core of the universe, what makes it not just unpredictable but destructive. Theologically we reach the conundrum that despite all faith allegations that the chaos of the universe has been overcome in the benign activity of deity, and despite the Aristotelian imperative — now theologically clothed — to study the universe to demonstrate that this is so, there is still sufficient evidence of the diabolic to make these allegations questionable, the conviction underlying them profoundly ambiguous. If we extend these celestial examples down to smaller levels, we find similar occurrences of destruction and unpredictability. An example of the former would be what happens in cataclysmic movements of the earth and sea, while one of the latter might lie in the consensus that electrons, far from being determinate particles of matter, are actually "packets" of energy that whirl indeterminately around a nucleus, jumping in and out of orbits in a dance of seemingly random spontaneity. But both these phenomena are really only specific expressions of the general one we know as change. And this we can observe all around us, without needing the sophistication of our science or technologies. When I look at some of the stars in the night sky, for example, their twinkling tells me of change. I know that in part this twinkling is due to chemical reactions and turbulence in the star, that destructive and indeterminate energies are at work there, and in part to the influence of our atmosphere upon my perception. But this is not what is important for my reflection. It is, rather, the way the light from these stars dances, the changing luminosity all around the night sky that speaks, once more, of the potential beauty enwombed in novelty.

❋　　❋　　❋

THE IDEA THAT the stars can speak to us, or, more accurately, educate us, is very old. We find it most thoroughly expressed in the maligned study of astrology. Here it is thought that the positions of stars (and planets), particularly at the moment of birth, provide an ineluctable destiny for us; that there is a force or power generated by the particular alignments of celestial bodies that determines what we become. Enough people apparently find sufficient coincidences between the facts of their own lives and predictions of astrologers that astrology is still a paid profession today. Part of the reason, I suspect, aside from the brute desire to know the future, is the hidden presumption that unless they play some role in determining human fate, the stars appear utterly useless, slight enchantments in the night sky that have no real value, like the cheap baubles with which we sometimes adorn ourselves. But this presumption we now know to be false. The issue here is one of immediacy, or how directly we wish to link the behavior of stellar motion, placement, or evolution with the contours our lives possess. It is well known, though still a source of embarrassment to some of his admirers, that Isaac Newton spent considerable time and energy in pursuing astrological "science."[22] But it may be that the linkages he sought between the stars and human life were more subtle and accurate than a tabloid account of his studies would imply — a type of prescience on his part that at the time had little data to lend it credence. For we now know that the stars contribute to our being in very basic ways: from the chemicals in our bodies born in the explosions of supernovae to the balance of our place in the galaxy. Johannes Kepler and his mentor Tycho Brahe had a similar passion for detecting stellar influences on the Earth, and before them a host of Christian theologians. Among these latter it was common doctrine that the stars maintained their place in the sky through angelic intervention, and Aquinas even thought that the soul before entering the body made a transit of the Sun.[23] It is unfair to dismiss such speculations as barbarously ignorant or the meanderings of superstitious minds, the way the Nobel laureate Richard Feynman once did.[24] It may be that these scientists and theologians had a greater appreciation than we of the beauty of the night sky, its apparent serenity and fidelity to a course of action, its praise of the creative generosity of God and, in more hope than fancy, believed that we might be influenced by celestial order. There is rapture for the stars here, a sense of intimacy in our relationship to them, that seems little different, say, from the rapture for numbers — attributing to them a special authority in the control of how things are — that we discover in a line extending from Pythagoras all the way to contemporaries like Paul Dirac.[25]

Who can plot the influences on us, many of which we know nothing of? The classic philosophical inquiry into this same issue takes the cleverly more pragmatic and specific form: Does a tree make noise falling in a forest if there is no one there to hear it? Many "hard" empiricists and idealists would say no — the empiricist because he or she refuses to bestow reality on anything that cannot be satisfyingly verified via sense-experience as influencing our existence, the idealist because he or she thinks that reality is bestowed on something only as it passes through the channels of conscious human thought. (The contemporary side-current of this idealism is the philosophy of deconstruction. In a corrupt interpretation by some of its representatives it argues that reality is achieved only as words describe it; the words, functioning autonomously from the one speaking, writing, or thinking them bestow the actual reality).[26] But those I would call philosophical realists would answer the question positively: yes, of course the tree makes a sound when it falls, even if there is no one to hear it. One of the realist's defenses of his or her position, therefore, is to ask what a working tape recorder would register if it was in the forest when the tree fell, and the answer is without doubt the sound of a tree falling. The empiricist or idealist might then say the tape recorder is merely an extension of human ears. But what if our mechanism was a video recorder that had no audio component? We would see the tree fall, watch it rake through the branches of its neighbors, then crash to the ground. Yet we would hear nothing nor be likely to think the word "noise." But if our eyes had seen the event, its entire gestalt — even if hearing or thinking "noise" were absent — that a noise would have occurred is spontaneously evident from what we've seen rather than heard or thought. A belligerent denial only tends to drag further discussion toward a *reductio ad absurdum,* and at that point to silence.

A theological component also enters such a discussion for each of the three participants — empiricists, idealists, realists — and we should provide a brief note of it. From the empiricist and realist viewpoint this component is easily and quickly described: when assessing whether events occur the role of God is superfluous. This does not always indicate atheism, but rather a conviction that in understanding how reality is constructed regard for God is not a factor. The common stance of deism is typically similar; it finds a role for God in the initiation of the universe but not in the precise and mathematically calculable unfolding of the remaining events in the universe's history. In each of these viewpoints, while God's role as creator might be acknowledged, a sustaining role is not. The idealist perspective is different, at least as it gets articulated by one of its foremost spokesmen, Bishop Berkeley.[27] He believed that reality occurs only as it is thought, but when confronted with an example like the tree falling in the forest had no desire to assert that nothing would have been heard. In what some consider a classic illustration of the "God of the gaps" maneuver he therefore argued that the sound would have occurred because it would have been received in the "mind" of God; if nothing or no one else, God witnessed the event. It is usual among empiricists and realists, along with those idealists not theistically alert, to have great fun at the expense of the Bishop's position, suggesting that under its influence just about any event, no matter how outlandishly imagined, could become real. There is some justification in this response, even if indecorously aimed at a great intellect. But Berkeley's position was not instigated by a desire to lend a patina of possible reality to imaginings we will never experience, but to assert the universal care of God over creation by insisting that whatever possesses reality does so because God, not we or anything else, has lent it notice. It is real because it is shared by God. To me, the profound theological truth of his position outweighs any inappropriate use to which it might be put, and we will be rehearsing it in later pages.

A further point we can draw from debates like this is that whenever impassioned philosophical (or, for that matter, scientific) stances are at stake, specific contradicting examples are seldom persuasive to either side — at least when compared to the inclusiveness of the vision in question[28] — until their number and seriousness mount to where they cannot be ignored. Consequently I would now like to cast our inquiry into the broadest terms I can think of, namely: Was there nothing going on in the universe until we appeared on the scene to observe it; or if something was going on, was it only a chaotic mess until our minds gave it order? My own answer to both these questions is no. Events would happen in the same way with or without an observer — unless, of course, the observer is in a position not just to observe but to intrude upon the events, such as what happens in our gardens when we allow one plant to grow but not others, or as always happens when observing quantum events at a very minute level where such things as electrons and photons perpetually interchange between the observed and whatever is observing.[29] Aside from such situations, though, the role of the observer is almost exclusively that of an interpreter of what is being observed, not a controller;[30] he or she is a provider of meaning — much, but not necessarily all of which (there may be established facts that cannot be ignored) can vary according to his or her given interpretive stance. There is a spiritual interlocking here between ourselves and the whole rest of creation that I find enormously appealing. And because of this, therefore, I do not share completely in the maligning judgment commonly made against astrology. To be sure, I have no interest in psychics who dupe a naive clientele into thinking that the future is largely discernible in the layout of planetary and stellar configurations; they remind me too much of arcane soothsayers who thought that the way stones fell from a bowl could predict a destiny. There is too much hocus-pocus in it all, an abandonment of rationality and disciplined forethought. But what does attract me — and this is where I think resides what merit astrology possesses — is its insistence on the way events can be appreciated in their mutuality: what I like to think of as the ecology of the universe, or what Francis Thompson was alluding to in his beautiful sentiment about troubling a star whenever we pluck a flower. The effects of this interlocking are predominantly cognitive in that what we observe in the universe influences how we think, not just about the universe itself, but about our own world and perhaps even ourselves — which in turn can give rise to aesthetic, moral, and religious effects. The crucial point is that the appreciation is there, and it bonds us spiritually to everything we can observe.

Thompson's poetic insight, however, is also the most concise and perhaps finest expression of what in the 1980s came to be called chaos theory, with obvious but somewhat misleading allusion to the myths earlier described.[31] Its argument, while mathematically complex, can be stated with brief precision: all things are linked not just in the poetic or logical structure of our thinking, in our spirituality, but in actual fact. Moreover, they are linked in *macroscopically* effective ways. The common example, cited in chapter 1, is usually cast in an agnostic context: there is no way we can be certain that when a butterfly flaps its wings in Bolivia it is not the decisive event that produces a windstorm in New York. This is the kind of theory that causes many physicists to pull their hair out, since it crosses the border from the indeterminacy of quantum mechanics at atomic and sub-atomic levels to the larger world we directly experience. For at heart many of them have kept alive the spirit of Einstein, who, as we've seen, never accepted quantum indeterminacy because it assaulted the decipherable and logical order he was convinced must prevail in the structure of the universe if it was to be reliably known, and friendly. Contemporary physicists have abridged his conviction so as to exclude the atomic and sub-atomic, since quantum mechanics and its experimental evidence requires it, but when it comes to the macroscopic world of daily life and the behavior of the universe as a whole, they have kept it warm, comfortable, and strong in their minds.

Macroscopic linkages in this macroscopic world are tolerated because they are accessible and confidently analyzable. But to slip into them the microscopic movement of quantum indeterminacy in a way that does not *always* overcome this indeterminacy through advance to macroscopic complexity[32] brings lack of analyzable and predictable order to the heart of their study. What is left is not certainty, which is their heart's desire, but statistics, which are sometimes workable for large groups, abstractly diagnosed, but always ambiguous for individuals. That a plucked flower might literally trouble a star troubles even more these scientists.

There is something else besides this uncertainty of confident predictability and its seeming prohibition of an ultimate order in the universe, though obliquely related to it. For the universe is also like a giant classroom in which history is the predominant discipline. This is due to the distances photons must travel before the source of their information becomes available to us. When you catch a brief glimpse of the Sun, for example, what you are seeing is the Sun eight minutes ago in its history. Or when you look at a stellar object 100,000 light-years away, you are seeing the history of that star as it was playing out 100,000 years ago. Our observational technologies are becoming sophisticated enough, especially those surrounding radio telescopes (the particles these telescopes record travel at the same speed as light), that we are closing in on objects which are apparently at the outer edge of the observable universe, thus making available data from very early in its history. The only way we could close this temporal gap would be by moving closer to the observed object. If we wanted to see what was going on right *now* on the Sun's surface, we would have to transport ourselves 93 million miles in the Sun's direction from where we currently are. Sending machines that close would do no good, since their transmissions would still take eight minutes to reach us. The other alternatives would be to develop observational technologies that could either overcome the speed-of-light barrier or that could identify such exotic speculative phenomena as tunnels and warps in spacetime: possibilities, as we've noted before, not taken seriously in the working (as compared to speculative) hypotheses of most scientists. But still, the thought is fascinating: if we could develop further our observational technologies to probe the edge of the universe, what wonders they might tell us of the composition and contours of the objects and forces emerging so much closer to the beginning of the universe's current spacetime continuum. We would observe the youth of all things and the grandeur of the night sky it produced over the eons.

For clarification we might now repeat that when we use the word "universe" in determining data about it, the qualification "observable" must always be implicitly or explicitly applied. The brute fact is that we have no way of knowing *exactly* how large or how old the universe as a whole is, and any technology described as bringing us back to its very beginning that ignores this qualification is misleading. All we can say with some reliability is that the universe we observe began developing some 12-20 billion years ago. This has profound repercussions on how thoroughly we wish to apply the legitimacy of our "natural laws," or what we called earlier in the chapter the constants of nature. For while most of us are familiar with the photon as the wave-like particle that carries electromagnetic force throughout the universe, especially in the form of light and radio transmission, it is as such also the primary carrier of information throughout the universe. If that information has not yet arrived from places and times beyond the current distance the photon can travel, we can know nothing about them, *nor* can they influence us. The most we have is an imagination of what they might be like, an intelligent imagination based on information we do have, but nothing more than that. We owe the basis of this insight, of course, to Einstein. In a famous thought experiment he realized, contrary to Newton, that if the Sun were suddenly to disappear, the orbit of the Earth would not be simultaneously affected; rather, it would take eight minutes for this affect to occur, and during this time the Earth would continue to orbit as if nothing had happened. Given this dependence of knowledge upon the finite transfer of data in the universe due to photon speed, it is therefore always a bit perplexing to study scientists, like James Trefil in his *Reading the Mind of God,* who nonetheless insist that there are certain constants that *must* apply — there is no choice, no exception — everywhere and at all times in the universe no matter how large or old it is.[33] How can he know this? He might surely hope it, but he cannot know it, not for certain. The universe is ultimately as limited by defining strictures on the knowledge it can release as any experiment in a laboratory is limited by its own strictures. It can enlighten us on only some of its past, less on its future, and this necessarily precludes sure knowledge of the whole. If it is a classroom, as we have suggested, then some of the lessons are there, available for our instruction — and we hope important ones — but not *all* of them; some information is revealed, but not *all* of it, just as in any classroom we may learn much, but never every single thing the teacher knows.

A momentary digression at this point might help connect these remarks to a parallel situation in theology. It is sometimes tempting to make partial knowledge, particularly when we are convinced of its certitude, universally applicable.[34] And we do so especially, as when we look through our telescopes, in making what we discover in the past the criterion for this applicability. In Christian theology this usually centers on the issue of biblical revelation, with the conclusion that knowledge of this revelation produces unerring confidence regarding God's will at all times and in all places. But how can we possibly be certain of this universality, any more than the scientist can regarding his or her knowledge of the universe, without inadvertently altering the certainty into a yearning expression of hope? We cannot. For God's will, too, like anyone else's, cannot be captured in its entirety by a partial knowledge of it. There will always be more to it that further study, insight, and experience in the world might reveal not as confirmation but as increase of the knowledge we already claim to possess — though at a certain point, like the limit imposed by photon speed, this available novelty also becomes inaccessible. The same sort of arrogance that theologians often lament when they read of scientists who claim to hold the whole of knowledge about the physical world within their possible purview sometimes repeats itself in their own attitude toward the will of God. In this context it is refreshing to encounter the humility of scientists like John Barrow,[35] or a theological confession like that of Schleiermacher in his later years: "The longer I live the less I am certain that we can know everything about God that we think we can." Age, along with a thorough devotion to one's object of study, has an uncanny way of revealing the truth of the Socratic maxim that wisdom shows itself first of all in an awareness of ignorance.

Still, there are many things we can learn with great confidence about the universe enfolding us, especially that which is close to home spatially and temporally. Scientists tell us, for example, that our own moon holds valuable data about the early formation of our solar system because it has not been appreciably altered either by seismic or volcanic activity or by the erosions of water or atmosphere. Consequently, its rocks and minerals appear to have remained remarkably stable since they were first formed. Moreover, the meteorite impacts that created the lunar "seas" can tell us what types of objects must have populated the system in its early eons. And even if those few are correct who suggest that the moon was not born with us, a small sister, but is a traveling rogue from far beyond our system which chanced too close to Earth's embrace, we would still be learning things of chemistry and gravity and mutual dependence. Mars, too, can teach us things, that gentle planet abused by a warrior god's name: what can we learn from flowing water long hardened into polar ice, an atmosphere dissipated into a meager presence, or perhaps of life as a failed experiment? Our other companions as well have their lessons: Venus, with its monstrous atmosphere and boiling temperatures; Jupiter, almost a star, perhaps still slowly compacting until it ignites; far distant Pluto, with its grand elliptical orbit telling of the enormous power of our star's gravity; Halley's comet, even more distant, speaking again of this power but also of others of its own kind. We can be educated by each of our companions in this system. Yet we must first be willing to learn, and this willingness must know no bounds.

There are more esoteric things to learn. Let us take just the single example of gravity.[36] We still do tend to think of the gravity holding the planets in orbit around the Sun as a force. Yet in chapter 2 we noted that within Einstein's general theory of relativity, confirmed by countless experiments, gravity is not strictly a force so much as a geometric phenomenon describing the bending of space around massive objects. Yet we also know that while this understanding of gravity has replaced the more familiar one given to us by Newton, where space is absolute and gravity is a true attractive force the way magnetism is, it has in fact not replaced Newton's inverse square equation regarding the strength of gravity's attraction, which is surely at least as important as its geometry. People are often defeated as soon as they hear the word "equation" in a context like this, finding it esoteric indeed, and frequently their response is justified.[37] But as with all equations when the effort is made, the inverse square equation can be expressed simply: if you take an object and move it three times as far away from another object, to discover how powerful the gravity then is, you simply square the three, which gives you nine, and then invert the nine, which gives you one-ninth. The gravity is one ninth as strong as it was before you moved the object. The reverse is equally true. If the distance between two objects is reduced to 1/3 of what it was, you simply square this, which gives you one-ninth, and then invert the nine, which gives you a gravity nine times stronger than before you moved the objects. We know further that the attraction is always concentrated at the center of the object and then dissipates with increasing weakness away from it; that it operates not just between two distinct bodies but among the components constituting each body itself; that gravity is indeed *always* attractive, never repulsive, save perhaps at some very tiny instant of time immediately after the Big Bang when its momentary repulsive force contributed to an unimaginably rapid expansion of the universe, an inflation bringing it from a size smaller than a proton to that of a grapefruit, or in numerical terms, an increase by a power of 10^{50}. Most amazingly of all, gravity is universal. This last point means that even two objects no more massive than a proton, separated by the whole breadth of the observable universe, will nonetheless still produce a mutual attraction, even though unimaginably small — and that this is one of those linkages between all things, a primary one, that promotes what I have designated an ecology of the universe. It is also something that can produce a theological twist in its interpretation, becoming a physically based and beautiful metaphor capturing the universal attractive love of God, no matter how far we may think ourselves from it. The whole of creation is in gravity's thrall, and this fact, with God's love, will finally determine what becomes of it.

The introduction of this theological twist allows us to twist it back in a description of science. We have repeatedly spoken of hope in this chapter, notably when discussing the idea of constants in nature, and we have implied as well the idea of faith as belief in the correctness of scientific theories that accounts for their hold on our minds. Yet if there is a single terrain of human concern where hope and faith have held strongest sway, it is not that of science but of religion. Christian religion is of particular assistance here, and in what now follows I will be synopsizing briefly matters that have concerned me at much greater length in other books.[38] In the Christian context hope is to be understood not as a device for escaping into imagined futures that will improve upon the present by divine intervention (heaven, a miraculously renewed Earth, etc.), but as commitment to a mission whose agents are ourselves. This mission is toward a human community that is motivated in its behavior toward creation by the witness of Jesus of Nazareth, expressed above all in his doctrine of love as fervent, unequivocal, and indifferent to reward as its seeks the cherishing of life. Faith is what enlivens this hope. But faith does not fall from the sky, nor, when it is passionately engaged, can it be given to us. Rather, it is born from obedience. This latter comes from two Latin words, the intensive prefix *ob-,* plus *audire,* meaning to hear. To be obedient is to practice intense and undistracted hearing, that is, to give oneself over in attentive ways — in contemplation, study, or prayer — to a proposal or experience so as to achieve a conviction regarding its legitimacy or truth. Presumably this conviction will then guide behavior.[39] The point I wish to make is that in its own hope science must share the same goal as Christian hope. Even in its most abstract musings about the universe, it must have at its heart something of a sense that in the knowledge procured life is being cherished. And in the faith that motivates this hope — that life *must* be cherished: physical life but also the life of the mind — science, like religion, must examine attentively all that can contribute, no matter how remotely, to faith's intelligence, persuasiveness, and strength. Otherwise it merely rambles around, unconvinced of its motives and tasks, or convinced, but with less noble goals.

Let me close this section with the following brief reflection. When I was 22 years of age I realized through tragic circumstances that logic, that crafty discipline wherein everything is neatly explained, regularly fails us. As mentioned in the last chapter, this is particularly true of inductive logic; we are easily seduced to believe that on the basis of a single or several experiences we can draw a general conclusion about all similar ones. So, because some people we know are kind and virtuous, we conclude that all people at heart are the same. But then we experience people who in fact are truly wicked, and this experience sends us into shivers of uncertainty. Our logic has failed us, and we have not yet learned that the premise of the logic determined eventual failure from the start. But when we achieve a taste of wisdom we finally become aware that experience is somewhat kaleidoscopic, that often it does not fit into the neat pattern of expectations outlined by our logic. In short, we come to appreciate the unexpected, whether in the events that populate our personal lives or those that populate the universe around us. At 22 years of age, then, being a Christian man, I also came to appreciate a dimension of the stories of Jesus which I previously did not: the dimension of surprise in certain teachings and incidents of his life. I saw anew his encounter with the rich young man and the arrogance of this man's behavior. He asks the Nazarene what he must do to fulfill the law, and the Master answers by enjoining submission to the fundamental commandments of Judaism. I can picture in my mind the young man's self-satisfaction as he announces that he has obeyed all these commandments, and then asking if there is anything more he should do, fully expecting Jesus to say no, nothing more, you are fully blessed. But instead the Master surprises him, saying yes, there is one thing more: go and sell all you have and give it to the poor. This was something completely unexpected as well as unacceptable for the young man, and the story concludes that he turned his back on Jesus and walked away, sadly and with tears. There is also the encounter with two others, disciples now, who ask him which of them will be the greatest in the coming Kingdom, clearly expecting him to name one or the other, or both. But instead he points to a small child and tells them that it is those who become like that child who will enter the Kingdom. Similarly, we can imagine the shocked outrage of the religious leaders when he taught that the Sabbath was made for human beings, not human beings for the Sabbath: a direct assault on the idea that we exist primarily, if not solely, to give praise and worship to the Creator. Yet the teaching perhaps most profoundly indicative of this unpredictability is the parable of the eleventh-hour workers we mentioned in the last chapter, wherein the landlord, prizing mercy over justice, awards the same salary to those who have worked one hour as to those who have worked twelve. But I can also

126

imagine the flabbergasted surprise those disciples must have felt who found a tomb empty one early morning three days after Passover, and that of those who experienced later visitations from the one crucified. And then there was my personal surprise when one day while meditating on the ancient Christian idea that all creation fell because of Adam but was redeemed because of Christ — and that this redemption proves itself singularly in the resurrection of the dead — I saw that this must mean that on the day of raising *all* that was alive will come alive again, not just human beings; that otherwise the rest of creation is trapped in a teleological absurdity that makes the claim about universal redemption itself absurd. Each of these examples speaks of education gained from the unexpected and the need to open our minds to its possibility in our lives. For the truly educated person is not the one who has simply amassed the wisdom and knowledge of others, but the one who has contributed to education itself by entertaining newness of thought about human experiences and the unexpected insights this can bring with it. The truly educated person is by definition an imaginative one, who knows to the bone that understandings of reality, whether in the life of the mind or the life of the universe, are always tentative, always open to novelty.

IN MANY OLD mythologies there are beautiful images of the Earth as the mother of human life and the Sun as its father. These images are not just aesthetically pleasing, they are also scientifically true. It is an overly obvious point, but one that might lead to less obvious truths, that if it were not for this planet and that star, we would not exist; it is their marriage to each other that brought us forward into the universe, from the moment the chasm was bridged between the conditions needed to produce life and life itself. There are, of course, more remote parents, just as there are in each of our own lives — grandparents, great-grandparents, etc. — and ultimate parentage finally belongs to the universe itself. As we have been arguing in several ways throughout the book, this fact should not be disparaged. Yet we are the easy prey of what I call the seduction of the immediate. By this I mean that we have a driving bias to foreshorten the importance of history and the influence of data more encompassing than what lies in our proximate surroundings. Our vision is clear when dealing with the at-hand; it tends to become increasingly myopic as we seek more distant sights. This concentration on the immediate produces not only seduction, however; it can also produce rapture. Love at its highest pitch, for example, is for many of us only found in the immediacy of the one we can touch; it becomes increasingly distilled the more we move away from this object, until it fades into an abstraction that might produce lively conversation but has little or no influence on how we live. We find it extraordinarily difficult to metamorphose this love for the one into a love for all, and even the encouragement of the greatest of our saints has produced scant headway among us. This is not perversion; it has something to do with the way our minds are put together, the concentration needed in primitive times, and inherited, on our immediate survival — we without claws or much speed or dexterity and needing to care for young who were long in coming to care for themselves. The saints are thus right when they say that to love all means a going against ourselves, a discipline that must overcome the powerful urgings of immediacy and live with scarce satisfaction for the effort. In the night sky we can see many stars, all of them remote and seemingly of little importance to us save for their abstract beauty. But in the day sky, save for when it first rises and just before it sets, we can see but one star, and its heat and light tell us of its intimate importance to us. It is this star that we know best, though in saying this we must also say that we still know little about it. Its enigmas are many, its behavior sometimes baffling, its influence on Earth, on all other bodies in the solar system, still being discovered.

Here are some generally proposed statistics about the Sun relative to Earth: it is roughly 93 million miles away (there is some variation since the Earth's orbit is not perfectly circular); its linear diameter is about 865,000 miles, the Earth's is a little under 8,000 miles; its mass is 332,000 times that of Earth, though its mean density is only about one-fourth of our planet's. And here are some generally proposed statistics about the Sun itself: it is around 5 billion years old, and has probably lived through half its lifespan as a medium-sized yellow star; its surface temperature is around 6,000 degrees centigrade, which, while hot enough to melt all known substances, is not nearly hot enough to cause fusion between hydrogen atoms to ignite the star — currently, therefore, an internal temperature of about 21,000,000 degrees centigrade is often suggested, definitely hot enough for an ignition; it is in one the spiral arms of our Milky Way galaxy, roughly two-thirds of the way out from the galaxy's center, and completing a full orbit around this center about once every 230,000,000 years; it is composed almost entirely of hydrogen (about 82%) and helium (about 18%), with very tiny traces of carbon, nitrogen, oxygen, and neon; it is the most chemically and physically active body in our solar system; finally, the Sun is by far the brightest source of light in the sky, even in the night sky, since it is what illuminates the moon.

The light from the Sun, along with its heat, is produced by nuclear fusion. The process is not difficult to describe, though there is some debate about details. I will offer what I think is a fair consensus of opinion.[40] The nucleus of a hydrogen atom is composed of a single proton (positively charged), with one electron (negatively charged) circling it. Ordinarily it will not fuse with another hydrogen atom because the similar respective charges of the protons and electrons in the other atom cause the two to repel each other. But under the extreme temperatures within the Sun this repulsion is overcome by the powerful kinetic (motion) energy of the atoms due to the extreme heat; they slam into each other with sufficient force and maintain close enough contact for a sufficient period of time that the so-called strong nuclear force between the protons activates and holds them together, with the electrons in tow. This force comes into play at a very tiny distance, about 10^{-13} centimeters, but is about 100 times as powerful as the electric repulsive force. The mediators of this force are called quarks, and every proton is composed of three of them, whimsically designated "up" (2) and "down" (1). It is the relationship between these quarks that creates the attractive energy that at the above distance binds protons to each other. These quarks are also the constituents of neutrons (1 "up" and 2 "down"), and bind them to each other and to protons. For while the neutron itself has no electrical charge, it is still subject to the strong force at the designated distance. An atom with one proton, one neutron, and one electron is called deuterium, and when two of these join there is helium. The proton and neutron both possess mass, as does, in a much smaller amount, the electron. Yet if you were to weigh the masses of two hydrogen atoms before and after their fusion into deuterium and helium, you would find a lesser amount after the process. Where does the missing mass go? Here enters the epochal contribution of Einstein and his renowned formula $E = mc^2$. The mass is converted into energy, almost exclusively in the form of the massless particles he was the first to call photons — which, among other things, carry what we experience as the Sun's light and heat. The formula tells us that a very tiny amount of mass can create a very large amount of energy (the mass multiplied by the square of the speed of light). With sufficient temperature still being generated in the star by the pressure of gravitational compaction, the helium in its own turn will then fuse to form still heavier elements, preponderantly carbon. As noted in chapter 1, this helium to carbon phase is especially critical, since through the massive energies it releases the Sun will eventually balloon into a red giant star whose circumference will extend beyond the Earth's orbit. At this point the Earth will either disintegrate entirely or through incineration be reduced to a scorched ember. Toward the end of this red giant phase, however, except in cases of very massive stars (where the evolution proceeds to the stage of a supernova explosion), the fusion process begins to weaken, since it takes a higher temperature, more gravitational pressure than the Sun can now generate to create heavier elements for further ignitions to occur. It will consequently begin to shrink and become a "white dwarf," still burning very brightly but even under continuing gravitational collapse unable to coalesce its atomic structures beyond a certain point (among other things, the so-called "Pauli exclusion principle" comes into play here, which states roughly that below a certain level of stellar mass — such as in our Sun — no two electrons can inhabit the same orbital position around a nucleus at the same time, thus limiting the degree of collapse).[41] Finally, over a period of billions of years it will gradually cool, with some intermittent but relatively insignificant detonations, until it eventually burns out and becomes simply a cold, dark lump of matter. These few observations, along with those in the previous paragraph, represent a fair consensus among scientists, some of them even unanimously affirmed, and I have put them here for the reader who may know little about our star so that he or she might better appreciate its magnitude, composition, and internal life and therefore enjoy more fully its presence. One consequence of this understanding, despite the conviction of ancient mythologies, is that the presence of the Sun, like that of the Earth, is not eternal.

The presence of our Sun, therefore, is obviously not merely a presence; it is one that generates effects. I suspect that for most people the preeminent effect is light, wonderful light that is the cause of so much of what we are and experience. Without the Sun's light we would likely have no eyes, for it is improbable that the stars in the night sky provide enough of it to give the evolutionary "nudge" needed for eyesight. And without eyes we would be moles, never seeing the beauty of contours and colors, nor the faces of each other. We would not imbue our poetry with its presence, nor our religion; there would be no reference in the old Christian creed to Jesus as "Light from Light,"[42] nor would we have developed the concept of an enlightened mind. There would be no photosynthesis and thus no green plants, probably no plants at all, and certainly no flowers. We would see no moon at night, no rainbows or auroras either. Darkness would prevail, that ancient symbol of evil and the dwelling place of demons, while its opposite, the equally ancient symbol of good and the abode of light and deity, heaven, would not be. Of course, it would be negligent of us not to note as well the negative effects this light can have. Were the light of the day star not tempered by night, think what would happen to rhythms of birth and growth among plants and animals, or to the consolation and wonder and knowledge gazing at the night sky offers us. Look at this light directly, too long and without filtering, and it always brings blindness.

"And God said, 'Let there be light.'" It is intriguing to realize that these words of Genesis recording the first object created by God[43] achieve a minor parallel in contemporary physics insofar as light would have been (to our eyes) the only perceptible constituent present in the earliest epoch we can reach in the evolution of the universe. This epoch lasted from 10^{-43} to 10^{-33} seconds after the Big Bang, and during it the universe can be characterized as a primal stew, one of whose primary ingredients were photons.[44] Light would have bathed the entire universe.[45] Electrons, among other elementary particles also present (quarks, neutrinos, gluons, etc.), would have collided constantly into each other at such speeds and temperatures that their mass would have been immediately converted into the energy-carrying photons. And these in turn, if maintaining sufficient energy in their constant motion,[46] would have collided and created the mass-carrying electrons, all together in a close and wondrous promenade of back-and-forth transfigurations, novelty upon novelty, that is the context for all creation. Only later, when these energies were reduced by distance and scattering as the universe expanded, would darkness become a characteristic of the universe, its dominant one to our eyes. Protons and neutrons would have formed from quarks, then together would have formed the nuclei of atoms, capturing electrons in the process, and all the while gravitating toward each other in enormous numbers until eventually igniting and concentrating most of the light in the assemblages of stars we call galaxies. It is this concentration of energy into mass — or in a looser description, light into matter — that is the primal act of creation. Chaos can certainly describe the primal stew, and while a scientist might prefer attending only to the secondary causes — the behavior of the elementary particles as they partnered themselves to each other — that altered this chaos into the intelligible and manageable forms that occupy his or her study, the theologian who wrote Genesis had the eminent right to identify a primary cause as the source of these secondary ones, and to speak of it as God. And while he may have been without our science, he was certainly not without insight, and his rendition of God's creative activity, whose first child was light, has stayed long alive, and vigorous, in human thought.

The twin of the Sun's light is its heat; we can scarcely think of them separately. This heat is enormous, powerful enough at some places and seasons on Earth as it circles the Sun on its tilted axis to raise the temperature well past 100 degrees Fahrenheit, despite the 93,000,000 miles separating the two bodies. It is true that unlike light, of which our planet has no natural source capable of anything near adequate illumination, the Earth does generate geo-thermal heat to the surface, principally through seismic and volcanic disturbances, which is then trapped by the atmosphere. But it is unlikely that it is sufficient to sustain anything except very primitive life-forms, like anaerobic tubeworms living near volcanic vents on the ocean's floor. In the radiant heat it throws at us, like its light, the Sun can also have both negative and positive effects. It can sear the water off large terrains, create a drought bringing death to plants, animals, and human beings. Fall asleep at the beach and it can wake you up with serious burns. Continue to thin out the ozone layer around the planet and it can produce far more massive forms of destruction, chemical and physical disruptions from thermodynamic anarchy. On the other hand, this heat brings not only warmth to nourish the stunning variety of life on this planet, but also the emotional and physical renewal relaxed sitting or reclining on a sunny day can bring to worried or worn-out human hearts and minds. And scientists tell us that one day solar heat, trapped by sophisticated technologies, may well provide a major source of power to run many of our machines. All of which means that the Sun's heat, like its light, must be received by us with a consistently careful gratitude and respect that we need show no other body in the heavens — except, of course, the Earth itself. We are also fortunate that our Sun is a remarkably stable star, pulsing its light and heat at us in fairly predictable patterns, and that this routine will apparently remain the same for another 5 billion years. The reliability of its orbit around the center of the galaxy and its steadiness as it spins on its axis contribute as well to an Earth that has nurtured continuing life to this day. It is a sunny August day as I write this, and I have just come in from reading outside, unshaded, for the past 30 minutes. My skin is tingling a bit, but it is a pleasant sensation, and my face is somewhat reddened, my hair slightly bleached. I can understand more profoundly Saint Francis's *Canticle of the Sun,* in which he gives thanks for much of the natural world surrounding him, but perhaps most eloquently for his brother, the Sun. It is a beautiful hymn of praise, and its sentiment has stirred easily in my mind today. I rarely have these feelings of nurturing and relaxed pleasure at night, though the night sky has its own enchantment and satisfactions, and I certainly never have them on bleak, thickly clouded days.

Aesthetics is the study of beauty, and while we normally think of it as heavy with subjectivity in its judgments, and thus the opposite of science, the best practitioners of the latter have always claimed that aesthetic appeal is a major factor in determining the persuasive power of a particular scientific theory, particularly when captured in simple, even austere mathematical equations. Perhaps no one captured this better than Paul Dirac when he said that "it is more important to have beauty in one's equations than to have them fit experiment."[47] Obviously he didn't mean that experimental results were unimportant, but only that a beautiful theory need not be rejected simply because it has remained experimentally undemonstrated. I have been defining beauty throughout this book as anything that gives pleasure to the senses or pleasurably elevates the mind; that it involves physical, moral, or spiritual loveliness. The bias of science, however, is like the bias of theology, namely, that there are some things that meet this standard so thoroughly that no one whose senses and mind are adequately alert could deny their beauty. Simplicity indeed seems a critical factor here; no one finds pleasurable, or pleasurable to the same degree, a complicated maze of equations or a convoluted theological discourse when it is possible to capture their meaning in more unadorned ways. This is the insight of all good teachers, as with Jesus when he chose parables rather than rabbinic disputation to convey his ideas. In art, too, we find the same idea. When viewed from a distance, Michelangelo's Last Judgment fresco in the Sistine chapel is an anarchy of colors, all interweaving in a complicated way, like a kaleidoscope that never stops moving, whose result more often than not is a headache. But seen up close, when the simplicity of the facial expressions, the folds in the clothing, the tempered posture of the bodies can be appreciated, it becomes a masterpiece of beauty. So much of life is like this; we seek the heart of our experiences, pruning their excrescent trivialities, because therein will their true beauty be found, if it is found at all. The Sun is like this, too. We might be impressed by much that goes into discussions of it, and perhaps even find beauty in them. But the profoundest beauty is experienced in the simple act of seeing its light and feeling its warmth.

For all we depend on it, then, and for the beauty we discover in its light and heat, it is not difficult to understand why the Sun was divinized in so many ancient cultures. We can appreciate better the aesthetic reasons for the revolution of Ikhnaton, an Egyptian pharaoh of the 14th century B.C. who sought to establish a monotheism with the deity represented by the disk of the Sun. And we can understand, while disapproving of it, the contemptuous vanity of Louis XIV when he allowed himself to be called *le Roi Soleil,* the Sun King, and the near deification it implied. In Christian piety something similar occurs, though there is nothing contemptuous about it, surrounding the mother of Jesus. She becomes identified with the woman "clothed with the Sun" described in the book of Revelation (12:1), and is proclaimed *Theotokos,* mother of God, by the Council of Ephesus in the 5th century. In some cultures the Sun is also worshipped in green plants, which are understood to be its children; in others it is worshipped in fire, the mirror of its light and heat. In folklore around the world we sometimes read of the great fear which eclipses of the Sun caused; in one of these tales a shaman describes an eclipse as the deity turning his back on the world. And then there were the sacrifices, human sacrifices included, which were thought to please solar deities through the "fragrance" they wafted toward heaven and thereby guarantee beneficent favor on the sacrificing group in times of killing drought.[48] Like the Sun's light and heat, therefore, our metaphors and mythologies about the Sun have both positive and negative aspects. The Day Star is too close to us, both physically and psychologically, for it to be any other way.

There are still other, more subtle metaphorical linkages between the Sun and notions of deity, qualities that we can reliably ascribe to the composition of our star (or any star) that find parallels in what several traditions — including a lengthy and revered one in Christianity — want to say about the "composition" of God. These comprise elementary statements from both astrophysics and theology, and interestingly bring us back to the elementary particle we previously discussed, the photon. Science asserts at least three characteristics regarding this particle that theology, at any rate those traditions I have in mind, also wants to assert about God. The first is that the photon is indivisible; so far as we know it has no component parts. In theology this is most often described as God's simplicity, and in both disciplines the characteristic means that we have reached an endpoint in searching out composite factors that might further our understanding of the item being investigated. In metaphysical parlance this is an *in ipso,* an "in itself" that limits all further investigation to effects the "in itself" produces. The second is that the speed of the photon, which is the speed of light, cannot be breached. One of the results this produces is that no information can be available to us beyond the limit this speed imposes. In theology this is most often depicted as God's unknowability, and in both disciplines it means that even the foregoing knowledge of effects is subject to an absolute limit. We cannot know at all times and in all ways what photons in the universe are doing, any more than we can know the same of God. The third is that the effects which the photon produces are not separable from their source, which resides in the mystery of its energy. In theology this is typically depicted as the difference between God's immanence and transcendence, and in both disciplines it means that the source is always distinct from, yet somehow always present in, its effects — which in a nice turn of a descriptive circle simply recapitulates and reaffirms the first two characteristics. Some scientists or theologians might find the foregoing parallels questionable, because of that bailiwick mentality we've noted before. But others, including myself, find that such connections pleasurably exalt the mind, and so, by the definition we have been using, represent not something suspect but something beautiful.

Finally, as I close this chapter, let me offer the following. In most English-speaking Christian groups the day set aside for special worship of the deity is called *Sun*day. Moreover, all the traditions agree that it is a day devoted not just to special worship but also to rest, analogous to the final day of the creation narrative in Genesis (2:1-3), the day Yahweh reposed after the work of bringing the universe into being. On at least one interpretation, therefore, what the Genesis account is telling us is that we are not the final act of creation, its pinnacle — a common enough belief — since we were created on the sixth day. Rather, this privilege belongs to the day of Sabbath rest, the wonder and serenity with which it blesses and encourages pleasure in the universe. I am enchanted by this viewpoint. I know it finds a home in my own mind, and in a culture which neither teaches nor encourages us to rest, where success is prized far more highly than serenity, where contemplation of the heavens comes far down a list from contemplating the stock market, I hope it also finds a home in yours.

V

Thoughts in the Late Hours

Sometimes during lonely nights, when sleep eludes me in a game of hide-and-seek turned nasty, I write; at other times, if the sky is clear, the temperature warm enough, and exhaustion still distant, I go out for a walk. Writing will often ease the feelings of luckless isolation, the hurting sense of being alone at the mercy of bad health, bad colleagues, or bad memories that have kept me awake. But walking under the night sky always does; tranquility arrives, slow or fast paced, simply from seeing the stars, letting my imagination roam freely, and regaining an awareness of proportion that soothes my mind and assesses more clearly the influence of what had been bothering me. I think that in this I have been fortunate, or at least receptive to the sight of the night sky in ways that many are not. Their acquaintance with it is at best perfunctory, a glance now and then, and they have other methods for dealing with their isolation and hurt, from television shows and reading in the early morning hours, a traveling of the mind away from the pain, to the crying consumption of alcohol, an attempt to deaden it. But for me it has always been the beauty of the night sky which has produced a turn toward companionship, or better, a cloaking, an embrace that holds me tight to creation and makes me feel a part of it. Then, after such experiences, I can turn back to my companions of flesh and blood, understand more thoroughly their own isolation, and seek to offer what presence and goodwill I can to help alleviate it. It is a therapy I'm talking about here, a way of coping in this often ragtag, badly rehearsed, semi-pornographic tragicomedy I call human life.

I have found such therapy, however, not just in the presence of the night sky but also in the presence of animals, those singular expressions of innocence which have been a part of my life as far back as I can remember: owls and ducks, dogs, cats, angel fish, rabbits, turtles, and more. I would guess, too, as I did in chapter 3, that others have had a similar experience, ancient minds who blended the consolation of the night sky with that of animals when they imagined singular or interwoven stars and nebular formations as portraying bears, canines, the head of a horse, a crab, a tarantula, and a swan linked to other formations named for human-like shapes and heroes like Hercules, Andromeda, the Water-Bearer, and the Archer. This last, also called Sagittarius, is particularly important to my mind because it captures all four of the major players in stories of creation: Sagittarius is a centaur, thus combining both animal and human forms; his bow, so essential to his definition, is made of wood and therefore incorporates plants; his mere existence as a constellation indicates both his celestial or cosmic identity as well as his source in the creative playfulness of the gods. Sagittarius is for me a symbol of an all-encompassing appreciation of the universe in which prevailing relationships interlock specific parts to each other and ultimately to the whole. Any vision based on this appreciation, therefore, any *Sagittarian* vision is one which has the whole universe as its concern, in the sense that there is nothing in the universe — no experience, no new insight or data, no source of wonder or beauty, no life — that it will not entertain in the pursuit of fuller knowledge, imagination, and love.

For us who live on this planet one of the specific, identifying parts of this vision is comprised of the animals which surround us, giving of their lives to feed and clothe us, and of their attention (when we allow it) to console our loneliness without cost and draw forth feelings of care and worry we might rarely or never experience for our own kind. In his magnificent volume *The Fate of the Earth,* Jonathan Schell thus describes our responsibility toward these other life-forms, the gratitude rather than greed and rapacity with which we should relate to them —

and above all, for the particular interest of his book, the concern that must prevent us from exploding our devastating nuclear devices. Some have accused Schell of a hysterical piety, the stuff of bad sermons; these people are fools, these self-designated hard-boiled "realists" whose viewpoint is worthy only of correction. Others have accused him more gently of naivete, hoping for a lasting peace with eyes closed to the innate, butchering, always chosen maliciousness of human beings; these people are pessimists, thinking of themselves, too, as the realists among us. Somewhere along this road of judgment there must be room for the optimist Schell actually is, and those like him — people who know of our depravity yet also our capacity for virtue, and who will not give up on the latter even when the pages of our history seem drenched, warped, and paralyzingly morbid with the stories of our indiscriminate bloodletting. Optimism must never be equated with an easy high-mindedness, or the attitude of the blind enthusiast who hums a tune of silly confidence while walking unaware straight into the mouth of hell. It is a hard and difficult set of mind to come by, optimism, because it never forgets or diminishes reasons for pessimism. And when it is the type that Schell desires, and the one I myself seek, it takes into account not just human beings, but the butterfly and panda bear, the human and non-human animal linked in the body of Sagittarius.

I remember once giving a series of lectures on cosmology and taking special pleasure in telling the students that cosmology is the mother of thought; since it is the study of the universe, everything that is, all other disciplines are its children. In doing so, I gave the study a broader compass than it usually possesses in order to impress the students with its importance.[1] For regarding this importance I have discovered that many of us travel too soon over Lethe, the sacred river of forgetfulness. During the course of one of the lectures I brought in some telescopic photographs of various celestial formations, concentrating especially on the Crab nebula, and asked the students to write down their initial impression upon seeing it. When I read these descriptions later in the evening I was stunned to find that a fair number of them said their first thought on seeing the nebula was of the explosion of a nuclear bomb. In the course of the following session when discussing this fact, their fear of nuclear war emerged sharply, along with a downcast sense of the in-

139

evitability of a nuclear exchange between nations. Where I had seen beauty in the photograph, they had seen only cataclysm of image-killing proportions, stone-melting, inexpressibly ugly, and indicative of what lay ahead for the Earth. And their fear, of course, has cause. In every silo, submarine, and aircraft harboring a nuclear device there is the potential of a little star-maker, whose cumulative capacity for destruction when all are exploded isn't very little at all. It might be the case that such a full-scale nuclear exchange would not obliterate all life from the planet — as mentioned in chapter 1, most reports indicate that some species of insects, algae, grasses, and deep ocean organisms would survive — but the devastation would likely be complete for our own species. So we are all aware, then, that we need not wait for the Sun to turn red, signaling our final end unless in some way we have protected ourselves from the event. We can accomplish fairly much the same effect by our own present power; and we learn, too, in a far more immediate fashion, that something else we must protect ourselves against in order to prevent this final demise is precisely ourselves. The sorrowing yet angry fear of my young students, all with life's enrichment ahead of them, thus became my sorrow and fear. And now I can no longer look at the photograph of the great nebula that caused their response without swiftly casting my eyes toward other portraits of the night sky, quickly passing over its form for some other.

I know this much about peace: I know that peace among us cannot exist unless there is peace within us.[2] I also know that there are such things as self-fulfilling prophecies, that a generation convinced of the inevitability of nuclear war has laid the seedbed within this conviction of the war's actuality. The peace needed within us to provide peace among us is therefore absent, killed by our sorrow and fear as surely as chronic suspicion or indifference can kill a kindly love, or faith in the tender mercies of God. Much, then, depends on how we discipline our thinking, the recognition along with the Decalogue's ninth and tenth commandments that while judgment of our virtue or vice is laid upon our deeds, the preceding thought (or lack of it) is intimately linked to these deeds: what we do is almost always controlled by how we think. And how we think is a question of learning. So we must learn of war and learn of peace in what Kierkegaard would call an "appropriation process" whereby decisions we make adequately express knowledge of the past, present concern, and forethought. Otherwise our individual lives, and our living with each other, can too easily take on the quality of a Mad Hatter's dance, constant movement with no guidance, gestures without direction, pointless maneuvers, a thinking of thoughts and doing of deeds that leave us dizzy and confused because of lack of wisdom and discernment; or more telling than a dance: life as a roulette wheel round upon round ending up finally as a gamble. But we cannot gamble on something like nuclear war. For the night sky teaches us that exploding stars might grace our sight with beauty, but should they move closer, should they come nearer our home, the less would be the beauty, the more would be the terror, until there was no beauty at all. The same must be the case with how we think of the exploding star-makers within our arsenals.

In a number of religious traditions, including Christianity, the state of final peace among us is portrayed in the image of a banquet.[3] It is an exquisite and allusive image, conveying not just the peace among them that brings people together to share a common table, but the peace within each that allows vivid and informed conversation — the second and sometimes more important form of nourishment that occurs at such a meal, the first, of course, being the nourishment of the body. All of us have had experiences like this, and we know the result is a closer bonding among the partners, a rejuvenation of spirit, and a deepening of knowledge and insight. The great Nordic myth of Valhalla, the banqueting feast of gods and great heroes when no word of scorn or contempt is spoken, no gesture of hostility done, no sullenness or pride engaged to silence the mirth or seriousness of ideas shared, all being served with grace and goodwill by the Valkyries, the maiden daughters of Odin: let us forget for a moment the patriarchal and bellicose religiosity that underlies this myth, the hero who achieves heroism by the slaughter of enemies, gods who are relentlessly savage, and look only on the feast itself. Perhaps we can learn again that even a brutal and murderous society of warriors, who praised the ax and hammer slamming into human skulls, the blood and entrails a well-placed spear disgorged from a hated opponent, could still imagine the peace of the banquet table, hold it of highest value, and call it heaven.

❀   ❀   ❀

I HAVE LEARNED from Whitehead that there are different types of adventures that can populate one's life. In his own case the dominant adventures were those pursuing ideas, but we can also think of spiritual and emotional adventures, physical ones as well, taking us to near and far-off lands, or perhaps just to our backyard, or the river or stream in the neighborhood. The great Loren Eiseley spoke of himself as a bone-hunter, and spent much of his life roaming the badlands and high deserts of this country looking for clues to past life in fossil remains; many of his adventures were thus outside himself, though he was a profoundly reflective man. Teresa of Avila we might describe as a huntress of the spirit, searching the corridors of her own psyche and the meaning of her prayers for clues to her beloved God, and often finding them where least expected; many of her adventures were thus within herself, though she was a profoundly apostolic woman. I like this image of life as a series of adventures, and I like thinking of this book as one of mine. What is the appeal here? I was mulling this question over on a night walk not long ago, and it came to me that the appeal lay not so much in the newness of experience which adventures bring into life as in the excitement they produce, something like the excitement we touched on in chapter 3 when discussing one of Rilke's short stories. That was the key, I decided, and I did some word searching (the reader knows by now my pleasure in discovering the root meanings of words we use). "Excitement" derives from two Latin words, *ex* + *citare,* meaning literally to move or be moved rapidly out of something, the implication being that the movement is out of what is ordinary or routine. I understood at once that this could be applied to anything from moving into a new home or school or job opportunity, to moving into a new relationship or a new set of values or ideas. Quickness or rapidity is also an integral ingredient to the experience, so that slow or easy-going movement tends to obscure, diminish, or simply prohibit excitement. I came to appreciate more fully, too, what philosophers like Schopenhauer and Lonergan were suggesting when they described the excitement of the experience of insight, the abrupt thought that occurs without being bidden or worried and effects major changes in one's patterns of perception and understanding. Of many examples I might give, one from my work as a theologian will be sufficient. It happened many years ago while reading an otherwise turgid book of biblical studies that I suddenly came to the author's analysis of the beautiful, honey-textured word "heaven" as commonly employed not to name a place but as a circumlocution or euphemism to avoid using the holy name of God. The meaning of many biblical passages changed immediately for me from that point forward, and a new, much richer flavor was given my contemplation of the night sky when I recalled that from ancient days it has been called "the heavens" or "the heavenly sphere." And what I experienced here I would readily call an adventure, now of the intellectual or spiritual kind, for the excitement it lent me and the changes it produced in how I thought of matters important to me. I have been fortunate in that similar experiences have continued throughout my life and have given it a personality, quality of surprise, and desirability it might otherwise not have possessed, or at least certainly not have possessed in the same ways.

As I noted above, writing this book has also been an adventure for me. I have deliberately stayed away as much as possible from technicalities of mathematics and physics, partly because I am not professionally trained in these fields, but mostly because I do not think that discussing them would have much place in the working out of meditations on cosmology for a readership likely composed of people with the same or even less training than myself — with the proviso, of course, that the meditations do not flagrantly contradict issues that science has generally settled. The adventure has been to discover data and theories about the universe, and then ways of bringing them into league with some of my concerns as a theologian. Sometimes I have discovered theories that have fascinated me enormously but which I have found no way of utilizing — like the "wormhole" theory of K. Thorne and M. Morris postulating accesses in the "fabric" of spacetime which would allow for rapid space and time travel[4] — save as an instance of human wonder and imagination about the universe. At other times I have discovered theories that neither fascinated me nor were of much usefulness to my own continuing education or insight, like the famous argument from design as it is presented by Thomas Aquinas and his inheritors,[5] or the speculations on creation offered by Karl Barth, that colossus astride twentieth-century Christian theology, or a boil on its backside, depending on your point of view.[6] But all have contributed to some degree, whether used or unused in the pages of this particular book, to my continuing adventure, now I might even say my love affair, with the night sky.

I suspect it is the adventure and excitement of discovery that is also the basis for the often dirge-like repetition of requests by scientists for state or federal funding of their projects. We need to be careful here, since the typical explanation for such requests is the broken-record refrain, "to learn about ourselves, about ourselves, about ourselves," skirting close to our bête-noire, that nemesis since earlier chapters, anthropocentric conceit. To study the solar system or the stars only for the sake of ourselves is not as fine a motive as studying them for their own sakes as well; it tastes of the double-mindedness of which Kierkegaard spoke (doing something for the sake of something else, a reward) as compared to single-mindedness, or in the telling phrase of Jesus, purity of heart (doing something solely for its own value). But I sometimes wonder if the human-centered explanation is a bit of a ploy for political and publicity reasons masking the more fundamental intent, which — like that of all committed thinkers — must also be the joy of scientists, namely, the simple pursuit of knowledge.[7] On the other hand, there is surely legitimacy in the complaint that funds spent gaining knowledge of planets and stars could be better spent (meaning in ethically more honorable ways) on the food, shelter, and medical care of deprived human beings. It is an old conundrum that individuals and nations, particularly wealthy ones, have always faced, and the immediate step toward its resolution must be an assessment of how needed items already available are being distributed in today's global village on a worldwide scale. If distributed well, and yet there is a lack which only additional funding can meet, then in my judgment we must give food to human bellies before we provide further knowledge for human minds. The planets and stars will survive for eons, but starving, unsheltered, medically neglected human beings die quickly and painfully. And I would make the same case for all other deprived life on this planet. The sight of a skeletal human infant, too weak to do more than whimper, covered with flies and lice feeding on open sores, or a battered and broken kitten trying to fend for herself because someone's brutal indifference threw her out alone into the world — these sights are not just horrifying, they are infinitely more compelling as catalysts for human attention and the behavior needed to correct them than the beauty of the night sky and implements for studying it. It is life that breathes and wounds and can do nothing to assuage its pain that is our primal responsibility, on this Earth or anywhere else where life has seeded its bounty. Knowing more of the night sky must wait upon this, though even so, in moments we spare, our sight can still turn toward it for the pleasure, challenge, and virtue which meditation can bestow, and be thankful.

The common wisdom is correct: events happen that can initiate all kinds of adventures in our lives, of various lengths of time, whose excitement can move us out of our normal routine into a myriad of experiences, some pleasing, others frightening, some beautiful, others abhorrent. The question is how many of these adventures one can handle intellectually or spiritually; and here each must know his or her own limits, including for critical consideration the extent of one's need for feelings of intellectual security. But I am convinced that one judgment is reliable: the more adventures, the fuller, more vital and interesting the life seems to be. All of us know people whose lives can be characterized in such ways, so that when other, reluctantly adventurous lives are examined, perhaps our own, they seem somewhat stunted, overly repressed, or bleak in comparison. The adventures, as I have said, can be predominantly internal or external, some weighted combination of both. Immanuel Kant, renowned and poked fun at for the predictability of his daily schedule, nonetheless enjoyed staggering adventures of the mind. On the other hand, Sir Richard Burton, the British explorer seeking the source of the Nile, could scarcely sit still until he was again trekking land and sailing waters. But Kant still did seek panoramas of "the starry sky above me" which Heidelberg did not afford technologically, and Burton still did take the time to write his marvelous journals. Any adventure, after all, loses something of its worth unless it is rehearsed in the mind, contributes to one's knowledge, and is shared with others.

There is a certain lyrical quality to contemplation of the night sky, and I am again reminded that the notion of the music of the spheres was not just an attempt at astronomical explanation but also expressed an

145

aesthetic appreciation for what these old scientists believed they were observing: the measured and melodic presence of the Creator. Other scientists, contemporary ones, are now telling us that sound does indeed travel throughout the universe, though like the hiss we hear as a remnant of the big bang wherever we direct our listening devices, it might be measured, but it is not melodious. And there is certainly no praise of God involved but only a compilation of inelegant and awkward theories regarding how this sound came to be, what behavior of energy vacuums and elementary particles triggered the primal ignition. We are in dark caverns of puzzlement here, or better, the lightened day of ideals, those goals of beauty, including the beauty of knowledge and understanding, that can never be fully achieved but that empower a diligent and life-long striving for them.[8] And this striving, the love of the night sky it represents: it is born only from time, dream, analysis, and romance, four parents these of any love.

❁   ❁   ❁

IN THIS AND the following section concluding the book I will continue my meditations writing strictly as a theologian and on a more personal note to each individual reader; take the words, as always, for whatever worth and application they have in your life. I will say that there is no privileged place where alone we can experience God, no church or temple where alone God's presence has been "caught." For God dwells within each of us, and within everything else that composes our universe, so that if we must still speak of a "place" wherein God is found, we must say that the place is creation, our own entire lives, all that we are, and all that everything else is. In short, our relationship to God is formed cosmologically; it is inclusive of all our experiences, and its boundaries are not those of particular times and places but of all that life holds out to us. Hope and faith and love, despair and pride and hatred, a sense of life's purpose and the purpose of the universe, God's presence and absence to us: all these thoughts and feelings are woven into our existence, and we are dependent on them. As such they provide the varying sources and many dimensions of our relationship to God, just as they provide the varying sources and many dimensions of a whole human self — a wholeness not of a single piece, however, but of many pieces, all interlocking to describe what God is, what we are, and how the two relate us to everything else that is. Our beloved night sky is the taste or symbol of this truth.

But while the physical/psychological components that shape our characters might be complex, the truth of what we are can be so simple that contradictions which this complexity raises within us become understandable. For these contradictions are not necessarily a reflection of the truth or falsity of our character in and of itself, its rationality and integrity, but rather of how we are going about experiencing life. To appreciate this, however, we must first learn to qualify our judgments and adjust our perspective to the point where we can view and accept *everything* we experience as formative elements of what we are, including our relationship to God. And we must appreciate, too, that though our reason is remarkably capable of comprehending through experience the fact that such and such is a reality of life, the difficulty confronting all of us is comprehending the accurate meaning which may be surreptitiously underlying the reality, and then relating it to the meaning of other realities we've experienced. In this context, then, reason is always circumscribed: we can delve rationally into some experiences of life only so far, searching out a certain and indubitable meaning to them, and then we must admit defeat. And yet: this very quality of reason is precisely what also sets us apart from — I will *not* say "above" — all else in this world and makes possible for us a unique relationship with God, since it is what makes us aware of the limitations upon which we are dependent, and thus open to what lies beyond them. It was the great philosopher/psychologist Karl Jaspers, in my judgment, who most incisively analyzed this function of reason, doing so within the context of what he called the "limit situations" of life. He described these as fundamental human experiences that are felt and thought "on the boundaries of our existence and whose common denominator lies in the fact that there is nothing firm, no indubitable absolute, no support (regarding them) which could withstand the test of (rational) thought." The basic realization in such limit situations, therefore, is that everything "is fluid, in the restless movement of its constantly being called into question. Everything is relative, finite, split into opposites; never the whole, never the absolute, never the essential."[9] Here reason must abdicate its power, affirm its weakness, and be still. But here wonder is also fully born, that companion of ours from the beginning pages of this book. For surely the night sky, and the universe which it represents, is one of these limit situations, where reason may never be fulfilled but wonder is generously nourished.

Yet the concluding word is not yet spoken, because it is exactly at these limit situations that our reason fails and we are confronted with the contradictions and unknowns of our existence, the ambiguities surrounding its certain meaning, that we begin to understand the completeness of our relationship to God. We begin to see that it opens and incorporates whole dimensions of our existence and our experience which can never be fully understood, and problems which can never be fully resolved.[10] A spirituality, even a very good one, can offer at best only a truncated description of these dimensions, a partial approach to these problems. Why is this so? One answer, a very good one, lies on the pages of that profound witness to Jesus of Nazareth that we call the gospel. It is an answer that every disciple of his knows, and knows to the bone. For when we look to Jesus for what it means to relate to God, we do not find a hard-and-fast definition; we do not find the relationship bounded or separated off from the rest of life like a closed compartment. No — what we find is a beautifully simple and direct description that takes into account the whole person, the whole of life itself, and the whole of our relationship to the universe we catch a glimpse of in the night sky. Jesus says: "You shall love the Lord your God with *all* your heart, and with *all* your soul, and with *all* your strength, and with *all* your mind" (Luke 10:27; Matthew 22:37). Yet — no one can ever capture the all of what he or she is.

To the extent that he himself lived this way, then, in a boundless love of God that knew no bounds in God's creation, the ancient designation of Jesus as cosmic in his meaning is true.[11] The cosmic Christ is not an individual presence, not even one raised from the dead, that fills the whole of creation, but rather a presence that is filled with the whole of creation. The fact that he himself was baptized and that he enjoined this experience upon his followers is in this context, then, not first an implied mandate for benign proselytizing but of an emulation of this same boundless love in oneself: to be baptized with the whole of creation as one's own, as one's name is one's own — to attend to it, learn from it, cherish it as one does oneself. In this way is the deity which Christians claim is present in a privileged way in Jesus made manifest, in the perfection of his love of God in the love of creation, and the ineffability of ever being able to capture the all of this. And while others may not be able to achieve the perfection of this love, all are called upon to seek it in a vast, universal absorption or embrace of all that is, each according to his or her talents in a Christlikeness that is not reserved for some but demanded of each. The Christ is not confined to just one, the Nazarene of two millennia ago. Each must strive with Paul toward that identity that confesses with joy, "It is now no longer I who live, but Christ who lives in me" (Galatians 2:20), so that the hope is not empty but possible, in an awareness that motivates life-cherishing deeds, that of a day God will be everything to everyone (1 Corinthians 15:28).

Let me conclude this section by recalling that throughout the book I have suggested in a variety of contexts that in any relationship there is more involved than just the sum of the partners, whether it be of electrons to each other, trees, dragonflies, stars and galaxies, or human beings in the common experiences they share. The communion that exists between them, the act or energy or word that unites everything to other things, is in some way before, between, and ahead of them, ahead of us. The plural must then become the habit of speech, the singular left behind in the knowledge that it is insufficient to explain this universal companionship — the single electron, tree, dragonfly, or human being, bereft and alone, by itself, makes no sense and is deprived of meaning. A pieta, a sculpture of a sorrowing Mary embracing mightily the body of her dead son, with eyes indescribably saddened on a face numb with disbelief, only appears to us as a singularity; we know that in reality it is composed of many relationships, of the molecules binding themselves to each other, the chisel and the marble, the artist's imagination and the finished product, ourselves and what we are seeing. Or when we spy a hummingbird outside our window, iridescent in reds and blues and greens, we again know that we are not viewing a singularity but a communion of relationships, wings to air and pigmentation to sunlight, to name just two. Our conclusion is thus a simple one: everything exists in

149

and is comprised by relationships. And this includes you and me. I cannot pretend, therefore, that I can take you out of your relationships to the world and what is alive around you and find an autonomous value and dignity in you. You have value and dignity, to be sure, but they exist only because of the relationships in which you dwell. These relationships, moreover, can never be completely compelled; to one degree or another they always happen of their own accord, somewhat like a wonder, somewhat like a gift, but always beyond the total control of the partners. And if we remain true to a suggestion made variously in these pages and call this power which unites everything that exists to something else that exists by the name of God — that God is found *in* the relationships, all for the cherishing of life — then it means that God is neither totally beyond the universe nor only indifferently involved with it, but instead is an elemental, integral, active, and free presence within it.

❈   ❈   ❈

THERE ARE SOME people, scientists and theologians among them, who are at their eloquent best when challenging God to account for certain behavior. The hesitation, stuttering, groping for words that may regularly punctuate their speech when addressing other human beings disappear in a flash. They speak with utter confidence, a certainty that truth is on their side (disagreement indicative of imbecility), and a rhetoric bordering on art. Where does all this confidence and certainty come from? Why in the singular instance of challenging God are their words at fever pitch, fluid, and unwavering? The answer is found in the ancient maxim of the law, that silence is consent, and in the knowledge that before all their accusations God will remain quiet. From the outset of the challenge they have already won the case because they are the only ones being heard. It sounds terribly unfair, of course, this taking silence as consent, but it is remarkable how freely we practice it when addressing God. It is the unfairness we feel when reading the accounts of Jesus before his accusers, when his silence too was taken as consent to their indictments. Why didn't he speak in his own defense, disarming his opponents with the subtlety and insight that had not only made them his enemies but had also gained him disciples? Where was the Jesus in the courtroom who in the fields could turn the most commonplace events into exquisite parable? His silence nailed him to a tree just as much as a soldier's arm swinging a hammer.

Sometimes our challenges against God are mere displays. We have a need to parade before our mind's eye the adroitness of our facility with words, the detail and cleverness of the arguments we launch. But in our hearts we don't really mean what we are saying, no matter how eloquently we say it, because our interest is not sincere; we know that God will not account for behavior, that victory in the contest is always ours. But the words pour forth simply because it makes us feel good. It is the same feeling we have when we berate a little child for accidentally breaking a vase we have treasured. The little child can only sit and stare at us in dumb inarticulateness. She says nothing, and we take this as the right to unleash our frustration on her with a verbal flourish that, were we facing an adult, would embarrass us and likely draw the other's contempt. It is all for display — to express, justify, or simply channel out of us anger that has welled up and needs expression. So we challenge God, as we might the little child, asking questions we know will go unanswered, voicing taunts that are meaningless, accusations that make no sense. We still, if nothing else, have our say, and then pick up the broken pieces of what had once been beautiful. *We* will not greet events with a silence that implies consent; we will speak out if only to let ourselves know that we disapprove.

When it turns more serious, the type of courtroom duel I have just described — wherein we imagine ourselves as having reduced our opponent to silence by the power of our impassioned words — can take on more the contours of an actual duel. Now it is no longer our goal simply to reduce to silence but to kill our opponent. And again we imagine ourselves as superior in this task: we have the gun drawn and are aiming a bullet between our opponent's eyes before he or she has even moved a hand. The opponent is at our mercy, and all we need do is decide whether or not to pull the trigger. It is this sort of duel I had in mind for this concluding meditation, and the decision confronting us whether or not we will indeed pull the trigger, put a bullet between God's eyes, and kill the religious consciousness. It is a decision, I think, worthy of a lifetime's reflection, and an examination of how others have decided. But let me hone down the meditation more thoroughly by noting that when we duel with God in such ways, despite the specific forms it may take, the duel is almost always centered on secrets the universe still holds from us, particularly those of suffering and death. It takes the form of any one of a number of challenging and unsettling questions of cosmology — such as Einstein's, which we have already noted twice, "Is the universe friendly or not?," or the more ancient inquiry, "Why are things the way they are, and where are they going?" — and our perception that God is unable or unwilling to offer adequate answers. This brings us, I have suggested, into the terrain of myth, that is, myth understood as a conceptual framework for understanding our experiences. More specifically, it brings us to myth as the way we articulate what we understand to be God's reply to experiences of uncertainty and confusion, suffering and death, so that it is ultimately these myths which we are judging adequate or inadequate as responses to the above questions. It has been and still is important for the reader to keep this definition in mind so that he or she does not confuse myth with fable or fairy tale *or* with unquestionable truth, and also realizes that everyone is a mythmaker in the sense that all of us try to provide a conceptual framework to give intelligent, coherent, and pertinent meaning to our experiences. And the discovery is quickly made that when these myths refuse to involve the presence of God, ignoring or expunging the religious consciousness as a positive and formative agent, they inevitably take the form of atheistic humanisms, triumphalistic ones like Nietzsche's, self-infatuated ones like Sartre's, or frantic ones like Camus'.

It is clear, then, that mythology (at least as I am describing it) plays a critical role in how we express the experiences that confront us in life and the intent or purpose of the universe and ourselves within it. Beginning with the ancient theorists of Mesopotamia and Egypt, and their vivid portraits of divine behavior, up to modern times and our myths of the dead and illogical God, we have consistently attempted to answer questions of cosmology with as educated and informed, critical and analytic a mind as it is possible for us to gain. And the study of these answers, these myths, is rich ground indeed, over some of which we have traveled in these meditations: an adventure, we said earlier, worthy of whatever pursuit we can give it. As a response to our experiences, however, myth-making must be kept clearly distinct from theology. For though their concerns may be similar, the very task of the theologian is to overcome storytelling and myth-making through some type of creative reasoning or analysis, while recognizing the limits of reason we spoke of just a short while ago. The motive for doing so — as thinkers like Bultmann, Ricoeur, Eliade, Marcel, Jung, and Campbell tirelessly encourage us — is to secure a divulgence of truth that will satisfy whatever standards of trustworthiness his or her theological viewpoint makes its own: something which myth-making in itself can obviously not do without becoming its own judge. Theology's claim to trustworthiness, like that of science or any intellectual discipline, thus involves insightful appropriation of past situations, intelligent appraisals of present ones, and foresight into what the future may hold so as to bring about effective awareness of what is no longer immediate or at-hand. In this way it gradually comes to replace myth as the more subtle and comprehensive method of expressing truths about our experiences. Yet it must also be said that in this very refinement of at-hand experiences theology continually broods its own potential failure. For although the theologian must change and challenge and build and abstract in order to be faithful to his or her trade, this effort is not guaranteed success, and can even become self-defeating. In fact, we usually find that the more abstract a theology becomes, the more prone it is to become mute or condescending toward concrete experiences such as suffering and death, wonder, excitement, and beauty which people have and which simultaneously ring the warning — the just lament — against its excessive, often bewildering detachment, its maddening irrelevance to the round of life. Certainly a theology must often involve the suppression or negation of myth, as in the literal rendering, say, of several portions of the creation stories in Genesis, in order to maintain its intellectual trustworthiness. But this process is also a potent source for misguidance and alienation when it loses contact with immediate reality, such as, for us, the night sky. Theology's detachment from myth, therefore, should not mean the refusal of myth. Rather, myth must remain a challenge to theology and retain the right to appraise it — as theology does myth in a mutuality of critical assessment — regarding its consistency, relevance, and illuminating power when addressing the full compass of human experiences.

And so we are at the end of this book, this escapade into myth and science and theology born from my love of the night sky. You have been my cherished companions here, and I hope I have been a worthy guide. And as we stand at the end, the trigger must not be pulled, no bullet sent between God's eyes. Instead, our foolish threat abandoned, we must run to God's embrace, with head thrown back and eyes smiling with wonder as they look home, and a heart and mind finally knowing the beauty, grace, and love of the one who has made it so.

Notes

NOTES TO CHAPTER I

1. The sentence in which this phrase appears occurs in the conclusion of *Critique of Practical Reason*. It reads: "Two things fill the mind with ever increasing wonder and awe, the more often and the more intensely the mind of thought is drawn to them: the starry heavens above me and the moral law within me." Kant was probably concerned in this statement, as he was throughout much of his more renowned and influential *Critique of Pure Reason,* with the intricacies of cause-and-effect relationships as they produce both physical and psychological (or spiritual) realities, and the extent to which these could be conclusively known. In this task his great companion, and frequent adversary, was David Hume, whose philosophy sought to cast into doubt the legitimacy of *all* cause-and-effect relationships as accesses to certain rather than just statistical knowledge. During the illness that finally killed him, however, this did not prevent Hume, in ironic contrast to his philosophy, from traveling widely seeking its certain cause and cure. Many scientists today, particularly those in quantum mechanics where the indeterminacy principle comes into play, would likely find themselves in sympathy with Hume. As we will suggest in chapter 4, however, this sympathy is frequently grudging and halfhearted.

2. For those who have not yet read Eiseley, I would recommend as a start the collection of his essays entitled *The Starthrower* (New York: Times Books, 1978). Of special pertinence to our interests in this book is "The Inner Galaxy," pp. 297-311.

3. Lynn White, "The Historical Roots of Our Ecological Crisis," *Science,* vol. 155 (1967), p. 1203. In this analysis he is dependent, wittingly or not, on a long line of exegetes stretching from Origen to Luther to Barth.

NOTES TO PAGES 3-6

4. For a more philosophically, less theologically oriented analysis of care than I will give in this book, see the superb volume by Robert C. Fuller, *Ecology of Care* (Louisville: Westminster/John Knox Press, 1992). Care also figures largely in Heidegger's *Being and Time,* though he confines his analysis preponderantly to the care one gives to oneself, including one's thinking processes, and to other human beings. With the notable exception of Nietzsche, very few of the existentialists show any interest in nonhuman life (save God), and none of them shows more than the vaguest interest in cosmology as the study of the universe.

5. A useful volume to catch the flavor of this excitement in professionals is A. Lightman and R. Brawer (eds.), *Origins: The Lives and Worlds of Modern Cosmologists* (Cambridge: Harvard University Press, 1990). This is a collection of interviews with 27 of the world's leading cosmologists. The questions are designed so that at some point in the interview each individual is given the opportunity to comment on the role of God in the practice of science.

6. See Jeffrey Sobosan, *The Turn of the Millennium: An Agenda for Christian Religion in an Age of Science* (Cleveland: The Pilgrim Press, 1996), *passim,* but especially chapters 1 and 5.

7. Some of this has already occurred in the works of scholars like Barbour, Peacocke, Polkinghorne, Berry, Santmire, Gustafson, and Scharper.

8. This is captured, among other places, in the ancient Latin maxim, "quidquid recipitur ad modum recipientis recipitur" which, roughly translated, means: whatever is received, is received according to the capacity of the receiver. In its Greek version, as employed, for example, by Aristotle, the maxim almost always pertains to a physical condition that affects one of the senses, in the manner, say, that eyes filled with tears or cataracts can affect how one sees an object. Later, however, it comes to represent an epistemological maxim indicating that before we actually undergo an experience we have already formulated prejudgments — no matter how consciously or not, accurately or not — regarding what the experience will be like, thus influencing the experience itself. Identifying these prejudgments, or biases, is one of the initial steps toward wisdom.

9. The history here is recounted in many fine books. One of the best, lucidly written and anecdotally engaging, is Timothy Ferris, *Coming of Age in the Milky Way* (New York: William Morrow, 1988), pp. 19-101. I would also recommend N. Spielberg and B. Anderson, *Seven Ideas That Shook the Universe* (New York: John Wiley & Sons, 1987), pp. 14-49, and Steven Toulmin, *The Fabric of the Heavens* (New York: Harper, 1961).

10. This hostility was due not exclusively but notably to an attempt to save the literal meaning of certain biblical texts. Among these perhaps the most notorious was Joshua 10:12-14, where it is said that at Joshua's request God made the

Sun stand still. The author, either in amazement or with a wink at the exuberance of the tradition he is recording, closes with the statement, "There has been no day like it before or since."

11. Tycho's geometry justifying this viewpoint was even messier than that of the Ptolemaic and Copernican systems preceding it. All three were filled with anomalies between theory and actual observations of planetary movement. It was Tycho's protégé, Johannes Kepler, who finally provided in his famous three laws of motion a viable system that resolved most of these anomalies and vindicated the essence of the Copernican argument for heliocentrism. For a lucid presentation of this history, along with a commentary on the personalities involved, see Timothy Ferris, *op. cit.,* pp. 61-82. No less an intellect than Immanuel Kant, who himself assisted astronomical science with his nebular hypothesis on the formation of solar systems and galaxies, considered Kepler "the most acute thinker ever born" (*ibid.,* p. 75).

12. Of the many studies on Darwin and the socio-religious repercussions of his theory of evolution during his own lifetime, one of the best is A. Desmond and J. Moore, *Darwin: The Life of a Tormented Evolutionist* (New York: W. W. Norton, 1991), especially pp. 391-677. For a richly documented and elegant assessment of his contributions to science, see Loren Eiseley, *Darwin's Century* (New York: Doubleday, 1958).

13. For further reflections on this point, see my book *The Ascent to God: Faith as Art, Risk, and Humor* (Chicago: Thomas More Press, 1981).

14. For an example of how this same conviction is honored in another work, even though applied much differently than in this one, see Wolfhart Pannenberg, *Toward a Theology of Nature: Essays on Science and Faith* (Louisville: Westminster/John Knox, 1993). The chapter "Contingency and Natural Law," pp. 72-122, is particularly insightful.

15. We use this awkward hyphenation, energy/mass, in recognition of Einstein's insight that energy and mass are equivalent, according to his famous formula, $E = mc^2$. In easily accessible images commonly employed by scientists — though by this fact lacking in precision — mass may be understood as "frozen" or "solidified" energy.

16. Two books recommend themselves on this issue: Stephen Weinberg, *Dreams of a Final Theory* (New York: Vintage Books, 1993), and especially John Barrow, *Theories of Everything* (Oxford: Clarendon Press, 1991).

17. I would name just two studies that support this impression. The first is John Farella, *The Main Stalk: A Synthesis of Navajo Philosophy* (Tucson: University of Arizona Press, 1984). The second is the magisterial work by Gladys A. Reichard, *Navajo Religion: A Study of Symbolism* (Princeton: Princeton Univer-

sity Press, 1990). The latter work is part of the Bollingen Series and demonstrates one of the most amazingly adroit uses of the works of Carl Jung with which I am familiar. A far more popular agreement with my impression can be found in the many novels of Tony Hillerman.

18. I will be reinforcing this dictionary definition primarily with a reliance on George Santayana, *The Sense of Beauty* (New York: Dover, 1955).

19. For an assessment of some of these theories, see J. A. Wood, "The Moon," in the *Scientific American* volume of collected articles called *The Solar System* (San Francisco: Freeman and Co., 1975), pp. 69-80. The ensuing years have not required any appreciable alteration of his analysis.

20. On this point see George Hendry, *Theology of Nature* (Philadelphia: Westminster Press, 1980), pp. 43-44, 127-28, 143-46, 170-72, 198f. This much neglected book is perhaps the finest I have read on its topic. The direct comparison between Goethe and Barth is my own. It should be noted, however, that Goethe, unlike Barth, did seem to provide at least some leeway for a more positive assessment of the relationship between science and theology — particularly when the former is understood as at root an aesthetic enterprise — when he ended his masterwork by having Faust, the stereotype of the Goethian scientist, redeemed.

21. Together with those already noted in endnote 7 above.

22. This longing is usually expressed quite subtly, though here and there quite vividly, among many of Einstein's published works and unpublished letters. For a sample, see his eloquent volume, *Out of My Later Years* (Secaucus, N.J.: The Citadel Press, 1956), especially pp. 41-115.

23. Tillich makes much use of these notions of finitude and fallenness throughout his *Systematic Theology* (Chicago: University of Chicago Press, 1951, 1957, 1963), especially in volume 1. His ontological/existential appraisal of them is now a commonplace in theological analysis. While he rarely uses the terms explicitly, few have attempted to apply their implications more thoroughly to the dialogue between science and theology than Arthur Peacocke. See especially his *Theology for a Scientific Age* (Minneapolis: Fortress Press, 1993), *passim,* but especially pp. 213-54, 321-31. Also recommended is Holmes Rolston, *Science and Religion* (New York: Random House, 1987), pp. 1-32, 297-347.

24. In this paragraph I am incidentally dipping slightly into the turbulent waters of a much debated issue among scientists, namely, whether we *discover* truths about the universe that are present independently of us, or *create* them through the way we texture our analysis of otherwise chaotic data. I have dipped only slightly into this debate because I think that this is all it is worth. The either/ or context in which it takes place seems to me to befuddle the more realistic ap-

praisal that science both discovers and creates valid statements about the universe.

25. Here wisdom means what it often does in biblical traditions, particularly those of the Old Testament: the ingenuity that permits the achievement of a purpose or goal through resourceful and effective activity. When applied to human behavior this achievement was deemed of special admiration when it occurred without breaking the law understood as a revelation of God's will.

26. For the interested reader, the suggestions occur in chapter 5 of the book.

27. The relationship between religious and scientific faith is examined nowhere with more remarkable insight than in Michael Polanyi, *The Tacit Dimension* (New York: Doubleday, 1966). See also his much shorter volume, *Science, Faith, and Society* (Chicago: University of Chicago Press, 1964).

28. Bacon is a perpetually interesting figure, and many consider him the founder of rigorous experimental method in science. Of numerous studies of his life and thought, one of the most profoundly appreciative is Loren Eiseley, *The Man Who Saw through Time* (New York: Scribner's, 1973).

29. Sartre's analysis can be found above all in his *Psychology and the Imagination* (New York: Philosophical Library, 1948) and *The Psychology of the Imagination* (New York: Rider, 1951). His analysis in both is directed preponderantly to the literary imagination and is heavily freighted with his love/hate relationship with Freudian psychology. As one counterpoint I would recommend Jacob Bronowski, *The Origins of Knowledge and Imagination* (New Haven: Yale University Press, 1978). For the role of imagination in the specific context of theology, see especially Ray Hart, *Unfinished Man and the Imagination: Toward an Ontology and Rhetoric of Revelation* (New York: Seabury, 1979) and R. Masson (ed.), *The Pedagogy of God's Image: Essays on Symbol and the Religious Imagination* (Chico, CA: Scholars Press, 1982).

30. I use dictionary definitions with some frequency in my writing since they are brief, presumably represent a consensus understanding of the meaning of concepts, and for many readers are more handy for further research than, say, the works listed in the previous endnote. In no way, of course, does this degrade the need of the serious student or scholar to pursue such other works.

31. For a layman's guide to the development and functioning of the brain, I would recommend the book by that master and competent popularizer, Isaac Asimov, *The Human Brain* (New York: Signet Books, 1965). For a technical guide to this development regarding specific components, there is Karl Popper and John Eccles, *The Self and Its Brain* (New York and Berlin: Springer-Verlag, 1977), especially Part II (by John Eccles), pp. 225-407. There is also Karl Pribram's

enormously interesting study on holographic processing in the brain, *Languages of the Brain* (New Jersey: Prentice-Hall, 1971), and the volume edited by G. Globus, *Consciousness and the Brain* (New York: Plenum, 1976). An excellent and fairly recent study is Antonio Damasio, *Descartes' Error: Emotion, Reason, and the Human Brain* ((New York: G. P. Putnam, 1994). The author, a renowned brain physiologist, makes plain how very little we know about the brain — we are not even sure, for example, how its cellular mechanisms account for why we can remember a telephone number. This makes brain physiology, from my viewpoint, along with cosmology, one of the two most exciting and imaginative fields of research in science today.

32. That science, however, is also dependent upon competent imagination is the keystone of Thomas Kuhn's classic study, *The Structure of Scientific Revolutions* (Chicago: University of Chicago Press, 1962). Kuhn's basic argument is that when controlling scientific paradigms begin to weaken as a result of anomalies that can no longer be ignored because of newly discovered flaws in their logic, which in turn are almost always due to new experimental or observational data, a period of time usually goes by before a new paradigm arises that is capable of resolving the anomalies. A classic illustration is the new paradigm of celestial motion that arose from the combined work of Copernicus, Galileo, Brahe, and Kepler as this issued in the mechanics of Newton. The intriguing point is that it is the imaginative effort of individuals that appears to be the impetus leading to these new paradigms, the ability of these people to cast old and new data into novel patterns that more simply and elegantly describe the issue under consideration. This imaginative effort is itself typically the result of some sudden, unbidden idea, some insight that springs to mind — a glitch in one's normally discursive reasoning — with an overwhelmingly powerful certitude regarding its correctness. In short, as in most other areas of thought, great advances in science that provide the groundwork for paradigm shifts are seldom the result of group work, but rather of the solitary thinker willing to allow imagination free rein in the meanderings of the mind. The mind dances until its hits upon the unforeseen insight, and then it goes to work.

33. Neutrinos are very, very small particles, though there are countless numbers of them in the universe; hundreds of billions of them pass through our bodies every second. Should each possess even the tiniest amount of mass (say, one millionth that of an electron), as some very recent experiments seem to be indicating, they would, by virtue of their enormous numbers, dominate the mass of the known universe. However, they cannot be much more massive than this (say, one ten-thousandth the mass of the electron), since then we would not be able to account for the observed structures of galaxies. The reason is that if there was *too*

much mass after the universe's inception, it would have begun contracting well before galaxies had time to form.

34. I am using "mass" and "matter" as interchangeable terms. Strictly speaking, mass is the amount of matter in a body as determined by a comparison of the changes in the velocities when one body comes close to another that is being used as a standard. Or, to put it differently, it is what results when you divide the weight of a body by its acceleration due to gravity.

35. In addition to the candidates just mentioned to account for this missing matter — since many scientists think that they are not sufficiently present in the universe (or, like the neutrino, too light and too swift) to bring about a contraction — some theorists hypothesize still other candidates, the foremost being black holes and the axion, a relatively slowly moving massive particle that is not only dark but transparent (neither absorbing nor admitting light). For a brief and lucid discussion of all these candidates, see George Johnson, *Fire in the Mind* (New York: Knopf, 1995), pp. 74-83. For further comments on the axion in particular, see J. Gribben and M. Rees, *Cosmic Coincidences* (New York: Bantam, 1989), pp. 114-17.

36. The actual amount of mass needed for these further stages must exceed the so-called Chandrasekhar limit (named after the physicist who first proposed the idea); it is 1.44 times the mass of the Sun. Below this limit what happens is that under gravitational pressure electrons get stripped from atoms and begin to form, along with the residue nuclei, a very dense "soup." Eventually the electrons are squeezed close enough together that their mere density exerts a sufficient pressure of its own to resist further gravitational compaction. This state of matter is formally termed "degenerate matter," just as the pressure bringing it about is called "degeneracy pressure."

37. The electron is negatively charged, the proton positively charged; when forced together they produce an electrically neutral particle, the neutron. The density at which this occurs is around 10 trillion kilograms per cubic meter. When density at the center of the collapsing star reaches a hundred quadrillion (10^{17}) kilograms per cubic meter it has enough pressure to stop the inward crush of gravity. The neutron star that results will have a radius of just a few miles and a surface gravity a hundred billion times that of Earth.

38. Stellar black holes are a major enigma in contemporary theoretical physics. From what I can garner the following points seem to share a general consensus. 1. The original star must have a mass at least 3 or more times that of the Sun if it is to eventuate in a black hole; the more the original stellar mass, of course, the larger the final black hole. 2. Since nothing can escape a black hole, no information regarding its internal components, if any, is avail-

able; time and space within them are unanalyzable; the black hole's presence is known only from its effects. 3. Gravity at the center of a black hole theoretically achieves infinite proportions, which become finite (or measurable) the further one moves away from this center. Among other ways that scientists use the word "infinite," it means that the appropriate equations do not issue in a terminal number but a series with an indefinite end, or a series always issuing in zero. 4. All black holes probably have some degree of spin. 5. Some of them, especially very tiny ones, appear to leak an esoteric type of energy at a slow rate, and so will one day dissipate; perhaps all of them share this leakage. 6. Black holes are probably quite commonplace throughout the universe, and one locale where large ones likely exist is at the centers of galaxies. 7. They have a lifetime, if not infinite, of many, many billions of years. One suggestion, though hardly a consensus, is that they may also form portals to and perhaps from other universes, or to and from various far distant points in this one. For a detailed and fairly clear discussion of this suggestion, see Paul Davies, *Other Worlds: Space, Superspace, and the Quantum Universe* (New York: Simon and Schuster, 1980).

39. On this point, especially regarding the way it might apply to the work of science, I would refer to the fine article by Langdon Gilkey, "Whatever Happened to Immanuel Kant?," in his volume, *Nature, Reality, and the Sacred: The Nexus of Science and Religion* (Minneapolis: Fortress, 1993), pp. 43-57.

40. If at this future time, however, it turns out that we are indeed more or less similar to what we now are biologically, and if the chosen planet is not itself hospitable to us, there are some interesting remarks on the engineering aspects of creating an artificial biosphere by Freeman Dyson in R. E. Marshak (ed.), *Perspectives in Modern Physics: Essays in Honor of Hans A. Bethe* (New York: Interscience Press, 1966), pp. 641-55.

41. This last option currently seems the most feasible one, and a few experiments have already been undertaken to discover if such self-contained habitats can provide enduring homes for us. The theory underlying this option is usually called arcology, and one of its outstanding interpreters has been Paolo Soleri. See especially his masterwork, *The City in the Image of Man* (Cambridge, Mass.: MIT Press, 1977). Obviously a self-contained habitat in space would have requirements that one on Earth would not. For what some of these might be in the very primitive habitat of a space station, see the report *Salyut: Soviet Steps toward Permanent Human Presence in Space* (Washington, D.C.: Congress of the United States, Office of Technology Assessment, 1983).

42. For a delightful rendition of the Milky Way as it would be experienced on a trip from its far distant corona through its halo and into its disk, with an

abundance of fascinating data along the way, see Joel Davis, *Journey to the Center of Our Galaxy* (Chicago: Contemporary Books, 1991).

43. One of the more difficult of these specifics to grasp is the so-called "false vacuum" that the inflationary period requires. For the most lucid discussion I can find, see James Trefil, *The Moment of Creation, op. cit.,* pp. 163-68.

44. The time period usually given for the inflationary period is from 10^{-35} to 10^{-33} seconds after the big bang. To illustrate just how large the growth was, if the initial object had been the size of a tennis ball, it would have grown to the size of the entire observable universe! There are many accounts of inflationary theory available. Just two that I have found helpful are *ibid.,* pp. 158-70 and George Smoot and Keay Davidson, *Wrinkles in Time* (New York: Avon Books, 1993), pp. 173-91.

45. As originally formulated by Guth, the inflationary period would have produced an extraordinary smoothness or evenness of matter and energy throughout the universe that would not have assisted the galaxy formation problem.

46. In addition to the work of Kuhn previously cited, two others should also be mentioned as classic studies of the phenomenology of insight: Karl Popper, *The Logic of Scientific Discovery* (New York: Basic Books, 1968), and Bernard Lonergan, *Insight: A Study of Human Understanding* (New York: Philosophical Library, 1958). Both of these works emphasize what we might call a period of gestation, worrying the resolution of a problem from as many angles as possible, letting it occupy the mind intensely and often protractedly, before insight is born. The suddenness of insight that we described previously thus emerges in a context of thought that itself may have occupied the individual for months or years. In this sense an insight is not so much a gift as a reward.

47. For a brief description of this long-lived idea (a few scientists were still supporting it at the beginning of the twentieth century), see G. Smoot and K. Davidson, *Wrinkles in Time, op. cit.,* pp. 2-8, 114-17.

48. Photons, of course, have been proven experimentally to exist; so far gravitons have evaded all attempts to isolate them experimentally. Gravitons, among other things, are necessary if Einstein's theory of gravitation, which we'll touch on in a later chapter, is to be unified with quantum mechanics. In quantum mechanics the three other fundamental forces (electromagnetism, the strong and weak nuclear forces) have all been shown to be transmitted by elementary particles (photons, gluons, vector bosons). It is presumed that gravity must be as well.

49. For a fascinating cross-cultural selection of primary sources, see Mircea Eliade, *From Primitives to Zen* (New York: Harper and Row, 1967), pp. 83-129.

50. This existence of a soul or spirit as capturing the presence of God throughout creation is one of the most beautiful and powerful concepts in the history of human thought. It has had particular influence over Christianity, which in its early years inherited the profound Greek analysis of the concept, including (1) setting it in a hierarchy that reserved the soul's most sublime activity (the ability to reason, appreciate beauty, form abstractions, contemplate God, etc.) to human beings, and (2) identifying it as what survives the body's death. To both these attributes I would offer the following two provisos. The first is that "the soul's most sublime activity" must never be used to demean the rest of creation, first because sublimity of thought may be a value but is scarcely a virtue in a Christian vision of life and secondly because we don't know very well what goes on in the souls of other life-forms here on Earth and nothing at all of possible life-forms elsewhere in the universe. The second proviso, which I will attend to more thoroughly in chapter 3, is that while I wholeheartedly agree that life succeeds death in the universe, this is true of everything that is alive and occurs more in accord with the way the resurrection of Jesus is described in the Gospels than with the traditional doctrine of an immortal soul as an entity that somehow escapes the body at death and yet still remains identifiable as distinctly human. This last idea is particularly traceable to Christianity's Greek heritage, far more, at any rate, than to its heritage in the Old Testament. For what is still the outstanding study of the development of the Greek notion of the soul, see Erwin Rohde, *Psyche,* tr. W. B. Hillis (New York: Harper and Row, 1966), 2 vols.

51. For an excellent analysis of this point, particularly with regard to animals, see Andrew Linzey, *Christianity and the Rights of Animals* (New York: Crossroad, 1987), pp. 7-51; for animal sacrifice specifically, see pp. 42-43.

52. On this point, see *ibid.* For a superb historical study of some major Christian traditions in their approach to the natural world, see Paul Santmire, *The Travail of Nature: The Ambiguous Ecological Promise of Christian Theology* (Philadelphia: Fortress, 1985), where he discusses the earliest traditions, up to and including Irenaeus and Origen, on pp. 13-54.

53. For this analysis I am relying on George Hendry, *Theology of Nature, op. cit.,* pp. 154-57. He offers a much fuller explanation of the characteristics I list.

54. The most intriguing of these are so-called virtual particles. Their existence is postulated on the basis of the indeterminacy principle underlying quantum mechanics. What this means in a specific and very simplified example is that we cannot determine for certain whether a particle of mass sitting by itself is not for very brief moments of time two particles, the original one "fluctuating" into a second one, and then, so to speak, returning to itself. These moments of time

must by definition be so brief that they cannot be measured, so that any energy the second particle "drains" from the first (and any mass it consequently has, according to Einstein's mass/energy conversion equation, $E = mc^2$) remains forever unmeasurable and so does not offend the law of the conservation of energy (the energy is not lost to the second, undetectable particle). The major reason why these virtual particles have become so important in nuclear and sub-nuclear physics is that they can be exchanged between two bodies of mass, let us say protons, providing adhesion between them and thus accounting for the strong nuclear force that overcomes the "natural" repulsion of protons for each other (all protons are electromagnetically positive). For much more exact detail on these virtual particles than I can give here, see James Trefil, *From Atoms to Quarks* (New York: Doubleday, 1994), pp. 47-52, 198-200. The point I wish to make is that these particles, by definition unseeable and unmeasurable, are nonetheless an active presence in science's current explanation of how the universe exists.

55. It is difficult to be precise about the dating of the big bang, since our technology itself starts losing precision the greater the distance (in space and consequently in time) we are examining; it is frequently difficult to know what exactly is being seen and to decipher accurately optical tricks that light traveling very great distances might be playing through reflection, refraction, gravitational bending, and so on. Sometimes this difficulty is also compounded by in-house bickering among astrophysicists. The reader may recall that a few years ago a very distant star was discovered that was aged by some scientists as older than the universe itself. This, of course, immediately captured the attention of the popular media and in the process common sense disappeared from many of the discussions. Obviously, no star can be older than the universe itself. If you have a star whose age can be reliably known (and at the distances involved this would be a superb achievement) and this age makes the star older than your assessment of the age of the universe, then the only available conclusion is that you have seriously underestimated the latter.

56. The physics underlying various theoretical proposals regarding the singularity are very complex. The best overall presentation I know of is Paul Davies, *The Edge of Infinity* (New York: Simon and Schuster, 1982). I will make just two further points about these proposals. The first is that while I have been describing the singularity that existed at the beginning of the universe, another type apparently resides at the center of massive black holes and has traits somewhat distinct from the primordial singularity preceding the big bang. The second and more important point is that the primordial singularity is *by definition* unfathomable. Even if we were able to breach experimentally the Planck time (10^{-43} seconds after the big bang) and the Planck length (4×10^{-33} centimeters), for both

of which smaller measurements at present make our notions of time and space meaningless, the singularity remains infinitely reducible to still smaller times and lengths. In other words, with the singularity we are always at a point of aporia, that is, a point beyond which thought cannot go. For a theologian this is not particularly disturbing, since the concept of God always issues ultimately in a state of aporia. Many scientists, however, not used to such a situation, are far less sanguine about it and at times even seem resentful that it exists. This can issue in an intellectual aggressiveness that simply but blindly refuses to acknowledge that some things are perpetually impossible for us; that the notion of impossibility is not always the fancy of a mind or talent currently at its limit, but can characterize reality ontologically, that is, in its very being.

57. To avoid a common misconception, this means the gradual dissolution, not increase, of heat: the death of heat, not death by heat.

58. These would include among the great theoretical physicists John Wheeler, George Ellis, and, to some extent, Stephen Hawking. Yet it is often difficult to pin these thinkers down; they regularly adjust their viewpoints on the basis of rapidly changing hard data from observations and what they judge persuasive new theoretical insights. Perhaps the safest thing to say is that these thinkers are willing to entertain the idea of a cyclically recurring universe as a definite possibility.

59. I am confining this indefiniteness to the future. Whether the cycles extend indefinitely into the past, or had to originate at some point, is not especially relevant in the context of the brute fact that we are definitely in a universe that is now expanding. On this point I take an attitude somewhat like Thomas Aquinas: there is no scientific evidence that the universe is not infinite in time, though the sentiment that it had an origin is so universally prevalent in our traditions (Aquinas, of course, emphasized what he took to be the revelatory nature of the Genesis account and the way it was being interpreted in his day) that in my judgment the notion needs to be respected. It is not, as I say, particularly pertinent to our discussion here, and even if it were, we could acknowledge that the creating word of God in Genesis could be one that is eternally, continually spoken, not spoken just once. We will be touching on this issue again in chapter 3.

60. Many physicists, for example, already accept not just as a hypothesis but as a proof the decades-old and rigorous mathematical demonstration of Henri Poincare that entropy cannot be an absolute law; *given enough time,* he argued, and a state of confinement, molecules must eventually reconvene to form the object that had dissipated, or something very much like it. In addition to this, a growing number of contemporary cosmologists are also arguing that the inevitable heat death of even an open universe is a fiction: that while entropy will in-

deed increase in an ever-expanding universe, the maximum amount of entropy the universe can accommodate will increase even more rapidly. With regard to an oscillating universe, a number of these same cosmologists argue — applying Poincare's demonstration, and presuming that the universe is in fact a closed or confined system — that while our own particular cycle is destined to increase in entropy, with each new cycle the parameters of the entropy are set anew, with no indication that these new parameters will themselves require a similar increase. This is obviously the position I am favoring here. For an excellent discussion of these issues, see John Barrow, *The Origin of the Universe* (New York: Basic Books, 1994), especially chapter 1. For a discussion of Poincare in particular, see P. Davies, *About Time* (New York: Simon and Schuster, 1995), pp. 37-38.

61. This issue of similarity between the cycles is a point of much disagreement. John Wheeler and George Ellis are sympathetic to it, while acknowledging that the similarity might in some cycles be quite remote. Paul Davies, on the other hand, thinks that black holes would accumulate throughout the cycles until they defined the entirety of what constitutes the universe. For a brief description of Wheeler's and Ellis's position, see Paul Davies, *The Edge of Infinity, op. cit.,* pp. 147-50 and 181 respectively. For Davies' position, see *ibid.,* p. 166. See also the previous endnote.

NOTES TO CHAPTER II

1. See, for example, T. S. Eliot in *Four Quartets: Burnt Norton,* II, where he is talking about "the still point of the turning world" and writes:

Except for the point, the still point,
There would be no dance, and there is
only the dance.

2. The Great Magellanic Cloud, along with its companion, the Small Magellanic Cloud, are our closest neighboring galaxies, being roughly 170,000 light-years away. They are clearly satellites to our own galaxy, held in its gravitational grip and unlikely to be separated from us by the expansion of the universe. They are visible to the naked eye, but only from the southern hemisphere.

3. Stars lying behind the dust and gas also contribute to this illumination. The various colors are due principally to the way different kinds of dust and matter absorb different wavelengths in the color spectrum.

4. See John Gribbin and Martin Rees, *Cosmic Coincidences, op. cit,* pp. 205-6. An interesting sidepoint on this extraordinary regularity of pulses is that when

they were first discovered a number of scientists thought they might be communication from intelligences elsewhere in the universe. While many people found this amusing, and called the interpretation the LGM theory (for "little green men"), it may be that just such regulated pulses, where no neutron star has been located, will be a primary means whereby such communication will occur. The premise that there is such intelligent life elsewhere in the universe will occupy us in chapter 3.

For stars initially around 3 or more times the mass of the Sun, the neutron star collapses further and becomes a candidate for evolving into a black hole. See our remarks on black holes in the previous chapter.

5. The notion that beauty, especially as linked to truth, is available only to an elect is one of the fundamental tenets of the philosophical/religious vision known as gnosticism. In science this often takes the form of an insistence that understanding intricate sets of equations can only occur for relatively few after many years of study. This, of course, is not true, and the claim is a continual source of irritation to many of us. For if something can be put into an equation, it can be put into prose, and prose can be written so as to make the equations understandable to many. The equations function only as compressions for what the prose would require greater length to explain. One of the most outrageous examples of scientific "gnosticism" is Frank Tipler, *The Physics of Immortality* (New York: Doubleday, 1994), where he claims that only a handful of people are fully competent to understand what he says. We need our educational professionals to seek continually to overcome this bailiwick mentality. Such an effort is what recommends so highly, among others I could name, the work of scientists like James Trefil, Paul Davies, John Gribben, Freeman Dyson, Steven Weinberg, and in his *The Quark and the Jaguar* (New York: W. H. Freeman, 1994), Murray Gell-Mann.

6. C. H. Dodd, *The Parables of the Kingdom* (London: James Nesbit & Co., 1935), pp. 21-22.

7. The notion of an "opening" in experience also provides the basis for one of the common metaphors describing revelatory moments in the Bible, namely, the auditory, sometimes visual epiphany described as the "opening of the heavens," such as we find in Matthew 3:16-17 where the context is Jesus' baptism. I would also like to note that in my judgment Schopenhauer is one of the most profound but neglected thinkers in post-Cartesian philosophy; he was, furthermore, the first European thinker of any stature to take seriously the scriptures of Hinduism and Buddhism that were then making their way into museums and universities, and in fact translated some of them. Neglect of his contribution may be due to his extreme antagonism toward his much more influential and popular

contemporary, Hegel. Schopenhauer's use of the notion of insight is found throughout his masterwork, *The World as Will and Idea*.

8. I have discussed this demand at some length in my book, *Christian Commitment and Prophetic Living* (Mystic, CN: Twenty-Third Publications, 1986), chapters 2 and 6.

9. We should note that this unexpectedness can be considerably controlled under certain abnormal conditions, such as bringing electrons very close to absolute zero in temperature.

10. For an excellent but fairly demanding scholarly presentation of the thought of these men, and of the atomists in general, beyond the nod being given here and by most contemporary cosmologists, see G. S. Kirk and J. E. Raven, *The Presocratic Philosophers* (Cambridge: Cambridge University Press, 1957), pp. 246-56, 400-426.

11. This is true even if we are not on the planet; wherever we are, we need to cloak ourselves in a terrestrial ecology in order to survive.

12. I want to exercise discretion on this issue. I am aware that we often find it necessary to take other lives to preserve our own, its quality and longevity. This always places us in the context of biblical tragedy, which describes any situation in which all the choices confronting us are evil, and we must choose. The point I wish to make has two parts. First, the evil that we choose must always be the least among the choices available. Second, we must never lose sight of the fact that we have still done evil and must therefore repent in some appropriate way; the fact that we have been forced to choose the evil does not thereby metamorphose it into a morally indifferent or morally good act. If we take the life of an animal to nourish ourselves, for example, we ought to repent this through the manner of care we give the animal before slaughter and the care we give other animals that are not food sources.

13. This is true only of hydrogen bombs and their descendants. The original "atomic bombs," such as those dropped on Japan, were fission devices. In a brief description, fission releases energy when atoms are "smashed" or blown apart, fusion releases it when atoms are joined.

14. Ben Bova, *The New Astronomies* (New York: New American Library, 1974), p. 35.

15. In this he is sometimes credited as being the first formulator of a theory of attractive and repulsive forces in nature. See George Hendry, *Theology of Nature* (Philadelphia: Westminster Press, 1980), pp. 78-79. See also Werner Jaeger's disagreement with this view in *ibid.*, p. 227.

16. A confession is needed. When I come across phrases describing the size of the universe at the moment of the big bang the way I just have — as that of a

proton or less — my imagination breaks down completely. Yet this is precisely the way many contemporary cosmologists describe its size; in fact, most describe it as many powers smaller than a proton. When I am driving through the Sierra Nevada mountains and try to imagine just the panorama I am seeing reduced to a proton in size, even then my imagination breaks down. And I suspect that if any of you were a companion seated next to me, the same breakdown would occur. I am, therefore, finally left with utter reliance on the legitimacy of the mathematical physics that says, despite this failure of imagination, the universe nonetheless was that small. Can imagination be so completely alienated from reality? Apparently so — though like a melody barely whispering in our minds but refusing to depart, denial won't fade completely away.

17. We should note that the word for create, *barah,* is actually quite rare in the Old Testament and is used exclusively with reference to God, probably to preserve some sense of the specialness of divine activity. As we will see, however, what the word is getting at is quite similar to terms drawn from analogy to human activity, especially making, forming, and generating. Very generally we may say that to create means to make or generate a recognizable form in what previously did not possess it.

18. Two points need to be made here. The first is that "formless matter" is the way I am translating the Hebrew *tohu-wabohu,* a notoriously difficult phrase which in many other translations is given as "without form and void." I prefer my own translation because the term "void" is too easily commandeered by Christian interpreters to mean nothingness, a conceptuality which, despite the difficulty in translating it, the phrase definitely does not contain. The second point is that while Genesis 1:2 designates the *earth* as being in a state of formless matter, I take this to mean not exclusively the planet but the universe, "earth" being a synonym for all of material reality.

19. The exception, as already noted, would be that infinitesimal part of the universe which is our planet and its immediate environs.

20. Even Barth recognized this, as when he writes that "within the sphere of ideas possible to us *creatio ex nihilo* can appear only as an absurdity" (*Church Dogmatics,* vol. II, part 1, p. 76). However, instead of allowing this judgment to initiate a reappraisal of the idea, he insists on the need to affirm it despite its absurdity, thus aligning himself with proponents of the "credo quia absurdum" ("I believe because it is absurd") school of theology. To me this position is reprehensible, making religious faith a type of mind game equating belief in God as creator with acquiescence to an idea of which we can make no sense at all. Faith becomes consent to non-sense.

21. See especially my *The Turn of the Millennium: An Agenda for Christian*

Religion in an Age of Science (Cleveland: The Pilgrim Press, 1996), particularly chapter 5. These issues will also occupy considerable attention in two other manuscripts I am currently completing.

22. For an excellent assessment of this point in a whole variety of contexts, see J. Fiscalini and L. Grey (eds.), *Narcissism and the Interpersonal Self* (New York: Columbia University Press, 1993). We may note that in its advertisements the cosmetic industry unashamedly panders to this equation between physical beauty and the control of others.

23. See Fromm's *The Anatomy of Human Destructiveness* (New York: Fawcett, 1973), *passim,* but especially pp. 226-31. See also F. Alford, *Narcissism: Socrates, The Frankfort School, and Psychoanalytic Theory* (New Haven: Yale University Press, 1993). Both books are particularly valuable in the way they analyze narcissism from a sociological/communal perspective. Both, of course, are profoundly dependent on Freud's work.

24. On this point, see the excellent study by Donald Capps, *The Depleted Self: Sin in a Narcissistic Age* (Minneapolis: Fortress Press, 1993).

25. With very rare exceptions, all acclaimed Christian mystics I have read, but especially Teresa of Avila, have emphasized this point. It is not, however, as prominent among Hindu, Buddhist, and Sufi mystics. It is an intriguing observation that in the popularity of books like F. Capra's *The Tao of Physics* and G. Zukav's *The Dancing Wu Li Masters,* it is these latter traditions that are almost exclusively employed in an attempt to relate science to the interests of mysticism. One might expect, given the prominence of the indeterminacy principle in physics coupled to someone like Teresa's emphasis on the need for attentiveness to the unexpected, that Christian mystical traditions would have figured much more prominently in these books.

26. The child's experience, then, is not unlike that of the mystic when the latter "passes into" God in a way that obscures awareness of the isolated self.

27. On this point, see my book *Act of Contrition* (Notre Dame: Ave Maria Press, 1976), *passim.* For the specific case of Narcissus, see pp. 47-54.

28. I have taken my inspiration for this description from Søren Kierkegaard, *Philosophical Fragments.* I am referring specifically to his famous parable of the king and the poor maiden. The king loves the maiden but is in a quandary regarding how to express this love in a way that does not make the maiden dependent on his favor the rest of her life; or differently: how to establish an equality between himself and the maiden when their differing social positions seem to require a perpetual inequality.

29. This centrality of gratitude in Christian living is perhaps indicated nowhere more clearly than in the fact that the central cultic act of all the Christian

churches, the eucharist, derives at least its name, if not always the spirit permeating it, from the Greek word meaning thanksgiving. For further comments on this virtue, see my article "Gratitude and The Spiritual Life," *Emmanuel* (October 1977), pp. 468-74.

30. This difference between a beauty that affects behavior and one that does not is the same as the difference between an abstract beauty and an ideal one. I have discussed this distinction at some length in my book *The Turn of the Millennium, op. cit.,* chapter 2. The word "ideal" comes from the Greek *eidolon,* which means precisely a beauty that becomes active in one's life, especially in the desire to know the ideal as thoroughly as possible and so allow it to determine the contours of one's existence: how one will spend time, finances, and emotional commitment in its pursuit. Two qualities of this pursuit are particularly pertinent: it never ends (ideals are not commodities that can be fully gained or possessed) and the pursuer asks for nothing in return for the pursuit; the pursuit itself is the satisfaction. Needless to say, ideals come in many shapes, from the person one perceives as beautiful to various forms of art, virtue, religious vision, and so on.

31. The critical event here occurred in 1965 when Robert Wilson and Arnold Penzias discovered the electromagnetic "hiss" or "murmur" pervading the universe in all directions as the residue of the big bang. It is located at a wavelength of 7.35 centimeters and is the radiation emitted at a temperature of about 2.9 degrees above absolute zero. This discovery established with near definitive certainty and unanimity among scientists the general outline of the big bang model of the universe's origin.

32. For a brief and lucid discussion of these solids and their use by Kepler, see N. Spielberg and B. Anderson, *Seven Ideas That Shook the Universe* (New York: John Wiley & Sons, 1987), pp. 41-45.

33. A brief description of this theory is provided by Einstein himself in his volume *Out of My Later Years, op. cit.,* pp. 45-48, though it should be read in the larger context of pp. 41-122. There are many popular descriptions of the theory available, though its precise details are accessible only to well-seasoned mathematical physicists. The conclusion Einstein wrote at the end of his presentation is still valid: "The general theory of relativity is as yet incomplete insofar as it has been able to apply the general principle of relativity satisfactorily only to gravitational fields, but not to the total field. We do not yet know with certainty, by what mathematical mechanism the total field in space is to be described and what the general invariant laws are to which this total field is subject" (p. 48).

34. In a famous experiment in 1919, this was demonstrated by Sir Arthur Eddington during a total eclipse of the Sun. There are many accounts of this ex-

NOTES TO PAGES 61-65

periment in books dealing with the history of science. For one of them, see N. Spielberg and B. Anderson, *Seven Ideas That Shook the Universe, op. cit.,* pp. 179-81.

35. For a further appraisal of this role of visualizing, see A. Lightman and R. Brawer, *Origins: The Lives and World of Modern Cosmologists, op. cit., passim.* As mentioned in a previous note, this book is a collection of interviews with 27 contemporary scientists and is fascinating reading. As a sidepoint to the issue at hand I might note that the one thing all of them were asked was to respond to Steven Weinberg's statement toward the end of his book *The First Three Minutes* (the context in which it appears has already been cited in the Preface): "The more the universe seems comprehensible, the more it also seems pointless." The majority of responses showed, if nothing else, a disturbing ignorance or disregard for the motives of many great scientists from previous generations when doing their craft, and even more for the motives of theologians. Efforts are badly needed today to encourage much more thorough interdisciplinary dialogue between theologians and scientists, through journals (such as *Zygon*), conferences, interdepartmental meetings at universities, endowed research, etc. Two organizations through which laudable steps in this regard have been made are the Templeton Foundation and The Center for Theology and the Natural Sciences (CTNS) in Berkeley.

36. It is estimated that at 10^{-43} seconds after the Big Bang the temperature of the universe exceeded 10^{33} degrees centigrade (few are willing to speculate just how much it may have exceeded this). At 10^{-33} seconds it was 10^{28} degrees, then diminishing over the eons until today it is just a few degrees above absolute zero. For a lucid discussion, see H. Fritzsch, *The Creation of Matter* (New York: Basic Books, 1984), pp. 223-36.

37. The pathos in this attitude — the attitude of the thoroughgoing conservative — is captured nowhere more succinctly than in Whitehead's remark that its adherent is fighting against the very essence of the universe, which is change. See Alfred North Whitehead, *Adventures of Ideas* (New York: The Free Press, 1961), p. 274.

38. For its immediate effect upon our well-being, the truth of this has perhaps been nowhere more evident than in the science of microbiology, where the delineation of such things as cellular and sub-cellular structures, viral and bacterial behavior through the use of microscopes has assisted so enormously our capacity for medical healing. Without the ability to actually see these phenomena, this healing would have proceeded, as it did in all pre-microscope generations, far more slowly and tentatively. In observations of the universe, of course, it is not the microscope but the telescope that provides us with the details we need for increased accuracy of observation and analysis.

39. For two excellent guides through this complexity, I would recommend Wolfhart Pannenberg, *Jesus — God and Man,* tr. L. Wilkins and D. Priebe (Philadelphia: The Westminster Press, 1968), *passim,* but especially pp. 34-41, 119-24, 302-57, and especially John B. Cobb, Jr., *Christ in a Pluralistic Age* (Philadelphia: The Westminster Press, 1975), *passim,* but especially pp. 71-94, 150-72. Cobb's analysis is particularly appealing in what he himself offers to an understanding of the term, drawing importantly from Andre Malraux's aesthetic theory and describing the logos as the "principle of creative transformation" in the universe. Countless other texts in christological studies also offer analyses of the term.

40. While he doesn't use the specific illustration and explanation I have just offered, in my judgment the most insightful analysis into the phenomenology of wonder, especially as it might pertain to Christian themes, still belongs to Sam Keen, *Apology for Wonder* (New York: Harper and Row, 1969). See especially pp. 201-12.

NOTES TO CHAPTER III

1. It is estimated, for example, that the meteor crashing into the Earth at the time of the dinosaur extinction roughly 65 million years ago measured somewhere between 3 and 5 miles in diameter. Many millions of years before that, during the so-called "Cambrian extinction," it is estimated that a somewhat larger meteor may have been a major player in the extinction of around 95% of life-forms on Earth.

A fact: there is a comet in orbit within our solar system called Swift-Tuttle (after its discoverers) that is about 5 miles wide at its solid core. It will barely miss collision with our planet in the late summer of 2126, but will be a definite threat in 3044. There is a presumption that missile or some other pertinent technology will have been developed by the fourth millennium to confront and overcome this threat.

2. These flares pack enormous electromagnetic energy, and even with our great distance from the Sun, they regularly interfere with radio and television transmissions. A large enough one, or a series of them, would have devastating effects on the normally protective blanket of our atmosphere and so on the life beneath it. One of the best studies describing this and other solar phenomena is John Gribbin, *Blinded by the Light: The Secret Life of the Sun* (New York: Harmony Books, 1991).

3. Tipler's discussion of these probes is found in *The Physics of Immortality* (New York: Doubleday, 1994), pp. 44-55.

4. See *ibid., passim,* but especially pp. 153-58.

5. See *ibid.,* pp. 217-68.

6. Something of this same intuition underlies James Trefil's essay "Models, Reality, and the Arrogance of Theoretical Physicists," in his *Reading the Mind of God* (New York: Scribner's, 1989), pp. 143-55. Trefil uses Kelvin as his case in point, and the way the latter's theoretical estimate of the age of the universe was maintained even while being flatly contradicted by facts garnered from geology. A theological assessment of the same intuition can be found throughout Langdon Gilkey's *Nature, Reality, and the Sacred* (Minneapolis: Fortress Press, 1993), but especially pp. 79-157.

7. I am reminded here of Kierkegaard, who in his great ethical treatise *Either/Or,* but more directly in his small classic *Purity of Heart Is to Will One Thing,* describes what he calls double-mindedness — doing the good for the sake of some personal reward. He contrasts it with single-mindedness, or what he also calls, borrowing from Jesus (Matthew 5:8), purity of heart, which is doing the good precisely because it is good, without consideration of beneficial or damaging effects upon oneself. In Christianity and most other religions purity of heart represents the highest and most implacably difficult stage to reach in the development of a consistent motivation for ethical behavior.

8. Whitehead isolates this pettiness or triviality as one of three fundamental sources of the evil we do, the others being discord and destruction, themselves frequently the result of triviality, especially as it gives something an importance it simply does not deserve. This can be a pettiness demanding commendation over some insignificant virtuous deed or damnation over some insignificant bad one. Jesus is making the same point when he talks about straining a gnat while swallowing a camel (Matthew 23:24).

9. For a detailed examination of *hubris,* see Douglas L. Cairns, *Aidos: The Psychology and Ethics of Honor and Shame in Ancient Greek Literature* (New York: Oxford University Press, 1993). The proper response to *hubris* is shame, just as honor resides in acknowledging one's limits and living with courageous virtue *(arete)* within them.

10. Thus, for example, Hawking does bring up the possibility of a universal, encompassing theory in his inaugural lecture as Lucasian professor of mathematics at Cambridge (1980). "I want to discuss," he says, "the possibility that the goal of theoretical physics might be achieved in the not-too-distant future: say, by the end of the century. By this I mean that we might have a complete, consistent, and unified theory of the physical interactions that would describe all possible observations." Yet in the very next paragraph he knowingly adds, "Even if we do achieve a complete unified theory, we shall not be able to make detailed predictions in any but the simplest situations." The lecture is reprinted in Ste-

phen Hawking, *Black Holes and Baby Universes* (New York: Bantam Books, 1994), pp. 49-68. The quotations are on pp. 49 and 50 respectively.

11. The most widely acclaimed presentation of the principle belongs to J. Barrow and F. Tipler, *The Anthropic Cosmological Principle* (New York: Oxford University Press, 1986). Since its publication Barrow has modified his position on some of its implications; Tipler also, but less so. For a lengthy theological appraisal of the principle, see M. A. Corey, *God and the New Cosmology: The Anthropic Design Argument* (Lanham, Md.: Rowman and Littlefield, 1993). For a philosophical appraisal, see E. E. Harris, *Cosmos and Anthropos: A Philosophical Interpretation of the Anthropic Cosmological Principle* (Atlantic Highlands, N.J.: Humanities Press International, 1991).

12. This notion of alternate universes, often called the "many worlds" theory, is an intriguing one. It is born from a wedding between quantum mechanics and probability theory. The classic illustration is that of Schrodinger's cat, which in a nutshell reads as follows. A cat is placed in a sealed box with a vial of gaseous poison. If the vial remains unbroken the cat will be alive when we open the box; if not, the cat will be dead. The argument is that until we actually open the box, however, both life and death remain actual simultaneous realities for the cat. In the same way, other universes must actually exist until we observe that they don't. But since this observation is not possible, their reality remains. On this whole issue, see the lucid discussion by John Gribbin, *In Search of Schrodinger's Cat* (New York: Bantam, 1984). See also the previously cited work by Paul Davies, *Other Worlds: Space, Superspace, and the Quantum Universe.* A much briefer presentation can be found in J. Gribben and M. Rees, *Cosmic Coincidences* (New York: Bantam, 1989), pp. 270-91.

13. For a different view of reductionism, especially its role in science, see Steven Weinberg, *Dreams of a Final Theory* (New York: Vintage Books, 1993), pp. 51-64. While I admire much of what Weinberg says elsewhere in this book, I am at odds with his analysis here. And I certainly am in disagreement with Frank Tipler's extreme view in his *The Physics of Immortality, op. cit.,* where he not only announces, "reductionism is true" (p. xiv), but goes on to describe the specific reductionism he has in mind: "Science can offer *precisely* (his italics) the consolations in facing death that religion once offered. Religion is now a part of science" (p. 339). The marriage I would recommend between science and religion is now replaced, as it is in all reductionism, by one partner, one viewpoint attempting to absorb and dominate the other(s).

14. For a taste of what these debates were like, see the superb biography by A. Desmond and J. Moore, *Darwin: The Life of a Tormented Evolutionist, op. cit.,* especially pp. 485-677. It is replete with primary documentation.

15. For further remarks on this relation between humor and humility, see my *The Turn of the Millennium* (Cleveland: The Pilgrim Press, 1996), chapter 4.

16. One of this century's most influential interpreters of Job, Carl Jung, offers a psychological interpretation of Job's silence that, while sympathetic, is unsatisfied. He therefore insists that he will speak when Job does not, answering God's question with questions of his own. The result is a magnificent display of Jung's incisive psychoanalytic talents, but it concludes that God's imperious questions and refusal to account for Job's suffering beyond the assertion that God is God and may do as God wishes indicate that deity is both good and evil. The reader is not surprised at this conclusion, however, since Jung presumes in his interpretation that we can only reliably say about God what we can say about ourselves. See Carl Jung, *Answer to Job,* tr. R. F. C. Hull (New York: Meridian Books, 1960).

17. There are many lucid descriptions available of the role of anti-matter in experimental and theoretical physics. See, for example, P. Davies and J. Gribben, *The Matter Myth* (New York: Simon and Schuster, 1992), pp. 153-62, 245-49; H. Fritzsch, *The Creation of Matter,* tr. J. Steinberg (New York: Basic Books, 1984), pp. 108-27; James Trefil, *The Moment of Creation* (New York: Collier Books, 1983), pp. 36-41, 171-75. When matter and anti-matter come into contact, their masses annihilate instantaneously and convert into energy. Naturally occurring particles of anti-matter appear to be very scarce in our part of the universe; in fact, none has yet been reliably detected. They are, however, regularly produced in the experiments of high-energy physics.

18. A clear and brief presentation of cosmic string theory can be found in J. Gribbin and M. Rees, *Cosmic Coincidences, op. cit.,* pp. 175-201. String theory is one of the most exciting proposals occupying cosmologists today. It is important to realize that there are actually two types of strings involved in the theories: the cosmic strings I have just described, and then the "superstrings" that proponents use to redefine the idea of the tiny particles that compose matter: instead of describing these particles as mathematical points of mass/energy in the image of billiard balls they are described as lines or loops of one-dimensional string, many times smaller than protons and neutrons. While I cannot go into the details here (and thus refer again to the above book), the excitement the theory causes is that blending the two types of strings together appears to hold the possibility of constructing a theory that will finally unite in a single sequence of equations all four of the fundamental forces of nature, including the recalcitrant renegade against all such theories so far, gravity. For further discussions of this theory, including some doubts about its viability, I would recommend: Freeman Dyson, *Infinite in All Directions* (New York: Harper and Row, 1988), pp. 14-19; John Boslough,

Masters of Time: Cosmology at the End of Innocence (New York: Addison-Wesley, 1992), pp. 98-112, 197-213; Paul Davies and John Gribbin, *The Matter Myth* (New York: Simon and Schuster, 1992), pp. 246-57.

19. For an analysis of these attractors, especially the one that is pulling our own galaxy toward it, see Alan Dressler, *Voyage to the Great Attractor* (New York: Vintage Books, 1994), pp. 238-64.

20. I first took up this issue of intelligent life elsewhere in the universe in *The Turn of the Millennium, op. cit.,* chapter 1, section 3. The rest of this chapter will offer much different and far more extended reflections on the issue, though the same basic attitude toward the possibility of this life prevails here as did in the previous book. Together these accounts provide to date the fullest scope of my appropriation of the issue for its theological pertinence.

21. The literature diagnosing intelligence is vast. I have found the following books of particular interest in my own research and would recommend them to the interested and diligent reader: R. Sternberg and Nathan Detterman (eds.), *What Is Intelligence?: Contemporary Viewpoints on Its Nature and Definition* (Norwood, N.J.: Ablex Publishing Corp., 1986); Howard Gardner, *Frames of Mind: The Theory of Multiple Intelligences* (New York: Basic Books, 1983); Nathan Brady, *Intelligence* (San Diego: Academic Press, 1992); Jean Khalfa (ed.), *What Is Intelligence?* (Cambridge: Cambridge University Press, 1994); Robert Howard, *All About Intelligence: Human, Animal, and Artificial* (Kensington, NSW, Australia: New South Wales Press, 1991). This last is particularly pertinent because it includes a discussion of intelligent life elsewhere in the universe.

22. I am currently uncertain regarding how pertinent this information is when it derives from those professing to have encountered such intelligence, that is, those claiming encounters with the inhabitants of UFOs. To my mind the most intriguing of these putative encounters occurred in Roswell, New Mexico, in 1947. The government claims that almost all pertinent documentation of this event at the time has been lost. This is very hard to believe. There are witnesses who claim the craft was inhabited; that two of the beings were killed on impact, but that three survived, at least one of whom subsequently died and was autopsied; that the craft was made of material whose composition is unknown; that engraved on this material was something like hieroglyphic language; that the official investigators initially acknowledged the craft as alien, 8 hours later insisting it was a weather balloon (to avoid massive panic) and, in 1993, that it was a device for spying on Russia. One has to approach such accounts as one wills, though government collusion in obscuring facts — if indeed this occurred — is reprehensible.

23. For what might be expected in scientific rather than moral/aesthetic

categories, see Frank Drake, *Is Anyone Out There?: The Scientific Search for Extraterrestrial Intelligence* (New York: Delacorte, 1992). See also our remarks in the following paragraph.

24. A fine essay in this regard, as on the more general issue of life elsewhere in the universe, can be found in Freeman Dyson, *Disturbing the Universe* (New York: Harper and Row, 1979), pp. 205-17. There are also the many places where Carl Sagan addresses the issue, including his intriguing novel *Contact*.

25. That there are planets circling other stars was finally confirmed in 1995 by using the advanced observational technology of contemporary, computer-dependent telescopes. The planet in question is circling the star Pegasus 51 in our own galaxy and is located about 40 light-years from us — by galactic standards, just down the block. It is small and very close to the star, much like our own Mercury, and could not sustain biological life as we know it. There is possibly another, much larger planet circling the same star, but in this case at too great a distance to sustain biological life. Yet another star much closer to us (19 light-years) was discovered a short time later with at least one very large planet — perhaps a so-called "brown dwarf" as described in chapter 1 — circling it. These discoveries are truly momentous scientific achievements; they provide a required first step toward needed physical conditions to allow the possibility of biological life (as far as we understand its empirical origins and sustenance) elsewhere in the universe.

26. In the early 1960s when there was one of those periodic upsurges of interest in nonterrestrial intelligent life, a number of serious proposals were made for detecting communication from it. A representative selection of these can be found in A. Cameron (ed.), *Interstellar Communication* (New York: Benjamin Publishing Co., 1963). Most of the chapters are still relevant on the topic, especially 11, 13, and 15. Despite the protest of many scientists, led by the formidable Carl Sagan, the United States government has abandoned its formal participation in the search for extraterrestrial intelligence, the SETI project. For an assessment of the government's involvement, see P. Morrison, J. Billingham, and J. Wolfe (eds.), *The Search for Extraterrestrial Intelligence* (Washington, D.C.: NASA Scientific and Technical Information Office, 1977).

27. However, on the particular issue of wormholes in this regard, see the intriguing article by M. Morris and K. Thorne, "Wormholes in Spacetime and Their Use for Interstellar Travel: A Tool for Teaching General Relativity," *American Journal of Physics* (May 1988), pp. 395-412; and by the same authors along with U. Yurtsever, "Wormholes, Time Machines, and the Weak Energy Condition," *Physical Review Letters* (September 26, 1988), p. 1446.

28. That these statistics can obviously not provide definitive *proof* of the ex-

istence of nonterrestrial biological life bears remembering, as in Freeman Dyson, *Disturbing the Universe, op. cit.,* p. 209.

29. In this method of communication, and possibly even in mathematics and music, the role of analogy would undoubtedly be pivotal, that is, the ability of the other life-forms to draw likenesses between what we are communicating and their own experiences, if not in the entirety of what is communicated, then in as many of its attributes as possible. The same is obviously true in any communications we might receive from them. Analogy as an epistemological method is discussed with profound erudition by David Tracy, *The Analogical Imagination* (New York: Crossroad, 1981). While his predominant context is philosophical theology, the appraisal of analogy itself is independent of any specific application (see especially pp. 408-24, 446-55).

30. John Barrow, *Theories of Everything* (Oxford: Clarendon Press, 1991), p. 87.

31. See Alfred North Whitehead, *Process and Reality: An Essay in Cosmology*. Corrected edition. Edited by D. Griffin and D. Sherburne (New York: Free Press, 1978), pp. 90-92. We have cited Whitehead a number of times in the book. For those not familiar with him, the magisterial introduction to his thought, as well as a brilliant interpretation of it, belongs to Thomas E. Hosinski, *Stubborn Fact and Creative Advance: An Introduction the Metaphysics of Alfred North Whitehead* (Lanham, Md.: Rowman and Littlefield, 1993).

32. For this etymology I have relied on George Hendry, *Theology of Nature* (Philadelphia: Westminster Press, 1980), p. 237.

33. For a thorough analysis of these images, with, however, a clear bias favoring a Jungian hermeneutic, see the magnificent study by Joseph Campbell, *The Masks of God,* vols. 1-3 (New York: Viking, 1962, 1964, 1969), *passim*.

34. The Bible, for example, throughout all its traditions, is filled with this idea. It lies at the heart of the creation narratives in Genesis, reaches exquisite expression in the poetry of Job and Psalms, and finds its denouement in the narratives of Jesus' resurrection.

35. On this point, see David Tracy, *The Analogical Imagination, op. cit.,* and especially the superb volume by Richard Swinburne, *Revelation: From Metaphor to Analogy* (New York: Oxford University Press, 1992).

36. In my book *The Turn of the Millennium,* I suggest that those passages in which Jesus does speak of punishment or abandonment (e.g., being "cast out") by God should be read not literally but as a pedagogical technique to indicate the seriousness of what he is teaching, in much the same way you might say to someone, "I'll kill you if you don't do as I say," without meaning the statement literally. Otherwise we are left with a grotesque inconsistency in his witness.

37. See *The Turn of the Millennium, op. cit.,* chapter 4. Aside from generosity, the other traits I describe here are obedience, mercy, poverty, and, as remarked in a previous note, humility.

38. While I depart from him in the interpretation just offered, I would nonetheless recommend for its thorough exegesis of this parable, as well as a fine existential application of it, Dan Otto Via, *The Parables* (Philadelphia: Fortress, 1967), pp. 147-55.

39. The date for hominid origin is very difficult to determine because of the scarcity of fossil remains and the cantankerous disagreements among paleoanthropologists in interpreting them. As far as I know, 4 million years would be the outer boundary assigned by some of these scientists.

40. From the Middle Ages on, for example, particularly with regard to animal experimentation, countless scientists have asserted their professional right to "put Nature to the question" in pursuit of knowledge and technologies for human betterment. What they don't tell us, of course, is that the phrase "to put to the question" originates in the savage torturing and blood-letting of political prisoners and heretics.

41. See Andrew Linzey, *Christianity and the Rights of Animals* (New York: Crossroad, 1987), pp. 42-51.

42. For a history of some of its more outstanding examples, see Paul Santmire, *The Travail of Nature: The Ambiguous Ecological Promise of Christian Theology* (Philadelphia: Fortress, 1985). For examples of efforts to overcome it, see this same work, as well as Andrew Linzey, *Christianity and the Rights of Animals, op. cit.;* Jay B. McDaniel, *Of Gods and Pelicans* (Louisville: Westminster, 1989); J. Sobosan, *Bless the Beasts* (New York: Crossroad, 1991); and, not to be left unmentioned, Albert Schweitzer, *Reverence for Life* (New York: Harper and Row, 1969), especially the title essay, pp. 108-17, and "Ethics of Compassion," pp. 118-26.

43. The notion of the music of the spheres is an ancient one, not just in Greco-Roman mythologies but also in the emergent sciences they influenced. The most famous rendition of the idea is found in Cicero's treatise "The Dream of Scipio Africanus the Younger." In it he describes the universe as a series of interlacing concentric spheres, with the Earth as the center. The sound which Africanus hears is the rush and motion among these spheres as they move. The music is not necessarily melodic.

44. See his poem "Under Ben Bulben," stanza 6. The phrase is drawn from an epitaph on a gravestone and epitomizes Yeats's unrelenting demand that we take into account the brute realities of existence when assessing our own.

45. There are countless studies of the resurrection of Jesus, and several

schools of thought about it. If asked to which school I belonged, I suppose it would be that represented by Wolfhart Pannenberg, at least to the extent that here and there throughout his writings he insists that this resurrection must mean more than (1) ghostly appearance or (2) simply keeping alive the memory of Jesus in the lives of his disciples. See W. Pannenberg, *Jesus — God and Man, op. cit.,* pp. 53-114. One very important purpose I have in the remarks that follow is to honor the Gospel accounts that the raised Jesus could be seen and heard and touched, and that the resurrection therefore involved a reincarnation in the strict sense, that is, reconstitution as a physical body. This will make my viewpoint unpopular with a large number of contemporary theologians, just as how I interpret the implications of this reconstitution will be unpopular with others. Furthermore, I am intent on suggesting that in the resurrection of Jesus we also discover the preeminent disclosure of God as cherisher of life, a disclosure so intense and commanding over the experience of those witnessing the raised Jesus that it can issue in the stunning confession of Thomas in John 20:28, "My Lord and my God."

46. The universal blessing or salvation of all human beings — let alone all creation — when understood as ever-renewed life in God's presence is at best a minor and ambiguous theme in the history of Christian theology. The following are some passages, drawn from biblical, patristic, and medieval sources that directly or indirectly support it. I can do no more here than list them, with only brief notes on several of them. From biblical material: Isaiah 11:6-7, 65:25, 66:22; Jeremiah 31:12; Ezekiel 47:1-12, especially 9-12; Wisdom 11:24, 26; Psalm 145:9-13; Matthew 10:29 and Luke 12:6 (can both be interpreted to imply universal salvation); Romans 8:18-21; 1 Corinthians 15:28 (that God may be all in all); Revelation 20:1, 5. From patristic material: Irenaeus, *Against Heresies,* 5.36.1 (though elsewhere he expresses a different view from that represented here; Origen, cited here, is similarly inconsistent); Origen, *Against Celsus,* 3.78 (included are his two meanings of the word "eternal") and 8.72 (the Logos in Christ will "remodel" everything so that each freely chooses what the Logos wills and will thus freely be saved); Origen, *Commentary on Romans,* 6.5 (only life in Christ can be eternal in the strict sense; death and punishment cannot); Origen, *On First Principles,* 1.6.1 ("the goodness of God, through his Christ, may recall all his creatures to one end . . ."), 1.6.2 ("the end is always like the beginning"), and 3.6.3 (universal restoration). From medieval material: John Scotus Erigena, *On Nature* (the *Periphyseon*), 5.25 ("the entire sensible creation" will be saved) and 5.27-28. For a brief but enlightening treatment of the patristic material, I would add J. Sachs, "Apocatastasis in Patristic Theology," *Theological Studies,* vol. 54, no. 4 (December, 1993), pp. 617-40.

47. The brief suggestions I am making here and in following paragraphs about resurrection life are being worked out in far greater detail — not just theological but scientific detail — in another manuscript I am currently writing.

48. It is very interesting to note in this regard that many biblical exegetes now suggest that the usual translation of Yahweh as the name of God, "I am who am" or "I am who I am," is far better translated as, "I am the One who causes what is to be." While he doesn't mention this last translation specifically, on other possible versions of the name's meaning as well as on other names for God in the Old Testament, see Robert Gleason, *Yahweh* (Englewood Cliffs, N.J.: Prentice-Hall, 1964), pp. 113-23.

49. It must be acknowledged that this may be due to the fact that in the resurrection hope predominating at the time among the Jews, particularly those influenced by Phariseeism, only one resurrection was postulated, lasting eternally and without succeeding deaths by God's intervening power; the evangelists may have simply presumed this. The idea first enters Christianity explicitly with St. Paul, himself a Pharisee (Acts 23:6), apparently for parenetic purposes (exhortation and consolation). The exhortative dimension would serve his concern that judgment by God after death (for reward *or* punishment) be permanent, so giving the pursuit of virtue in this life its dominant motivation; the consoling dimension would recognize that for many people (especially in the social/psychological circumstances of his own day, particularly for persecuted Christians) the idea of another life perhaps similar to the one they are now living is horrifying; or from a different consideration, that death itself is so frighteningly anticipated that the idea of one death is all that can be borne. I acknowledge that for most people the consoling effect of the Pharisaic/Pauline view is probably more persuasive than the speculation I have just offered. It is certainly the view that has controlled the doctrinal traditions of the Christian churches. Yet it emphasizes the seeking of permanent personal happiness in a way that does not accord well with the teachings of Jesus, especially, as we've noted, his doctrine of single-mindedness or purity of heart.

50. I am thus using the notion of infinity here somewhat in the same sense that the great mathematical physicist Hermann Weyl used it when he said, "It (i.e., infinity) remains forever in the status of creation." Cited in P. Davies, *The Edge of Infinity, op. cit.,* p. 24. If some might still object to my using the notion as imputing to time (i.e., spacetime) an attribute, infinity, that properly belongs only to God, then in the context in which I am now using it — resurrection from the dead — the substitute "eternity of time" or "endlessness of time" would be just as suitable. Nonetheless, I have earlier addressed this issue by offering what I believe to be an accurate appraisal of the opening two verses of the Genesis ac-

count of creation, especially as they support the ancient and, to my mind, obvious philosophical maxim that nothing comes from nothing. The fact that some theoretical physicists currently speak about the feasibility of a creation out of nothingness should be assigned to indeliberately sloppy language. They do not mean *absolute* nothingness, but that the duration and movement of mass/energy at the moment the universe began is immeasurable, in somewhat the same manner as the virtual particles discussed in chapter 1, endnote 54.

51. One objection to this suggestion, a faulty one, has to do with theories of chance. The common example is that each time you toss a pair of dice there is a much larger chance that seven will result rather than two or twelve, and that the percentages never vary. This is true. But it is true only when each individual toss is isolated from all others, and becomes false when groups of tosses are taken into account as the standard of measurement. In an infinity of time, no matter how remote the odds are that a particular event will occur — not, as I have steadily insisted, identically, but rather identifiably (the dice will always come up identifiably as a number between two and twelve, but they can never land more than once on identically the same spot at identically the same time with identically the same motion, etc.) — the chance that it will occur, and occur countless times, becomes certain. In this context a maxim I first set out in *The Turn of the Millennium* (p. 25) achieves its full importance for the suggestion we are making: Once a possibility becomes an actuality, the actuality from that point on remains a possibility. The possibility that might concern us, then, is not *that* resurrection will occur — this, as I say, is virtually certain — but *precisely* where, when, and how it will.

52. My view of resurrection or reincarnation is therefore different from what we discover, say, in Plato or Hindu traditions. Both of them postulate a spiritual substance or "soul" *(psyche; atman)* that separates from the body at death, and then after a period of time (Plato suggests 1,000 years) gets reincarnated into another body — whose characteristics are largely determined by how one previously lived. The focus of both these viewpoints, however, is on stopping these reincarnations by achieving at some point in their cycles a high enough pitch of sanctity (according to the respective moral visions) to enter into an eternal beatific vision (Plato, *Phaedrus; Republic* 10) or Brahman (see H. Obayashi [ed.], *Death and Afterlife: Perspectives of World Religions* [New York: Greenwood Press, 1992], the article by T. J. Hopkins, "Hindu Views of Death and Afterlife"). On the notion of a soul separable at death, see chapter 1, endnote 50. To the remarks there I would now add that the suggestion I am offering postulates a soul only in the sense that the particles composing us possess something akin to memory that allows their continuing resurrection or reconstitution into identifiable forms, and that in this process there is something of God's cherishing of life in them.

53. See particularly chapter 1, endnotes 58-61. This notion of the identifiability of succeeding universes, coupled to the comment in the preceding endnote on memory, is also receiving increasingly serious attention in complexity theory, especially in those versions that postulate the existence of so-called "strange attractors." Most of the work being done here is in evolutionary biology, and commonly goes under the name "structuralism." The basic idea is that, contrary to classic Darwinism, where evolution proceeds by chance mutations whose occurrence is entirely unpredictable, evolution appears to be guided (at least mathematically or statistically) by the existence of certain patterns of development (the strange attractors) that confine evolutionary development along certain pathways. Because of this, one conclusion that many structuralists reach is that carbon-based life like our own — or, for that matter, life originating on *any* chemical basis — once it begins to develop, will continue to develop more or less in identifiable ways. In this suggestion, the structuralists are not far from a key ingredient in Whitehead's philosophy: that possibilities within creation are not helter-skelter, but guided, or, as he prefers, persuaded. My own view, like Whitehead's, identifies the source of this persuasion, the attractor, as God. Additionally, in the context of this note, I would want to argue that if such attractors do indeed exist, now not merely as mathematical but as metaphysical realities (though mathematicians tend to identify the two), they persuade not just the evolution of biological life, but of the universe as a whole, and that they do so throughout its rhythmic existence. For a clear and intriguing discussion of these attractors, as of many other topics in contemporary science, see George Johnson, *Fire in the Mind, op. cit.,* pp. 95-103, 269-77. See also, for the role of attractors in specifically biological development, the critically acclaimed volume by S. Kauffman, *At Home in the Universe* (New York: Oxford University Press, 1995), *passim.* The importance of Kauffman's work here can scarcely be underestimated. For a discussion of Whitehead's notion of the "lure" of possibility as the lure of God, see Lewis S. Ford, *The Lure of God* (Philadelphia: Fortress Press, 1978), where he is particularly concerned with providing biblical foundations for the idea, and Thomas E. Hosinski, *Stubborn Fact and Creative Advance: An Introduction to the Metaphysics of Alfred North Whitehead, op. cit.,* pp. 84-114, 157-79.

54. On the singularity, see our discussion in chapter 1, especially endnote 56.

55. In *The Edge of Infinity,* p. 5, Davies makes the more tentative proposal: "The singularity may represent the limits of science itself — the interface between the natural and supernatural."

NOTES TO CHAPTER IV

1. Marcel's analysis of mystery has been appropriated widely by theologians, since it overcomes the conceptual mistake that commonly views mystery as simply an unsolved or unsolvable problem. For one example, see George Hendry, *Theology of Nature* (Philadelphia: Westminster Press, 1980), pp. 33-34. Hendry also rightly relates this analysis of mystery to Marcel's further analysis of presence; one's own existence in the experience of mystery endows what is being experienced with reality, at least for oneself.

2. See the discussion of black holes in chapter 1, especially endnote 38. We will take them up again later in this chapter.

3. In this he was deeply influenced by his colleague Eudoxus, less so by his student Callippus. For a lucid rendition of Aristotle's argument, see Joel Davis, *Journey to the Center of Our Galaxy* (Chicago: Contemporary Books, 1991), pp. 36-58, especially pp. 45-52. That the orbits had to have the form of a circle satisfied the concept of perfection so prevalent at the time, namely, that perfection was synonymous with immobility, and that circular motion was thus the least imperfect since one always returned to the exact same spot by the exact same route. It was Kepler who conclusively overcame this bias — which previously he had strongly shared — when he demonstrated that the planetary orbits were in fact elliptical, thus wobbling slightly as their (gravitational) relationship to the Sun altered in distance at various points on the ellipse. It was Newton, of course, who actually demonstrated this alteration, and how much of it occurs, as due to the inverse square law of gravitational attraction.

4. Einstein's special theory of relativity permits the existence of tachyons, but forbids them from ever going *slower* than the speed of light, thus making them and whatever effects they might produce, if any, unavailable for observation. For some intriguing speculations on tachyons, see John Gribben, *Unveiling the Edge of Time* (New York: Crown, 1992), pp. 194-97.

5. This is especially true if one of the most debated consequences of inflationary theory (cf. chapter 1, including endnotes 43-45) proves correct, namely that our observable universe in fact constitutes just a tiny "bubble" in the universe as a whole, and that other bubbles are not only denied us currently by the speed of light limit, but permanently by unbreachable walls of primal energy from the big bang as well as the likelihood that each has laws of physics of its own. For a good discussion, see Alan Dressler, *Voyage to the Great Attractor, op. cit.*, pp. 292-95.

6. Stephen Hawking argues that such tunnels or wormholes would not only be many times smaller than the smallest atom, but would be completely dis-

rupted by the approach of anything like a spaceship. See the discussion in John Boslough, *Masters of Time* (New York: Addison-Wesley, 1992), pp. 189-91, 206-9 and in Stephen Hawking, *Black Holes and Baby Universes* (New York: Bantam, 1994), pp. 115-125, especially p. 120. Hawking's specific context is the "umbilical" or "wormhole" that links a parent universe to his theoretical proposal of an offshoot or baby universe deriving from it through quantum fluctuations.

7. However, see chapter 3, endnote 27.

8. Perhaps no one has analyzed this character of predictability more thoroughly and distinctly than Karl Popper, *The Logic of Scientific Discovery* (New York: Basic Books, 1968), *passim*. He is particularly concerned here with establishing the principle of falsifiability. His argument is that when a new discovery is made scientists usually deduce from it an explanatory hypothesis, and then from this deduce further hypotheses that can in turn be experimentally checked. These further hypotheses are the predictions, and if any of them prove to be false, the explanatory hypothesis has to be accordingly altered, or, if the falsification is serious enough, rejected. A good theory, therefore, is one that is highly susceptible to falsification, and so can be tested in a whole variety of ways. If these tests are consistently passed, then confidence in the theory can grow. The point of his discussion is that it is falsifiability rather than verifiability that really counts; or, to put it differently, it is more deductive than inductive reasoning that tends to produce scientific advance. The most reliable context in which hypotheses are proven false is provided by the presumed constants of nature.

9. See Jeffrey G. Sobosan, *Christian Commitment and Prophetic Living* (Mystic, CN: Twenty-Third Publications, 1986).

10. Even in alchemical practices, as with Paracelsus, valid discoveries were made not because of but despite the arcane rituals surrounding them; or perhaps better, because legitimate experimental techniques were embedded in the rituals. For a fascinating study of Paracelsus and his contributions to medical science, see Walter Pagel, *Paracelsus* (New York: Karger, 1982).

11. This faithfulness is at the very heart of Judeo-Christianity. In Judaism it undergirds the relationship with God as that of two adults under covenant with each other; in the teachings of Jesus it warrants the relationship with God as that between parent and child. Both traditions agree that in the respective relationships it is God who is always the completely faithful one, unlike the human partners.

12. Nonetheless, you still do find the concept employed now and then by scientists because it can function in much the same way as the unknown but needed quantity, "x," in an equation.

13. Stephen Hawking, *A Brief History of Time* (New York: Bantam Books,

1988), p. 175. This is the concluding paragraph of the book, and it is worth citing: "However, if we do discover a complete theory, it should in time be understandable in broad principle by everyone, not just a few scientists. Then we shall all, philosophers, scientists, and just ordinary people, be able to take part in the discussion of the question of why it is that we and the universe exist. If we find the answer to that, it would be the ultimate triumph of human reason — for then we would know the mind of God."

14. The concepts of symmetry and symmetry-breaking are now fairly commonplace in theoretical physics to describe the very early stages of the universe as elementary forces and particles broke apart and, with declining temperature, "froze" to become the ones that populate the universe today. For a good description, see James Trefil, *The Moment of Creation* (New York: Collier Books, 1983), pp. 87-101, 148-155, 218-28, or P. Davies and J. Gribben, *The Matter Myth* (New York: Simon and Schuster, 1992), pp. 245-56.

15. This is not to say that Plato had no interest in these areas; he did, and indications of it appear now and then throughout the Dialogues. But his interest appears more like that of an intermittent hobby, whereas for Aristotle it had the character of a vocation. Even in the previous example I provided of Aristotle's insistence that planetary orbits had to follow a circular path as a perfect geometric form (Plato was, after all, Aristotle's teacher), his enthusiasm here was linked to his empirical observations of these orbits and their experimental justification in the motion of solids, even though these eventually proved mistaken.

16. Many fine studies are available comparing Buddhism (and often, Hinduism) with biblical and Platonic traditions. A great upsurge began in the 1960s, including the many popular books by Alan Watts, especially *The Way of Zen,* and Harvey Cox's *Turning East.* But preceding these, with a concentration on Hinduism as the matrix out of which Buddhism was born, is the extraordinary analysis by S. Radhakrishnan, *Eastern Religions and Western Thought* (London: Oxford University Press, 1940).

17. For a classic analysis of this experience as it achieves philosophical and theological reflection, see Mircea Eliade, *Cosmos and History: The Myth of Eternal Return,* tr. W. R. Trask (New York: Harper and Row, 1959). Among those well-known in modern times, it is Nietzsche in philosophy and Spengler and Toynbee in historical studies who have been most sympathetic to this notion of continual return, or what the latter two would be more comfortable calling periodicity. As long as great caution is exercised in the comparison, something similar to this notion is also present in the suggestions I offered regarding resurrection in the final section of the previous chapter.

18. On the development of the mythology of these Fates and its repercus-

sions in philosophy, theology and science among the Greeks, see the still superb book by F. M. Cornford, *From Religion to Philosophy: A Study in the Origins of Western Speculation* (New York: Harper and Row, 1987), *passim,* but particularly pp. 40-72.

19. See, for example, Barbara Tuchman's vivid and well-researched account, *A Distant Mirror: the Calamitous 14th Century* (New York: Ballantine, 1979). Of particular interest is her portrayal of the recurrent emergence of the bubonic plague, but also the unconscionable deprivation forced on populations by princes, bishops, and kings, frequently from motives of a bellicose and sadistic piety. See also the classic study by Johan Huizinga, *The Waning of the Middle Ages* (New York: Doubleday, 1954), especially pp. 9-66, 138-50.

20. Even a cursory reading of Aquinas's work, for example, shows this blending repeatedly (especially as the Platonism got sifted through the writings of Augustine), as does the work of others like Albert the Great and Duns Scotus. For an excellent one-volume study of all three of these men, see F. Copleston, *A History of Philosophy* (New York: Doubleday, 1962), vol. 2, part II, "Albert the Great to Duns Scotus."

21. See Hesiod, *Theogony,* lines 1-153. The first line reads (my translation): "Before all else, Chaos existed, next fulsome Earth, our fixed and lasting home, then Eros, the loveliest of the ever-living gods. . . ." The notion of a primordial chaos is cross-cultural in religious mythologies. For brief samplings, see Mircea Eliade, *Cosmos and History, op. cit.,* pp. 9-20, 54-71. For a superb phenomenological analysis of these mythologies, concentrating on the tale of Tiamat and Marduk from the Babylonian creation epic (the *Enuma elish,* from the first two words, "When on high . . ."), see Paul Ricoeur, *The Symbolism of Evil,* tr. E. Buchanan (Boston: Beacon Press, 1969), pp. 175-91.

22. As an example: when chided by Halley as an old man for his belief in astrological principles, he replied, "Evidently you have not looked into astrology; I have." Cited in Nicholas Devore, *Encyclopedia of Astrology* (New York: Philosophical Library, 1947), p. xi. It is interesting to note that while Newton's interest in astrology is usually diminished in biographies, a discussion of his abiding interest in alchemy is now commonplace. And it makes for fascinating reading. See the excellent accounts in Richard S. Westfall, *The Life of Isaac Newton* (New York: Cambridge University Press, 1993), pp. 133-59, and Gale Christianson, *In the Presence of the Creator: Isaac Newton and his Times* (New York: The Free Press, 1984), pp. 203-37. For the relationship between alchemy and astrology, see, for example, *ibid.,* p. 209: "Moreover, each major (alchemical) process was related to a different sign of the zodiac, requiring the alchemist to command an intimate knowledge of astrology."

23. See the excellent study by Max Wildiers, *The Theologian and His Universe,* tr. Paul Dunphy (New York: The Seabury Press, 1982), pp. 49-56, in particular p. 54.

24. He mocked the ancient but incorrect idea that to keep a planet in orbit it was necessary to provide a force to push it along its path, thus requiring the need for angels to follow behind it, flapping their wings. Cited in James Trefil, *Reading the Mind of God* (New York, Scribner's, 1989), p. 8.

25. On Dirac's view in particular, see endnote 47 below and its reference in the main text.

26. To demonstrate the extreme of this position, I once heard a lecture in which a deconstructionist philosopher said of his recently published book, "I didn't write it; it wrote itself." This is giving a degree of autonomy to the use and power of words whose only parallel I know of is the metaphorical usage of *logos* (word) in the prologue of the Fourth Gospel. Deconstructionism is a major school in current philosophy and literary criticism. For various appraisals, see Jonathan Loesberg, *Aestheticism and Deconstruction* (Princeton: Princeton University Press, 1991); Christopher Norris, *Deconstruction Theory and Practice* (New York: Methuen, 1982); and from the man considered by many its founder, Jacques Derrida, *A Derrida Reader: Between the Blinds,* ed. Peggy Kamuf (New York: Columbia University Press, 1991). For an attempt at a theological application, see Mark C. Taylor, *Deconstructing Theology* (New York: Crossroad, 1982).

27. See his major work *Treatise concerning the Principles of Human Knowledge*.

28. Einstein offers a stunning illustration of this point. When once asked how he would respond if a specific experiment testing his general theory of relativity disagreed with it, he replied with neither hesitation nor distress, "So much the worse for the experiment. The theory is right!" Cited in Paul Davies, *The Mind of God* (New York: Simon & Schuster, 1992), pp. 175-76.

29. This interchange lies at the very heart of quantum indeterminacy insofar as it demonstrates that we can never be certain if we are seeing the object as it actually is or as it has been sullied (particularly in its position or momentum) by our participation in the observation. Neils Bohr tried to give this rather unnerving conclusion a degree of consolation when he spoke of a "principle of complementarity" whereby we recognize that at these minute levels we are simultaneously spectators as well as participants in the phenomena of nature. For his various discussions of the principle, see Neils Bohr, *The Philosophical Writings of Neils Bohr,* 3 vols. (Woodbridge, CN.: Ox Bow Press, 1987). Volume 1 deals with his theory of atomic structure (the so-called Copenhagen model); volumes 2 and 3 attempt, among other things, to search out the ramifications of this theory for

application to human knowledge. For one appraisal, see Henry J. Folse, *The Philosophy of Neils Bohr: The Framework of Complementarity* (New York: Elsevier Science Publishing Co., 1985).

30. I use the phrase "almost exclusively" out of recognition that many physicists argue — and I have noted before my basic agreement with them — that the above principle of complementarity applies not just in large degree at the minute levels of nature, but to some degree (particularly in its participatory characteristic) at all levels of nature. To some extent, even if only infinitesimally small, the behavior of everything everywhere in the observable universe affects everything else. See the comments on chaos theory in the following paragraph.

31. Of the many studies available on this theory, I would especially recommend the following three: Arun V. Holden (ed.), *Chaos* (Princeton: Princeton University Press, 1986); T. Mullin (ed.), *The Nature of Chaos* (New York: Oxford University Press, 1987); James Gleick, *Chaos: Making a New Science* (New York: Viking, 1987). The first two are quite technical, the third less so.

32. This is commonly described as the "smoothing out" of the indeterminacy in the movement from sub-atomic to molecular dimensions. See also the comments on the "strange attractors" of chaos theory in chapter 3, endnote 53.

33. See James Trefil, *op. cit., passim*. He gathers these constants together as illustrations of what he calls "the principle of universality."

34. This is what is going on, for example, in Huston Smith's book, *Forgotten Truth* (San Francisco: HarperSanFrancisco, 1992). He argues with notable condescension that while this universal vision or truth can never be available to science, it very likely is to his own peculiar brew of philosophical/mystical theology (e.g., the appendix of the book is titled "The Psychedelic Evidence," and deals with the use of drugs to achieve this vision). In its attitude toward science this book provides a counterpart to Frank Tipler's attitude toward theology in *The Physics of Immortality*.

35. See his *Theories of Everything* (Oxford: Clarendon Press, 1991), *passim*.

36. There are many fine discussions of gravitational theory available, and in previous notes I have cited some that would be accessible to the interested but nonprofessional audience. But perhaps the clearest discussion I have read — for both its comfortable prose and abundant examples — belongs to John A. Wheeler, *A Journey into Gravity and Spacetime* (New York: Scientific American Library, 1990). Wheeler is himself one of the world's leading theoretical physicists.

37. On this point, see chapter 2, endnote 5.

38. See particularly *The Ascent to God* (Chicago: Thomas More Press 1981), pp. 65-128, and *The Turn of the Millennium, op. cit.*, pp. 84-97.

39. For an extended discussion of this understanding of obedience, particularly in the context of disobedience and the experience of guilt when one goes against his or her convictions, see my book *Guilt and the Christian* (Chicago: Thomas More Press, 1982), chapter 1, especially pp. 42-47.

40. There are a huge number of books detailing what this paragraph only briefly describes. I have relied on many of them, but principally on the lucid article by E. N. Parker, "The Sun," in the *Scientific American* volume of collected articles called *The Solar System* (San Francisco, Freeman & Co., 1975), pp. 27-37, as well as J. Gribben, *Blinded by the Light: The Secret Life of the Sun, op. cit.;* T. Ferris, *Coming of Age in the Milky Way, op. cit.,* pp. 246-71; and F. Golden, *Quasars, Pulsars, and Black Holes* (New York: Scribner's, 1976), pp. 112-25.

41. This principle is violated in the case of very massive stars, where the gravitational pressure of collapse is indeed strong enough to overcome the electron barrier, crushing the electrons into the protons, making neutrons and untold numbers of particles called neutrinos. As noted earlier in the chapter, this crushing is what produces a supernova, and the resultant object is called a neutron star. If still more mass was originally present, and in an extremely complicated process, the neutron star could itself collapse under further gravitational pressure, achieving an interior density beyond 150 billion tons per cubic centimeter and crushing the neutrons down into still smaller particles called hyperons. At this point classical physics cannot describe what happens and the relativistic physics of Einstein must be employed. What is eventually spawned is a black hole, and nothing, so far as we know, can collapse a black hole. It is the terminal point in the evolution of all very massive stars, having at its heart what is perhaps the most exotic item yet theorized about the universe, a singularity. See our brief remarks about singularities in chapter 1.

42. For what this phrase meant in the theological context of its formulators, see George Hendry, *Theology of Nature, op. cit.,* pp. 160-61.

43. The very first words of Genesis, "In the beginning God created the heavens and the earth" (Genesis 1:1), might seem to contradict this. Yet it would be a mistake to read this verse as indicating a temporal act, since the implication (especially when other Old Testament creation theologies are taken into account) is that from as long as there has been a universe God has been continually engaging in the act of creation, which we have been interpreting to mean the formation and/or transformation (the Hebrew *barah:* to create) of the material elements (the heavens and the earth) of the universe. This is sustained by the very next verse, which describes these elements ("earth" now being used in its wider, more generic application as a synonym for the universe) as initially "without form and void" ("void" being essentially a redundancy of "without form," but

also denoting anything void of meaning, that is, anything that we cannot identify from our experience). Verse 3, then, is saying that the first thing actually formed into being that we could identify is light. It might be suggested in this context that St. John's stunning claim, "God is light" (1 John 1:5), might simply be his way of saying that from the time light was formed into being, God too began to become manifest in creation.

44. See Harald Fritzsch, *The Creation of Matter*, trans. J. Steinberg (New York: Basic Books, 1984), p. 225.

45. See Steven Weinberg, *The First Three Minutes* (New York: Basic Books, 1988), p. 30.

46. The type and amount of mass photons can create are directly dependent upon how much energy they possess. The photon is a massless particle, which means, among other things, that in varying circumstances it shows the characteristics of both a particle and a wave. The energy of a photon is usually described as part of its wavelike character. The closer the waves are to each other (picture the peaks and troughs of an ocean wave), the more energy the photon contains. Of the countless variety of experiences we have that are due to the rapidity with which these waves occur, or we could also say their vibrations, one of these is color. For red light there are 4×10^{14} of these vibrations per second; for blue there are 7.5×10^{14}. Blue light is therefore more energetic than red. This provided perhaps the basic clue in establishing the famous "red-shift" measurement determining that the universe is expanding. When clusters of galaxies are moving away from each other, the light they generate appears distinctly red to observers because their motion is dissipating its energy. Within these clusters, however, when galaxies are approaching each other, their light appears distinctly blue to observers because its energy is "bundling up" on the approach (this is a very crude description). Our own nearest companion galaxy, the Andromeda, shows this blue shift, and thus is on a collision course with us.

47. Many scientists consider Dirac second only to Einstein in his brilliance as a theoretical physicist. While he doesn't say it, but like others using beauty in a similar mathematical context, he means by the term (1) simplicity of expression and (2) comprehensiveness of application. See Paul Dirac, "The Evolution of the Physicist's Picture of Nature," *Scientific American* (May 1963), p. 47.

48. We've already noted in the last chapter that Christianity never practiced such sacrifice, even when seeking to placate the God "of the Sun and stars and the whole of the firmament" during times of drought. While human sacrifice in the Old Testament existed in the form of the "first-fruits" sacrifice — including the firstborn child — as a means for such propitiation in times of duress such as drought, it gradually disappeared from the common practice centuries before Je-

sus was born. The sacrifice of animals, however, did not. I would like to say that when a great prophet like Jeremiah records Yahweh as saying, "Your burnt offerings are not acceptable, nor your sacrifices pleasing to me" (6:20), it was because of the barbarity of slaughtering the animals involved. But it was not. The prophet was complaining about the faithlessness of the people offering these sacrifices, not the sacrifices themselves. A description of how some of these sacrifices were to be carried out can be found in Leviticus 1:1-17.

NOTES TO CHAPTER V

1. For me the study of cosmology involves three primary facets. The first is the scientific analysis of the origin, present manifestations, and future of the universe. The second is the religious appropriation of this science coupled to claims made about God. The third is the articulation of the science and religious appropriation and claims in a fashion that elicits beauty defined as what gives pleasure to the mind, or spiritually exalts it through challenge and/or consolation.

2. The most profound, almost rapturous meditation on this point I have ever read is in Alfred North Whitehead, *Adventures of Ideas* (New York: Free Press, 1967), the chapter titled "Peace," pp. 285-96. "Peace carries with it a surpassing of personality. . . . It is primarily a trust in the efficacy of Beauty" (p. 285).

3. In Christianity this is linked above all with the eschatological understanding of the eucharist. For the finest study on this topic with which I am currently familiar, see Geoffrey Wainwright, *Eucharist and Eschatology* (New York: Oxford University Press, 1981).

4. See chapter 3, endnote 27.

5. As Aquinas formulates it, this argument is so thoroughly entrenched in medieval notions of order and immutability in the universe, along with certain scholastic biases regarding God, and so inescapably unaware of the results of modern observational technologies and experimental results drawn from science, that its usefulness in describing the universe is today quite bankrupt. However, the basic idea of an underlying design or order in the universe, freed from this medieval baggage, is still enormously appealing, and in fact is the *arche* or energizing motive for why many scientists engage their craft. On the other hand, the so-called "cosmological argument" is one that we have been sympathetic toward in a number of places throughout the book, especially in our remarks on God and the primordial singularity. This argument, however, is actually a composite of three, and it is only the first two that have drawn our sympathy: (1) from contingent causes to a first cause; (2) from contingent being to necessary being; and

(3) from motion to an unmoved mover. We have not been able to sympathize with the third argument because we have suggested several times throughout the book that motion is integral to our definition of life, and that this must include understandings of divine life. For some recent appraisals of the cosmological argument, see William Rowe, *The Cosmological Argument* (Princeton: Princeton University Press, 1975); William L. Craig, *The Cosmological Argument from Plato to Leibniz* (New York: Barnes and Noble, 1980); M. A. Corey, *God and the New Cosmology: The Anthropic Design Argument* (Lanham, Md.: Rowman and Littlefield, 1993).

6. See our comments on Barth in chapter 1.

7. On this point, for example, see Steven Weinberg, *Dreams of a Final Theory* (New York: Vintage Books, 1993), pp. 277-82, where the specific context is whether or not a hugely expensive super-collider should continue to be built (funding for it was cut off by the House of Representatives in June 1993) for the purpose (among others) of approximating more closely conditions in the universe soon after the big bang.

8. For an extended discussion of the role and function of ideals, see my *The Turn of the Millennium, op. cit.,* chapter 2.

9. The quotations are cited in Kurt F. Reinhardt, *The Existentialist Revolt* (New York: Ungar, 1960), p. 194.

10. On this same point, see Wolfhart Pannenberg, *Toward a Theology of Nature, op. cit.,* pp. 50-122, and especially the eloquent reflections on pp. 135-37.

11. For some understandings of this cosmic dimension to the person of Jesus other than those I will offer here, see Matthew Fox, *The Coming of the Cosmic Christ* (San Francisco: Harper and Row, 1988), pp. 75-128, where he analyzes biblical, patristic, and medieval material. The rest of the book is an attempt to offer an application of this dimension to contemporary concerns, concentrating, much as Thomas Berry also does, more on Earth-centered ecological issues than on cosmology proper.

Select Bibliography

(Not all books in the endnotes are listed here; only those I found of particular assistance, pro and con, in composing the analyses in the text.)

Alexander, Richard D. *The Biology of Moral Systems*. Hawthorne, N.Y.: de Gruyter, 1987.

Barbour, Ian. *Issues in Science and Religion*. New York: Harper & Row, 1971.

———. *Religion in an Age of Science*. San Francisco: Harper and Row, 1990.

——— (ed.). *Earth Might Be Fair: Reflections on Ethics, Religion and Ecology*. Englewood Cliffs, N.J.: Prentice-Hall, 1972.

Barrow, John. *Theories of Everything: The Quest for Ultimate Explanation*. Oxford: Clarendon Press, 1991.

———. *The Origin of the Universe*. New York: Basic Books, 1994.

Bateson, Gregory. *Steps to an Ecology of Mind*. Northvale, N.J.: Avonson, 1987.

Becker, Ernest. *The Denial of Death*. New York: Macmillan, 1973.

Berry, Thomas, and Thomas Clarke. *Befriending the Earth*. Mystic, Conn.: Twenty-Third Publications, 1991.

Bohm, David. *Wholeness and the Implicate Order*. London: Routledge & Kegan Paul, 1980.

Boslough, John. *Masters of Time*. New York: Addison-Wesley, 1992.

Bowman, Douglas. *Beyond the Modern Mind*. Cleveland: The Pilgrim Press, 1990.

Brooke, John Hedley. *Science and Religion*. Cambridge: Cambridge University Press, 1991.

Brueggemann, Walter. *The Prophetic Imagination*. Philadelphia: Fortress Press, 1978.

Buber, Martin. *Good and Evil*. New York: Scribner's, 1953.

Campbell, Joseph. *The Masks of God*. 4 vols. New York: Viking, 1970.

Capra, Fritjof, and David Steidl-Rast. *Belonging to the Universe*. San Francisco: HarperCollins, 1991.

Carnley, P. *The Structure of Resurrection Belief*. Oxford: Oxford University Press, 1987.

Choron, Jacques. *Death and Western Thought*. New York: Collier Books, 1963.

Cobb, John B., Jr. *A Christian Natural Theology*. Philadelphia: Westminster Press, 1965.

————. *God and the World*. Philadelphia: Westminster Press, 1969.

————. *Christ in a Pluralistic Age*. Philadelphia: Westminster Press, 1975.

Cobb, John B., Jr., and David R. Griffin. *Process Theology: An Introductory Exposition*. Philadelphia: Westminster Press, 1976.

Cohen, Jack, and Ian Stewart. *The Collapse of Chaos*. New York: Penguin Books, 1994.

Collingwood, R. G. *The Idea of Nature*. Oxford: Oxford University Press, 1945.

Commoner, Barry. *Making Peace with the Planet*. New York: Pantheon, 1990.

Cornell, James (ed.). *Bubbles, Voids, and Bumps in Time: The New Cosmology*. New York: Cambridge University Press, 1989.

Davies, Paul. *Other Worlds*. New York: Simon and Schuster, 1980.

————. *The Runaway Universe*. New York: Penguin Books, 1980.

————. *The Edge of Infinity*. New York: Simon and Schuster, 1981.

————. *God and the New Physics*. New York: Simon and Schuster, 1983.

————. *The Last Three Minutes*. New York: Basic Books, 1994.

————. *About Time: Einstein's Unfinished Revolution*. New York: Simon and Schuster, 1995.

————. *The Mind of God*. New York: Simon & Schuster, 1992.

————, and J. R. Brown (eds.). *The Ghost in the Atom*. Cambridge: Cambridge University Press, 1993.

————, and John Gribbin. *The Matter Myth*. New York: Simon and Schuster, 1992.

Dawkins, Richard. *The Blind Watchmaker*. London: Longmans, 1986.

de Rougemont, Denis. *Love in the Western World*. Translated by M. Belgion. New York: Pantheon Books, 1956.

de Surgy, P. (ed.). *The Resurrection and Modern Biblical Thought*. New York: Corpus Books, 1970.

Dressler, Alan. *Voyage to the Great Attractor*. New York: Vintage Books, 1995.

Dyson, Freeman. *Disturbing the Universe*. New York: Harper and Row, 1979.

————. *Infinite in All Directions*. New York: Harper & Row, 1988.

Ebeling, Gerhard. *The Nature of Faith*. Translated by R. G. Smith. Philadelphia: Fortress Press, 1967.

Einstein, Albert. *Out of My Later Years*. Secaucus, NJ: Citadel Press, 1956.

Eiseley, Loren. *The Star Thrower*. New York: Times Books, 1978.

Ferris, Timothy. *Coming of Age in the Milky Way*. New York: W. Morrow, 1988.

Ford, Lewis. *The Lure of God*. Philadelphia: Fortress Press, 1978.

Fritzsch, Harald. *The Creation of Matter*. Translated by J. Steinberg. New York: Basic Books, 1984.

Fromm, Erich. *The Anatomy of Human Destructiveness*. Greenwich, CN: Fawcett Publications, 1973.

Fuller, Robert. *Ecology of Care*. Louisville: Westminster/John Knox Press, 1992.

Gell-Mann, Murray. *The Quark and the Jaguar*. New York: Freeman, 1994.

Gilkey, Langdon. *Nature, Reality and the Sacred*. Minneapolis: Fortress Press, 1993.

Gillispie, Charles. *The Edge of Objectivity*. Princeton, NJ: Princeton University Press, 1960.

Goodenough, Ursula. *The Sacred Depths of Nature.* New York: Oxford University Press, 1998.

Gribben, John. *In Search of Schrodinger's Cat.* New York: Bantam, 1984.

———. *Blinded by the Light: The Secret Life of the Sun.* New York: Harmony Books, 1991.

———. *Unveiling the Edge of Time.* New York: Crown, 1992.

———, and Martin Rees. *Cosmic Coincidences.* New York: Bantam, 1989.

Gustafson, James. *A Sense of the Divine.* Cleveland: The Pilgrim Press, 1994.

Harrison, Edward. *Darkness at Night.* Cambridge, Mass.: Harvard University Press, 1987.

Haught, John. *The Cosmic Adventure.* New York: Paulist Press, 1984.

Hawking, Stephen. *A Brief History of Time.* New York: Bantam Books, 1988.

———. *Black Holes and Baby Universes.* New York: Bantam Books, 1994.

Heffner, Philip. *The Human Factor.* Minneapolis: Fortress, 1993.

Heisenberg, Werner. *Physics and Beyond.* New York; Harper & Row, 1971.

Hendry, George. *Theology of Nature.* Philadelphia: Westminster Press, 1980.

Hoffman, Frederick. *The Mortal No: Death and the Modern Imagination.* Princeton: Princeton University Press, 1964.

Hosinski, Thomas. *Stubborn Fact and Creative Advance: An Introduction to the Metaphysics of Alfred North Whitehead.* Lanham, MD.: Rowman & Littlefield, 1993.

Jantzen, Grace. *God's World, God's Body.* Philadelphia: Westminster Press, 1984.

Jastrow, Robert. *God and the Astronomers.* New York: Norton, 1978.

Johnson, George. *Fire in the Mind: Science, Faith, and the Search for Order.* New York: Knopf, 1995.

Jones, C., G. Wainwright, and E. Yarnold (eds.). *The Study of Spirituality.* New York: Oxford University Press, 1986.

Kaspar, Walter. *Jesus the Christ.* Translated by V. Green. New York: Paulist Press, 1977.

Kauffman, Stuart. *At Home in the Universe: The Search for the Laws of Self-Organization and Complexity.* New York: Oxford University Press, 1995.

Keen, Sam. *Apology for Wonder.* New York: Harper and Row, 1973.

Kierkegaard, Søren. *Works of Love.* Translated by Howard and Edna Hong. New York: Harper & Row, 1962.

Krishnamurti, J., and David Bohm. *The Ending of Time.* New York: Harper & Row, 1985.

Layzer, David. *Cosmogenesis.* New York: Oxford University Press, 1990.

Leopold, Aldo. *A Sand County Almanac.* New York: Oxford University Press, 1949.

Lepp, Ignace. *The Psychology of Loving.* New York: New American Library, 1965.

Lewis, C. S. *The Allegory of Love.* New York: Oxford University Press, 1958.

Lightman, Alan, and Roberta Brawer. *Origins: The Lives and Worlds of Modern Cosmologists.* Cambridge: Harvard University Press, 1990.

Linzey, Andrew. *Christianity and the Rights of Animals.* New York: Crossroad, 1987.

MacIntyre, Alasdair. *After Virtue.* Notre Dame: University of Notre Dame Press, 1984.

Macquarrie, John. *Principles of Christian Theology.* 2nd ed. New York: Charles Scribner's Sons, 1977.

May, Rollo. *Love and Will.* New York: Dell, 1969.

McFague, Sallie. *Models of God: Theology for an Ecological Nuclear Age.* Philadelphia: Fortress Press, 1987.

————. *The Body of God.* Minneapolis: Fortress Press, 1993.

McDaniel, Jay. *Of God and Pelicans.* Louisville: Westminster/John Knox Press, 1989.

————. *Earth, Sky, Gods, and Mortals.* Mystic, Conn.: Twenty-Third Publications, 1990.

McKibben, Bill. *The End of Nature.* New York: Doubleday, 1989.

McLaren, Robert. *Christian Ethics: Foundations and Practice.* Englewood Cliffs, N.J.: Prentice-Hall, 1994.

Marcuse, Herbert. *Eros and Civilization.* New York: Knopf, 1961.

Menninger, Karl. *Whatever Became of Sin?* New York: Hawthorn Books, 1973.

Moltmann, Jurgen. *Theology of Hope.* Translated by J. Leitch. New York: Harper & Row, 1967.

————. *Hope and Planning.* Translated by M. Clarkson. New York: Harper & Row, 1971.

————. *The Crucified God.* Translated by R. A. Wilson and J. Bowden. London: SCM Press, 1974.

Munitz, Milton. *Cosmic Understanding.* Princeton: Princeton University Press, 1986.

Murray, John Courtney. *The Problem of God.* New Haven: Yale University Press, 1964.

Nygren, Anders. *Agape and Eros.* Translated by P. Watson. Philadelphia: Westminster Press, 1953.

O'Collins, G. *The Resurrection of Jesus Christ: Some Contemporary Issues.* Milwaukee: Marquette University Press, 1993.

Overbye, Dennis. *Lonely Hearts of the Cosmos.* New York: Harper-Collins, 1992.

Pais, Abraham. *Subtle Is the Lord: The Science and Life of Albert Einstein.* New York: Oxford University Press, 1982.

Panikkar, Raimon. *The Cosmotheandric Experience.* Maryknoll: Orbis Books, 1993.

Pannenberg, Wolfhart. *Jesus — God and Man.* Translated by L. Wilkins and D. Priebe. Philadelphia: Westminster Press, 1968.

———— (ed.). *Revelation as History.* Translated by D. Granskou. New York: Macmillan, 1968.

————. *Toward a Theology of Nature: Essays on Science and Faith.* Louisville: Westminster/John Knox Press, 1993.

Peacocke, Arthur. *Theology for a Scientific Age.* Minneapolis: Fortress Press, 1993.

Pelikan, Jaroslav. *The Christian Tradition.* 5 vols. Chicago: University of Chicago Press, 1971-83.

————. *Jesus through the Centuries: His Place in the History of Culture.* New Haven, Conn.: Yale University Press, 1985.

Perkins, Pheme. *Resurrection: New Testament Witness and Contemporary Reflection.* New York: Doubleday, 1989.

Peters, Ted (ed.). *Cosmos as Creation*. Nashville: Abingdon Press, 1989.

Polanyi, Michael. *Science, Faith, and Society*. Oxford: Oxford University Press, 1946.

Polkinghorne, John. *Reason and Reality: The Relationship between Science and Theology*. Philadelphia: Trinity Press International, 1991.

————. *The Faith of a Physicist*. Princeton: Princeton University Press, 1994.

Price, Huw. *Time's Arrow and Archimedes' Point*. New York: Oxford University Press, 1996.

Prigogine, Ilya, and Isabelle Stengers. *Order out of Chaos: Man's New Dialogue with Nature*. New York: Bantam Books, 1984.

Ricoeur, Paul. *Fallible Man*. Translated by C. Kelbley. Chicago: Regnery, 1967.

————. *The Symbolism of Evil*. Translated by E. Buchanan. Boston: Beacon Press, 1969.

Rolston, Holmes. *Science and Religion*. New York: Random House, 1987.

Russell, Robert; Murphy, Nancey; Isham, J. C. (eds.). *Quantum Cosmology and the Laws of Nature*. Vatican City/Berkeley: Vatican Observatory Publications/The Center for Theology and the Natural Sciences, 1996.

Santayana, George. *The Sense of Beauty*. New York: Dover, 1955.

Santmire, Paul. *The Travail of Nature*. Philadelphia: Fortress Press, 1985.

Sawicki, Marianne. *Seeing the Lord: Resurrection and Early Christian Practices*. Minneapolis: Fortress Press, 1994.

Schell, Jonathan. *The Fate of the Earth*. New York: Knopf, 1982.

————. *The Abolition*. New York: Knopf, 1984.

Schweitzer, Albert. *Reverence for Life*. Translated by R. Fuller. New York: Harper & Row, 1969.

Smedes, Lewis. *Love within Limits: A Realist's View of 1 Corinthians 13*. Grand Rapids: Eerdmans, 1978.

Smoot, George, and Keay Davidson. *Wrinkles in Time*. New York: Avon Books, 1993.

Sobosan, Jeffrey. *The Ascent to God*. Chicago: Thomas More Press, 1981.

————. *Christian Commitment and Prophetic Living.* Mystic, CN.: Twenty-Third Publications, 1986.

————. *Bless the Beasts.* New York: Crossroad, 1991.

————. *The Turn of the Millennium: An Agenda for Christian Religion in an Age of Science.* Cleveland: Pilgrim Press, 1996.

Soelle, Dorothee. *To Work and To Love.* Philadelphia: Fortress Press, 1984.

Sorokin, Pitirim. *The Ways and Power of Love.* Chicago: Regnery, 1967.

Tillich, Paul. *Theology of Culture.* Edited by R. C. Kimball. London: Oxford University Press, 1959.

Tipler, Frank. *The Physics of Immortality.* New York: Doubleday, 1994.

Toulmin, Stephen. *The Return to Cosmology.* Berkeley: University of California Press, 1982.

————, and June Goodfield. *The Fabric of the Heavens.* New York: Harper and Row, 1961.

————. *The Architecture of Matter.* New York: Harper and Row, 1962.

————. *The Discovery of Time.* New York: Harper and Row, 1965.

Trefil, James. *The Moment of Creation.* New York: Macmillan, 1983.

————. *Reading the Mind of God.* New York: Scribner's, 1989.

————. *From Atoms to Quarks.* New York: Doubleday, 1994.

Via, Dan Otto, Jr. *The Parables.* Philadelphia: Fortress Press, 1967.

Wildiers, N. Max. *The Theologian and His Universe.* New York: Seabury, 1982.

Weinberg, Steven. *The First Three Minutes.* New York: Basic Books, 1977.

————. *Dreams of a Final Theory.* New York: Vintage Books, 1993.

White, Michael, and John Gribben. *Einstein.* New York: Dutton, 1993.

Whitehead, Alfred North. *Science and the Modern World.* New York: Macmillan, 1926.

————. *Adventures of Ideas.* New York: Macmillan, 1933.

————. *Religion in the Making.* Cleveland: Meridian Books, 1960.

————. *Process and Reality: An Essay in Cosmology.* Corrected edition by David R. Griffin and Donald W. Sherburne. New York: Free Press, 1978.

Wilber, Ken (ed.). *The Holographic Paradigm and Other Paradoxes.* Boulder, Colorado: Shambhala Publications, 1982.

Will, Clifford. *Was Einstein Right?* New York: Basic Books, 1986.

World Commission on Environment and Development. *Our Common Future.* New York: Oxford University Press, 1987.

Worthing, Mark. *God, Creation, and Contemporary Physics.* Minneapolis: Fortress Press, 1996.

Index

aesthetics, x, 133-34
aether, the, 27-28
Albert the Great, 189n.20
alchemy, 189n.22
Alford, F., 171n.23
analogy, 189n.29
Anderson, B., 156n.9, 172n.32, 173n.34
animals, 138-39; treatment of, 93-94, 95, 169n.12, 181n.40, 193-94n.48
Anthropic Principle, 75-78, 85, 88
anthropocentrism, 11, 85, 88, 144
anthropology, 56
anthropomorphism, 2
anti-matter, 79, 177n.17
aporias, 72, 75, 166n.56
Aquinas, Thomas, 95, 116, 143, 166n.59, 189n.20, 195n.5
Aristotle, 4, 27-28, 66, 101, 106, 111, 112, 113, 156n.8, 186n.3, 188n.15
Asimov, Isaac, 159n.31
astrology, 115, 118-19, 189n.22
astronomy, 3, 6, 8, 33
astrophysics, 3, 8, 33, 135, 165n.55
Athanasius, 73
atomism, ancient Greek, 42-43, 169n.10

Augustine, 105, 189n.20

Bacon, Francis, 16, 18, 103, 159n.28
Baillie, John, 78
Barbour, Ian, 156n.7
Barrow, John, 85, 122, 157n.16, 167n.60, 176n.11, 180n.30
Barth, Karl, 11-12, 13, 95, 143-44, 155n.3, 158n.20, 170n.20, 195n.6
beauty, x, 9, 11, 24, 53, 56, 59, 66, 90, 91, 133-34, 141, 146, 168n.5, 172n.30; as strangeness of proportion (Bacon), 16, 18, 103; and truth and goodness, 24; of the universe, 39, 46
Beckett, Samuel, 87
Berkeley, Bishop George, 117-18
Berry, Thomas, 156n.7, 195n.11
Bible, the, 47
big bang theory, 32, 34, 172n.31
Billingham, J., 179n.26
biology, 43
black holes, 22, 79, 106, 161n.35, 161-62n.38, 192n.41
blindness, 62-63; experimental, 62-63; moral or intellectual, 63

Bohr, Niels, 190n.29
Bonhoeffer, Dietrich, 11
Boslough, John, 177n.18, 187n.6
Bova, Ben, 169n.14
Brady, Nathan, 178n.21
Brahe, Tycho, 6, 116, 157n.11, 160n.32
Brawer, R., 156n.5, 173n.35
Bronowski, Jacob, 159n.29
brown dwarfs, 19-20
Brunner, Emil, 11
Buddhism, 111-12, 168n.7, 188n.16
Bultmann, Rudolf, 11, 95, 153
Burton, Richard, 145

Cairns, Douglas L., 175n.9
Calvin, John, 95
Cameron, A., 179n.26
Campbell, Joseph, 153, 180n.33
Camus, Albert, 152
Capps, Walter, 171n.24
Capra, F., 171n.25
Chandrasekhar limit, 161n.36
Center for Theology and the Natural
    Sciences (CTNS), the, 173n.35
chaos (in experience), 112-14
chaos theory, 28, 119
cherishing of life. See life, cherishing
    of
Christ, the cosmic, 148-49. See also Je-
    sus
Christian tradition, the, 22, 95
Christianity, 4, 67, 89, 94, 113, 135,
    141, 175n.7, 193n.48, 194n.3
Christianson, Gale, 189n.22
Cicero, 181n.43
Cobb, Jr., John B., 12, 110, 174n.39
Coleridge, Samuel Taylor, 2
complementarity, principle of (Bohr),
    190n.29, 191n.30
complexity theory, 185n.53
constants, universal, 85, 105-7, 121
control, 72-75

Copernicus, 6, 75, 160n.32
Copleston, Frederick C., 189n.20
Corey, M. A., 176n.11, 195n.5
Cornford, F. M., 189n.18
cosmic strings, 79
cosmogony, 29
cosmological argument, 194-95n.5
cosmology, xi, 7, 25-26, 29, 60, 62, 139,
    143, 152, 194n.1
Cox, Harvey, 188n.16
Craig, William L., 195n.5
creation, artistic, 31-32; dance of, 37;
    doctrine of, 11-12; out of nothing-
    ness, 29, 32, 47, 48-50, 170n.20,
    184n.50; religious myths of, 29-33,
    36, 47. See also God, creative activity
    of
creativity, as image of God, 69

Damasio, Antonio, 160n.31
Dante, 18
dark matter, 19, 34
Darwin, Charles, 6, 76, 84, 157n.12,
    176n.14
Davidson, Keay, 163nn.44,47
Davies, Paul, 162n.38, 165n.56,
    167nn.60,61, 168n.5, 176n.12,
    177n.17, 178n.18, 183n.50, 185n.55,
    188n.14, 190n.28
Davis, Joel, 163n.42, 186n.3
death, as format of life, 101-2
deconstruction, 116, 190n.26
deism, 14, 117
Democritus, 42
Derrida, Jacques, 190n.26
Desmond, A., 157n.12, 176n.14
Detterman, Nathan, 178n.21
dignity, human, 6-8
Dirac, Paul, 116, 134, 190n.24, 193n.47
Dodd, C. H., 41, 168n.6
dogmatism, 5, 76
domesticity, 41

Drake, Frank, 179n.23
Dressler, Alan, 178n.19, 186n.5
Dyson, Freeman, 162n.40, 168n.5, 177n.18, 179n.24, 180n.28

Earth, the, 23, 45, 127
Eccles, John, 159n.31
ecological awareness, 7
ecology, 30, 56
Eddington, Arthur, 172n.34
education, 56-57
Einstein, Albert, 12-13, 14, 15, 49, 51, 61, 75, 85, 98, 101, 106, 113, 119, 121, 123, 130, 152, 157n.15, 158n.22, 163n.48, 165n.54, 172n.33, 186n.4, 190n.28, 183n.47
Eiseley, Loren, 2, 18, 142, 155n.2, 157n.12, 159n.28
Eliade, Mircea, 153, 163n.49, 188n.17, 189n.21
Eliot, T. S., 167n.1
Ellis, George, 166n.58, 167n.61
Emerson, Ralph Waldo, 2, 69
Empedocles, 46
empiricism, 116, 117
Enlightenment, the, 4
entropy, law of, 35, 166-67n.60
Ephesus, Council of, 135
epistemology, 5
Erigena, John Scotus, 182n.46
ethics of humility, x
evolution, 185n.53
excitement, 142-43
existentialism, 156n.4
experience, and thought, 5, 89
extraterrestrial life, xi, 79-87, 93-94

faith, 124, 125
false vacuum, 163n.43
falsifiability (Popper), 187n.8
Farella, John, 157n.17
fatedness and destiny, 44-45

Ferris, Timothy, 156n.9, 157n.11, 192n.40
Feynman, Richard, 116
fields of force, 27-28
Final Theory, a, 8, 13
Fiscalini, J., 171n.22
Folse, Henry J., 191n.29
Ford, Lewis S., 185n.53
Fox, Matthew, 195n.11
Francis of Assisi, 30, 63, 95, 133
freedom, 7
Freud, Sigmund, 7, 53, 171n.23
Fritzsch, H., 173n.36, 177n.17, 193n.44
Fromm, Eric, 53, 54, 171n.23
Fuller, Robert, 156n.4
fusion, nuclear, 21, 46, 129

galaxies, 24-27, 167n.2
Galileo, 160n.32
Gardner, Howard, 178n.21
Gell-Mann, Murray, 168n.5
Genesis, Book of, 30-33, 47, 95, 131, 132, 136, 153, 180n.34, 192n.43
geocentrism, 11
geometry, 60-61
Gilkey, Langdon B., 162n.39, 175n.6
Gleason, Robert, 183n.48
Gleick, James, 191n.31
Globus, G., 160n.31
gnosticism, 168n.5
God, 8, 14-15, 31, 33, 41, 42, 47, 48-49, 63, 71, 72, 77, 78, 81, 88, 89, 96, 97, 99, 100-102, 109, 117, 118, 122, 131, 132, 135, 143, 146-49, 150, 154, 180n.36, 185n.53; as always cherishing life, 100, 101, 150, 182n.45, 184n.52; creative activity of, 31, 32, 77, 100-102, 131-32, 166n.59, 170nn.17,18, 192-93n.43; as in the relationships, 8, 15, 49, 99, 150; immanence and transcendence of, 136, 150; life-giving generosity of, 88, 90;

and the primordial singularity, 49, 102; our relationship to, 146-49, 187n.11; simplicity of, 135; as substrate of the universe, 8, 49; as universal constant, 109, 110; unknowability of, 136. *See also* singularity and God

"God of the gaps," 109, 117

Goethe, 11, 158n.20

Golden, F., 192n.40

Golding, William, 32

goodness, 24, 54

gratitude, 58

gravitons, 28, 163n.48

gravity, 25, 61, 123-24, 163n.48

great attractors, 79

Grey, L., 171n.22

Gribbin, John, 161n.35, 167n.4, 168n.5, 174n.2, 176n.12, 177nn.17,18, 178n.18, 186n.4, 188n.14, 192n.40

Gustafson, James, 156n.7

Guth, Alan, 26, 163n.45

Harris, E. E., 176n.11

Hart, Ray, 159n.29

Hawking, Stephen, 75, 106, 110, 166n.58, 175-76n.10, 186-87nn.6,13

heat (of the Sun), 132-33

heat death (of an open universe), 34, 35, 166n.57, 166n.60

Hegel, G. W. F., 169n.7

Heidegger, Martin, 156n.4

Hendry, George, 158n.20, 164n.53, 169n.15, 180n.32, 186n.1, 192n.42

Hesiod, 189n.21

hierogamy, 30, 32

Hillerman, Tony, 158n.17

Hinduism, 37, 46, 55, 168n.7, 184n.52, 188n.16

Holden, Arun V., 191n.31

hope, 124, 125

Hopkins, T. J., 184n.52

Hosinski, Thomas E., 180n.31, 185n.53

Howard, Robert, 178n.21

hubris, 52, 74, 175n.9

Huizinga, Johan, 189n.19

Hume, David, 155n.1

humility, 4, 25, 57, 77, 78, 85

idealism, 53, 116, 117

ideals, 172n.30

Ikhnaton, 134

imagination, 17-19, 56, 64, 81, 96

indeterminacy, quantum, 43, 119, 120, 164n.54, 190n.29

infinity, 102, 183-84n.50; and chance, 184n.51

inflation, theory of, 26, 124, 163n.44, 186n.5

insight, 41, 43, 142-43, 160n.32, 163n.46, 168-69n.7

intelligence, 79-80

Irenaeus, 164n.52, 182n.46

Isaiah, 108

Isaiah, Second, 91

Jaeger, Werner, 169n.15

Jaspers, Karl, 147

Jeremiah, 194n.48

Jesus, 21, 30, 40-41, 42, 47, 53, 54, 63, 66, 67, 68, 89, 92, 93, 95, 98, 99, 100, 125, 126, 131, 134, 144, 148-49, 150-51, 175nn.7,8, 180n.36, 183n.49; resurrection of, 98-99, 101-2, 164n.50, 180n.34, 181-82n.45

Job, 78, 177n.16, 180n.34

John the Baptist, 47

John, Gospel of, 60

John, St., 193n.43

Johnson, George, 161n.35, 185n.53

Judeo-Christian tradition, 14, 48, 60, 109, 187n.11

Jung, Carl, 153, 158n.17, 177n.16

kairotic moments. *See* time, as *kairos*
Kant, Immanuel, 2, 22, 145, 155n.1,
  157n.11
Kauffman, Stuart, 185n.53
Keen, Sam, 174n.40
Keller, Helen, 65, 66
Kelvin, Lord, 175n.6
Kepler, Johannes, 38, 60, 116, 157n.11,
  160n.32, 172n.32, 186n.3
Khalfa, Jean, 178n.21
Kierkegaard, Søren, 140-41, 144,
  171n.28, 175n.7
Kirk, G. S., 169n.10
knowledge, limitations of, 75, 78, 107,
  121-22
Kuhn, Thomas, 160n.32, 163n.46

Laplace, Pierre Simon, 75
laws of nature, 85-86, 106, 121
Leucippus, 42
Lewis, C. S., 97
life, biological, 38, 39, 92, 127; as characterizing all that is, 16, 28, 48, 101;
  cherishing of, 8, 16, 48, 66, 100-103,
  125
light, 131-32
Lightman, A., 156n.5, 173n.35
linkages, 27, 35, 36, 124, 135-36
Linzey, Andrew, 164n.51, 181nn.41,42
Loesberg, Jonathan, 190n.26
logic, failure of, 125-26
logos (word), 67-68, 174n.39
Lonergan, Bernard, 142, 163n.46
Louis XIV, 135
love, 53, 125, 128; divine, 8, 124;
  erotic, 53
Luther, Martin, 95, 155n.3

Malraux, Andre, 174n.39
"many worlds" theory, 176n.12

Marcel, Gabriel, 105, 153, 186n.1
Marduk, 29, 189n.21
Marshak, R. E., 162n.40
mass, definition of, 161n.34
Masson, R., 159n.29
mathematical physics, 13
McDaniel, Jay, 12, 181n.42
McFague, Sallie, 12
meditation, 66-67
Mesopotamia, 29
metaphor, 88-90, 100-101, 135
metaphysics, 88, 89-90, 101; of the
  cherishing of life, 100-103
Michelangelo, 134
Moltmann, Jurgen, 12, 110
moon, the, 10-11
Moore, J., 157n.12, 176n.14
Morris, M., 143, 179n.27
Morrison, P., 179n.26
Mullin, T., 191n.31
myth, 152-53

narcissism, 53-55, 57, 58; cultural, 56
narcissistic spirit, x, 18, 22
Narcissus, myth of, 50-58, 63, 66, 67,
  68, 74, 75
nature, 86
Navajo, the, 8-9
Nemesis, 55
neutrinos, 160n.33
neutron stars, 21-22, 38, 161n.37,
  192n.41
Newton, Isaac, 13, 14, 60, 75, 115, 121,
  123, 160n.32, 186n.3, 189n.22
Niebuhr, Reinhold, 57
Nietzsche, Friedrich, 63, 152, 156n.4,
  188n.17
Norris, Christopher, 190n.26
novelty in the universe, 12-13, 98, 115
nuclear weapons, 45-46, 139-41

Obayashi, H., 184n.52

obedience, 66, 125
obsession, 51-52, 53
Old Testament, 31
Oppenheimer, J. R., 46
optimism, 139
order of the universe, 12-13, 106, 107, 119-20, 194-95n.5
Origen, 95, 155n.3, 164n.52, 182n.46
origin of the universe, as kairotic moment, 43-44, 47, 48; religious myths of, 29-33. See also universe, origin of
Ovid, 50, 55, 57

Pagel, Walter, 187n.10
Pannenberg, Wolfhart, 12, 157n.13, 174n.39, 182n.45, 195n.10
pantheism, 15, 49
Paracelsus, 187n.10
paradigm shifts, 160n.32
Parker, E. N., 192n.40
pathetic fallacy, the, 2-3
Paul, St., 54, 99, 100, 102, 149, 183n.49
Pauli exclusion principle, 130
peace, 140-41, 194n.2
Peacocke, Arthur, 156n.7, 158n.23
Péguy, Charles, 9, 50
Penzias, Arnold, 172n.31
philosophy, 4, 108-9
photons, 21, 28, 121, 131-32, 135-36, 193n.46
physics, 3, 8, 35, 75, 102, 105, 119, 131, 165n.54; laws of, 49
Planck length, 165n.56
Planck time, 165n.56
Plato, 111, 112, 184n.52, 188n.15
Platonism, 112-13, 114, 189n.20
Poincare, Henri, 166-67n.60
Polanyi, Michael, 159n.27
Polkinghorne, John, 156n.7
Popper, Karl, 159n.31, 163n.46, 187n.8
possibilities, 44, 98, 184n.51, 185n.53
Pribram, Karl, 159n.31

Prometheus, 22
prophecy, biblical, 108
providence, divine, 24, 48, 109
pulsars, 38
Pythagoras, 116

quantum indeterminacy. See indeterminacy, quantum
quantum mechanics, 42, 43, 106, 119, 176n.12
quarks, 129

Radhakrishnan, S., 188n.16
rainbow, lunar, 40
randomness in the universe, 98-99
Raven, J. E., 169n.10
realism, 116-17
reason, limits of, 147-48
red giant (stars), 22, 130
red shift, 193n.46
redemption, 127
reductionism, 76, 77, 176n.13
Rees, Martin, 161n.35, 167n.4, 176n.12, 177n.18
Reichard, Gladys A., 157n.17
Reinhardt, Kurt F., 195n.9
relationship, 149-50; of care, 3; to non-human creation, 2
relativity, general theory of, 61, 123, 172n.33; special theory of, 186n.4
religion and science, 110, 176n.13, 194n.1. See also theology and science
religious consciousness, 151-54
resurrection, of all that is alive, 99, 101-2, 127, 184nn.51,52; traditional Judeo-Christian idea of, 183n.49. See also Jesus, resurrection of
revelation, 122
rhythms in the universe, 35-36
Ricoeur, Paul, 153, 189n.21
Rilke, Rainer Maria, 86, 87, 142
Rohde, Erwin, 164n.50

Rolston, Holmes, 12, 158n.23
Rousseau, Jean-Jacques, 32
Rowe, William, 195n.5

Sachs, J., 182n.46
Sagan, Carl, 179nn.24,26
Santayana, George, 158n.18
Santmire, Paul, 156n.7, 164n.52, 181n.42
Sartre, Jean-Paul, 17, 152, 159n.29
Scharper, Thomas, 156n.7
Schell, Jonathan, 45, 138-39
Schleiermacher, Friedrich, 122
Schopenhauer, Arthur, 41, 142, 168-69n.7
Schweitzer, Albert, 181n.42
science, xi, 19, 28, 33, 68, 101, 106, 107, 109-10, 125, 135, 143; and aesthetics, 133-34; and morality, 3. *See also* religion, and science; theology, and science
Scotus, Duns, 189n.20
Seraphim of Moscow, St., 63
Shakespeare, 19, 20
Shiva, 37, 46
simplicity, and beauty, 134; divine, 135
singularity, 34, 47, 49, 102, 165-66n.56; and God, 49, 102, 185n.55, 194n.5
Smith, Huston, 191n.34
Smoot, George, 163nn.44,47
Soleri, Paolo, 162n.41
soul, 30, 43, 164n.50, 184n.52
space, 61
speculation, 102-3
Spengler, Oswald, 188n.17
Spielberg, N., 156n.9, 172n.32, 173n.34
Sternberg, R., 178n.21
stars, 1-2, 20-24, 46, 57, 192n.41; evolution of, 38
strange attractors, 185n.53
string theory, 79, 177n.18

structuralism, 185n.53
Sun, the, 22-24, 46, 92, 127, 128-36, 174n.2
supernovas, 37-39
Swinburne, Richard, 180n.35
symmetry-breaking, 111, 188n.14

tachyon, the, 106, 186n.4
Taylor, Mark C., 190n.26
Templeton Foundation, the, 173n.35
Tennyson, Alfred, 2
Teresa of Avila, 142, 171n.25
theology, 13, 24, 56, 88, 109, 134; Christian, 7, 15, 48; and myth, 153-54; and science, xi, 3-4, 7-8, 11-12, 14, 16, 23, 48-49, 98-102, 108, 110, 117, 122, 135-36, 143, 166n.56, 173n.35
Theory of Everything, 75, 175n.10
thermodynamics, 35
Thompson, Francis, 28, 119
Thorne, Kip, 143, 179n.27
Tiamat, 29, 189n.21
Tillich, Paul, 57, 158n.23
time, as *chronos,* 41, 43; as *kairos,* 41-42, 43-44, 48
Tipler, Frank, 72, 74, 168n.5, 174n.3, 176nm.11,13, 191n.34
Toffler, Alvin, 95
Toulmin, Steven, 156n.9
Toynbee, Arnold, 188n.17
Tracy, David, 180nn.29,35
tragedy, biblical, 169n.12
Trefil, James, 121, 163n.43, 165n.54, 168n.5, 175n.6, 177n.17, 188n.14, 190n.24, 191n.33
truth, 24
Tuchman, Barbara, 189n.19

unexpected, the, 37, 38, 40, 126-27. *See also* time, as *kairos*
universal salvation, 182n.46

universe, the, 8, 36, 71-72, 78, 79, 97, 98, 103, 120, 121-22, 138; closed, 34; expanding, 34; origin of, 29, 33-34, 43, 47, 48; oscillating, theory of, 34-35, 43-44, 48, 102, 166n.59, 167n.60; "steady state" theory of, 34; unpredictability of, 73

universes, alternate, 76, 176n.12; parallel, 79

Valhalla, 141
Via, Dan Otto, 181n.38
virtual particles, 164-65n.54
Vishnu, 55
visual tradition, the (in relation to reflection, imagination, and wonder), 59-69
Von Neumann probes, 72

Wainwright, Geoffrey, 194n.3
Watts, Alan, 188n.16
Weil, Simone, 87
Weinberg, Steven, ix, 157n.16, 168n.5, 173n.35, 176n.13, 193n.45, 195n.7
Westfall, Richard S., 189n.22
Weyl, Hermann, 183n.50

Wheeler, John, 166n.58, 167n.61, 191n.36
White, Lynn, 3, 155n.3
white dwarfs, 22, 130
Whitehead, Alfred North, 21, 46, 85, 106, 107, 110, 142, 173n.37, 175n.8, 180n.31, 185n.53, 194n.2
Wilders, Max, 190n.23
will, expansivity of, 44
Wilson, Robert, 172n.31
wisdom, 66, 122; biblical, 159n.25
Wolfe, J., 179n.26
wonder, 66, 68, 148, 174n.40
Wood, J. A., 158n.19
Wordsworth, William, 2
"wormholes," 107, 143, 186-87n.6

xenophobia, 82

Yahweh, 31, 32, 114, 136, 183n.48, 194n.48
Yeats, William Butler, 98, 181n.44
Yurtsever, U., 179n.27

Zukav, G., 171n.25
Zygon, 173n.35